WRX vs. EVO
THE COMPLETE HISTORY

WRX vs. EVO

THE COMPLETE HISTORY

HUW EVANS

671 Press

Copyright © 2010 by Huw Evans

Visit www.wrxvsevo.com

Published by:

www.671press.com

All rights reserved. With the exception of quoting brief passages for the purposes of review, no part of this publication may be reproduced without prior written permission from the publisher.

The information in this book is true and complete to the best of our knowledge. All recommendations are made without any guarantee on the part of the author or publisher, who also disclaims any liability incurred in connection with the use of this data or specific details.

We recognize, further, that some words, model names, and designations mentioned herein are the property of the trademark holder. We use them for identification purposes only. This is not an official publication.

Version History
1.0 published March 2010

Evans, Huw
WRX vs. Evo: The Complete History

ISBN 0-9821733-4-2
ISBN-13 978-0-9821733-4-3

Design and Layout by Tom Heffron
Cover photo by Mike Maez
671 Press logo design by Micah Edel

DEDICATION

This book is dedicated to the memory, and the family and friends, of two of the greatest rally drivers of all time, Colin McRae and Richard Burns, both of whom inspired a generation of motorsports fans and car enthusiasts, including me.

CONTENTS

Publisher's Note		9
Acknowledgments		11
Foreword		13
Preface		15
Chapter 1	ORIGINS	17
Chapter 2	ARRIVAL	39
Chapter 3	THE ROAD TO STARDOM	75
Chapter 4	GLOBAL SUPREMACY	147
Chapter 5	STARS N' STRIPES	215
Chapter 6	GROWING UP	297
Appendix A	WRC WORKS RALLY RECORD	335
Appendix B	SPECIAL EDITION CARS	367
Appendix C	SPECIFICATIONS	391
Bibliography		421

PUBLISHER'S NOTE

Among performance cars, models like the Porsche 911, Ford Mustang, and Chevrolet Corvette have earned an honored place among the world's greatest. Accordingly, they have been glorified in hundreds of books and thousands of magazine articles over the years.

This book demonstrates that the Subaru Impreza WRX/STI and Mitsubishi Lancer Evolution deserve to be held in similarly high regard.

Consider the evidence. First, these two rally-inspired cars are among fastest in the world on real-world roads. They're no slouches on the track or autocross course either. And, of course, both have reached the very pinnacle of rallying competition, the form of motorsport that requires more versatility than any other.

These two cars have had an enormous influence upon automotive enthusiasm around the world. Currently, they are among the most popular performance cars on nearly every continent (Antarctica remains in question).

Their turbocharged engines endear them to hot rodders who dare to push the performance envelope. Their all-wheel-drive systems and competent chassis dynamics ensure that pavement-scorching horsepower translates into forward thrust, while delivering incredible cornering and braking capabilities. The emergence of the WRX and Evo displaced the once-ubiquitous Hondas as the compact performance cars of choice and spawned healthy aftermarket industries.

Sure, the WRX and Evo are based on lowly economy cars, but this doesn't disqualify them from the pantheon. Might I remind you of the Ford Falcon, Porsche's roots in the Volkswagen, or the slow boulevard cruiser that was the first Corvette?

Huw Evans is the ideal author for this book, after his lifelong exposure to car cultures around the globe and years of experience driving and writing about cars. I'm extremely pleased that we are able to put this book in print and share the result of Huw's hard work with automotive enthusiasts everywhere.

Peter Bodensteiner, founder and partner, 671 Press
Hugo, Minnesota
February 2010

ACKNOWLEDGMENTS

Although my name appears on the front of this book, many other people were crucial to making it happen. I'd like to say a big thank you to Peter Bodensteiner and Lee Klancher at 671 Press for giving this project the green light; to Susan Elliot at Mitsubishi Motor Sales Canada for providing me with some very rare and hard-to-find factory photos, as well as sample cars to evaluate; Marie-Claude Simard and Elaine Griffin at Subaru Canada for helping me find a vast array of factory and motorsport images, not to mention also providing me with cars to evaluate; Derric Slocum for providing much of the U.S.-based photography; members of the Central New York Subaru club (CNYSubies), for their enthusiasm in providing cars to feature in this book; the folks at Fuji Speedway and representatives from Nitto Tire (Japan) and Nitto Tire (USA) for their wonderful hospitality and camaraderie during my trip to Tokyo; and Craig and Amanda Dabbs for their great company and Craig for supplying his knowledge and expertise, not to mention the foreword for this book.

I'd also like to thank my mom, dad, and brother Owain, for their encouragement and support over the years. And last but not least, my loving wife Andrea, for having the patience to put up with me during the course of this project.

FOREWORD

I started my career in motorsports like many other people, riding motorcycles and eventually running in AMA Pro road racing during the 1990s. I later became an instructor at the Bob Bondurant School of High Performance Driving and more recently became lead instructor of advanced driving techniques at the Barber Driving Experience in Ventura, California.

Craig Dabbs gets ready to race a Crawford Performance Impreza STi in US Time Attack.

Over the years I've had the privilege of driving many of the world's great-handling cars, from a simple, gutted-out, turbocharged Honda to Lamborghinis and Ferraris. I must confess, however, that the kinds of cars that have put the biggest smile on my face have to be all-wheel drive turbo cars, and the Mitsubishi Lancer Evolution and Subaru WRX rank at the top of the list. I watched the battle rage between these two for a number of years in the World Rally Championship and on the street in other parts of the world. Then in 2002, something wonderful happened—these high strung, all-wheel-drive legends became available here in the United States. Many enthusiasts, including myself, were champing at the bit to get our hands on these machines.

Just as Chevy and Ford have their loyal followers who will debate and argue which is better, so do Mitsubishi and Subaru. Both the Evo and STI are four-door, AWD, four-cylinder turbo cars that have a similar weight. The Subaru devotees will say that the WRX is a more refined and classier vehicle, while the Mitsubishi followers will argue that the Evo is more of a purist's performance vehicle, citing less weight and sharper handling as its virtues. Magazines and their statistics may say one is better than the other, but it really comes down to personal preference.

I've had the opportunity to drive both cars on the street and road course, from bone stock configurations to examples in all-out competition trim with well over $200,000 invested. And, I have to say, I love them all.

With decent stock power, either will out-perform just about any car twice the price, and with their four doors and relatively large trunk space, it's easy to justify either one as a daily driver.

For track driving, these AWD cars are hard to beat in stock form, but the highly modified versions are setting new track records all the time. One of the biggest issues facing most race cars is being able to put the power to the ground without spinning the tires upon exiting a corner. Both the Evo and WRX have addressed this issue very well. With one of the highly modified STIs I drive, I love rotating the car into the corner while trail braking and being able to just mash the power back on and slingshot out onto the straight. The feeling you get exiting a corner when the turbo spools up to generate 500-plus hp in a car with all-wheel drive is simply unmatched. This book highlights the amazing story surrounding two of the most incredible cars I've ever driven, and I hope you find it a welcome addition to your library.

Craig Dabbs
March 2009

PREFACE

There are few automotive rivalries that have been as hotly contested as that between Mitsubishi and Subaru regarding their Lancer Evolution and Impreza WRX, however much Chevy, Ford, and Holden fans might beg to differ. These two cars were built with one primary mission—to conquer the FIA's World Rally Championship. Perhaps what neither manufacturer envisioned was the league of fans they would attract in the process.

Today people all over the globe enthusiastically purchase, cherish, modify, and race these cars, in all manner of different events and circles. With both Mitsubishi and Subaru unveiling new versions of these icons recently, we felt it was high time a book covered the dynamic rivalry between the Evo and WRX from their inception to the present day and beyond. To that end, I hope you enjoy reading it as much as I have enjoyed researching and putting it together.

Huw Evans
Barrie, Ontario, Canada
February 2009

CHAPTER 1

ORIGINS

It isn't surprising that the Mitsubishi Lancer Evolution and the Subaru Impreza WRX became such great rivals. The parent companies of both brands have a long history with quite a bit in common.

MITSUBISHI

Mitsubishi, a word that means three four-sided stars in Japanese, was the first of the two companies to come into existence. In 1870, businessman Yataro Iwasaki established a shipping company, called Tsukumo Shokai. A year later, the company secured a big contract with the Japanese government to ferry troops to Taiwan and later to expand shipping routes between Yokohama and Shanghai in China. In 1873, the company was renamed Mitsubishi, after Iwasaki's family crest, which incorporated the now-famous three-diamond logo.

Mitsubishi soon emerged to become one of Japan's zaibatsu (giant, industrial enterprises) and started building its own ships, which were equal to anything else in the world at the time. By the 1910s, wealthy Japanese were showing interest in automobiles; in response, Mitsubishi built its first cars in 1917. However, the project wasn't successful, and the massive company turned its attention elsewhere, to commercial and

WRX vs. EVO

Probably Mitsubishi's most famous product in the first half of the 20th century was the A6M Reisen fighter aircraft, built for the Imperial Japanese Navy. Dominant in 1941-42, it was outclassed by 1945 despite the addition of a more powerful engine and improved armor, like on this late-build A6M5. Yasukuni

military trucks, ship building, and aircraft manufacturing, particularly aero engines.

During the 1930s, the power and wealth of the zaibatsu grew further still. While some rivals pushed forward with car production, Mitsubishi continued to concentrate on commercial and military projects, including aircraft. Among the most significant were the Mitsubishi G3M and G4M medium bombers and the A6M Reisen (Zero) fighter. Built for the Imperial Japanese Navy, which dominated the Pacific skies in 1941 and 1942, the A6M proved a serious foe for the Allies, particularly at Pearl Harbor, the Battle of the Coral Sea, and Midway, until an intact example was captured and the weaknesses of its design, especially its light airframe construction, was discovered.

By the end of World War II, Japanese industry, having suffered from widespread bombing raids, was in ruins. A rebuilding process began slowly, largely with American assistance. In an attempt to limit their power and influence, the surviving zaibatsu were broken up into smaller companies, including Mitsubishi. At this time, plans were finally put in place for Mitsubishi to start building cars, though the first examples were little more than CKD (complete knocked down)

ORIGINS

Mitsubishi's first 'modern' car was the Colt 1000, a conventional sedan that featured a water-cooled, front-mounted, four-cylinder engine and rear drive. It went on sale in 1963. Beginning in 1967 the company started campaigning them in Pacific Rim rally events, notably the Southern Cross in Australia. Mitsubishi Japan

versions of various American Kaiser-Willys products, including Jeeps and the compact Henry J sedan.

A decade and a half later, with Japan's postwar economy enjoying a full-scale recovery, Mitsubishi released its first indigenous automobile—the 500. Somewhat similar to the Fiat of the same name, it employed a 500cc, two-cylinder engine mounted behind the rear wheels. The following year an even smaller 360cc car was released, but in 1963, the first of the conventional Mitsubishi passenger automobiles made its debut—the Colt 1000. This was a small sedan powered by a 1-liter, inline, water-cooled four-cylinder engine driving the rear wheels. Simple and tough, it proved quite popular at home, as well as a suitable platform for motorsport. This car would spearhead Mitsubishi's initial rally efforts, including the grueling Southern Cross in Australia. Other variations of the Colt soon followed, including a wagon and an interesting fastback coupe. In 1964, Mitsubishi launched a larger car that followed the same front-engined, rear-drive form, the opulent Debonair, powered by a relatively large inline six.

In January 1973, Mitsubishi introduced its first Lancer in two-door coupe, four-door sedan, and Celeste fastback forms. A choice of 1.2-, 1.4-, and 1.6-liter engines was available, the latter in a semi-sporting model, the 1600 GSR. The following year one of these cars, bought privately by Kenyan rally driver Joginder Singh, was entered in the grueling East African Safari. It won the event, crossing the finish line in 11 hours and 18 minutes, ahead of Bjorn Waldegaard's Porsche 911! Mitsubishi Japan

This car, styled by Hans Bretzner, was never exported, but its styling was clearly influenced by Detroit offerings of the time, most notably the compact Chevy II and full-size Impala.

In 1969, at the Tokyo Motor Show, Mitsubishi introduced what would become one of its most significant products ever—the Colt Galant. Available in two-door coupe or four-door sedan form, it shared much of its engineering with the old 1000, but it boasted contemporary coke-bottle styling. By the early 1970s, the Galant was being exported in significant numbers, particularly to the United States, where Chrysler, having purchased a stake in Mitsubishi Motors, sold the car as a Colt through its Dodge dealer network.

In Japan, a slightly smaller counterpart to the Galant, dubbed the Lancer, was launched in 1973. With a range of four-cylinder engines

ORIGINS

Mitsubishi continued to expand its rally efforts during the 1970s. Helping the cause were Scotsman Andrew Cowan (shown here, left) after winning the 1976 Southern Cross and Kenjiro Shinozuka. Mitsubishi Japan

and body styles, including the FTO (Fresh Touring Origination) coupe, semisporting 1600 GSR, and the interesting Celeste fastback (sold in North America as the Plymouth Arrow), the first-generation Lancer proved quite popular. With minor facelifts, it lasted until 1979, when a more modern, boxier design, dubbed the Lancer EX (with much improved multilink rear suspension), replaced it.

By the late 1970s, Mitsubishi was already quite a veteran of the international rally circuit, with a decade of Southern Cross rallies (in Australia) under its belt and also several grueling Safari events (in Africa). Scotsman Andrew Cowan had made a name for himself in the Southern Cross and won the event outright in 1973, 1975, and 1976. In the Safari, Mitsubishi Lancers also racked up wins in the 1974 and 1976 events. The 1974 Safari running was quite spectacular: Kenyan driver Joginder Singh, who drove a privately purchased Lancer 1600 GSR four-door sedan, defeated some very stiff competition from the likes of Porsche, Lancia, and Peugeot to win the event. Cowan and

Singh, driving two different GSRs, also finished a spectacular 1–2 in the 1977 Ivory Coast Rally in West Africa.

THE FIRST TURBOS

By the early 1980s, along with the second-generation Lancer EX, Mitsubishi had introduced Silent Shaft engine technology on its four-cylinder engines. Using balance shafts driven off the crank, the result was a powerplant far smoother than most anything on the market and one that rivaled some inline sixes (particularly those from BMW). At the same time, with the world experiencing its second fuel crisis in a decade, Mitsubishi also began looking at turbocharging as a way of extracting real performance from small-displacement engines.

On the Mitsubishi stand at the 1980 Tokyo Motor Show in September, the World Rally Championship claimed the spotlight as the company unveiled the Lancer EX–based 2000 Turbo. Conceived

Mitsubishi introduced a new, second-generation Lancer in 1979, dubbed the EX. It was a boxy four-door sedan, still with rear drive. The famed 4G63 made its first appearance as the 2-liter engine option on this car. Turbocharging it resulted in the Lancer EX 2000 Turbo, intended for World Rally Championship homologation. Mitsubishi Japan

ORIGINS

as a homologation machine for the WRC's then-current Group 4 class, it caused quite a stir, and a production version went on sale in export markets during the spring of 1981. With boy-racer styling touches and 174 bhp from its fuel-injected, 2-liter hair-dried powerhouse, the Lancer EX Turbo could rocket to 124 mph, which made it a serious performer in its day. In Japan, because of legislative and tax requirements, a tamer 135-hp 1.8-liter GSR turbo model was launched a few months later; it was also intended to boost somewhat flagging sales in the home market.

Despite a string of rally victories in the 1970s, Mitsubishi still wasn't considered a major player in WRC circles. By the early 1980s, the company was actively looking to change that. After establishing a European center for rally operations in 1980, it got to work to make the second-generation Lancer competitive. The WRC counterpart to the Lancer 2000 Turbo made its official debut as a works car at the 1981 Acropolis Rally, where two examples were entered, one driven by former Opel driver Anders Kullang, the other piloted by longtime Mitsu driver (and 1976 Safari winner) Andrew Cowan. The 1981 season proved fraught with teething problems, and the best finish a Lancer could muster was ninth in the RAC in Britain.

After a somewhat disappointing start, the Mitsubishi Rally team started making inroads. By 1982, many of the car's teething troubles had been overcome. This is Anders Kullang in the '82 San Remo. Mitsubishi Japan

The following year, 1982, marked a significant turning point in the WRC as rule changes instigated new Group A, B, and N classes in place of the previous 1–4. This paved the way for the mid-engined Group B monsters. As a small operation, Mitsubishi found the new regulations a bit tougher to contend with than some of the other teams. Still, it proved to be a more successful season for the Lancers. Finn Pentti Airikkala joined the team as a works driver and managed to finish third in the 1000 Lakes that year. Just as the car was starting to prove competitive, more changes in the rules for 1983 relegated the Lancer redundant as a WRC car, leaving Mitsubishi to focus on the new Starion coupe for its top-flight rally effort—first as a radical AWD contender in 1984 and 1985 aimed at Group B and then as a more conventional, production-based Group A machine beginning in 1986.

On the street in Japan, meanwhile, the Lancer had been joined by the smaller, front-drive Fiore in early 1982 (essentially a four-door sedan version of the contemporary Mitsubishi Mirage hatchback). Late in 1983, a second-generation Fiore, with more modern, angular styling, arrived on the scene, along with a similar-looking Mirage hatchback counterpart. Ultimately, this front-driver supplanted both the original Fiore and the larger, second-generation rear-drive Lancer EX, though the latter held on a while longer in Japan (until early 1988, in fact, by which time sales were very marginal). The new, second-generation Fiore was offered as a four-door sedan and, from 1985 on, in wagon form.

Also sold in export markets as the Mitsubishi Colt, Lancer, and Dodge Colt (North America), the second-generation Lancer Fiore could be ordered with a wide range of four-cylinder engines, up to and including a 1.6-liter 'Saturn' Turbo with electronic fuel injection, packing 120 bhp and a five-speed manual gearbox. Yet, despite the formation of the Ralliart competition arm in 1984 dedicated to building rally and homologation specials, Mitsubishi continued to push with the Starion in the WRC, so the Lancers of this era are little more than a footnote among most enthusiasts and are considered semi-sporting at best.

ORIGINS

Changes in the rules saw Mitsubishi switch to the Starion coupe for its rally efforts beginning in 1984. This is the AWD version, campaigned with limited success in 1984-85. A more conventional, Group A works car arrived for 1986. Mitsubishi Japan

A true third-generation Lancer, with front-wheel drive, was launched in June 1988. This car featured smoother, more grownup styling than the Fiore, but it was a version of this car's bigger brother, the thoroughly redesigned sixth-generation Galant (also debuting for '88), that planted the seed for the Mitsubishi Lancer Evolution.

GENESIS

After very limited success with the Starion in WRC, Ralliart decided to focus on a version of the new Galant for its Group A endeavors during the 1988 season—the all-wheel-drive, turbocharged VR-4. Naturally, to qualify for WRC, this car had to have a street counterpart (which interestingly, unlike many of the Lancer homolgation specials to follow, was sold in the United States between 1989 and 1992). With the arrival of the Galant VR-4, the Japanese finally became a serious force in World Championship Rallying. During the car's inaugural season, the works Group A VR-4s were dogged by reliability issues,

WRX vs. EVO

The birth of the Lancer Evolution's AWD sedan configuration can be traced back to the formidable Galant VR4, introduced in 1988. With all-wheel drive and all-wheel steering, it was quite the performer. In Group A rally trim, it showed tremendous promise off the bat. Here, works driver Pentti Airikkala gets airborne on his way to victory at the 1989 RAC in Britain. *Mitsubishi Japan*

but Ari Vatanen put in a strong performance at the RAC toward the end of the year, hinting at the car's potential.

Things improved considerably for 1989. Rally legend Jimmy McRae (father of future WRC champ and rival Subaru driver Colin) took one of the works cars to a fourth-place finish at the Acropolis in Greece, while another finished first in Australia. Finn Pentti Airikkala took the checkered flag at the RAC in November, fighting off fierce competition from the Mazda 323s, Lancia Deltas, and works Castrol Toyota Celicas.

In 1990, a familiar name debuted behind the wheel of a Galant in the Rally of New Zealand—Tommi Makinen. On his first outing, in a privateer Group N car, he finished first in class and sixth overall—a very good effort that proved a harbinger of things to come. In the meantime, another Japanese contender started showing tremendous promise in the WRC—Subaru, with its new Prodrive Legacy Group

ORIGINS

A car. Carlos Sainz and Toyota clinched the championship that year, but Mitsubishi wasn't about to take that lying down.

Ralliart had been making improvements to the car diligently, including its AWD system. In time for the 1991 Acropolis rally, it dished up an updated WRC machine: the Galant Evolution. With a larger intercooler, boosting power from 295 to more than 300 bhp, it proved fast, but despite strong performances neither of the works drivers—Kenneth Eriksson nor Timo Salonen—finished. Salonen managed to take third place in the 1000 Lakes, in a battle with Tommi Makinen (now a works Mazda driver), but he was ultimately disqualified, the result being awarded to Makinen instead.

Australia proved much better with second- and fifth-place finishes by Eriksson and Salonen, respectively. By the end of the year, the team had secured enough overall points to finish third in the WRC.

Nineteen ninety two proved to be a bit of a letdown in many respects—the only bright spot being a win (the second year in row) by Japanese driver Kenjiro Shinozuka on the tough Ivory Coast Rally in Western Africa.

Mitsubishi did well on the Ivory Coast Rallies in the early 1990s. Kenjiro Shinozuka won the event in 1991 (seen here) and 1992, though by then the VR4 was becoming outclassed as a competitive Group A rally machine. Mitsubishi Japan

WRX vs. EVO

By this stage the days of the Galant as the primary Ralliart WRC platform were numbered. The car was simply too big, too heavy, and too complex to be competitive. Mitsubishi decided that in order to advance its position in the highly competitive World Rally arena, it needed to field a different Group A machine from 1993 onward—one that was smaller and more nimble. It would prove to be the right choice.

SUBARU

Fuji Heavy Industries, the parent company of Subaru, got its start in 1917 as the Nakajima Aircraft laboratory, taking its name from founder Chikuhei Nakajima, an Imperial Japanese Navy officer with a background in aeronautics. After visiting Europe to supervise the sale of French aircraft to Japan, Nakajima realized that his country was far behind Western nations when it came to military technology and that aerial superiority would be of crucial importance in future conflicts (this would prove especially true two decades later in the World War II Pacific conflict, where the United States and Japanese fought many air battles without either side's ships coming in direct contact). With wealthy backing, Nakajima left his navy ties behind and set up shop in an old factory to start building airplanes. Teaming up with Kiyobe Kawanishi, the company secured army and navy contracts for aircraft.

However, the men had different ideas about engine development that caused Kawanishi to end all involvement (his company went on to build seaplanes and flying boats for the navy). Despite this setback,

Subaru's parent company, Fuji Heavy Industries, started out as the Nakajima Aircraft Laboratory. It turned out some of the best Japanese military aircraft of 1940s, though some, like the excellent Ki 84 Hayate, came too late to make a significant impact on the outcome of hostilities. Japanese public domain

ORIGINS

Nakajima managed to secure more backing, just as Japan began a massive rearmament program in the 1930s. The Nakajima Aircraft Company Limited, as it was now known, ended up building some of the most famous Japanese military aircraft of all time, including the B5N torpedo bomber that was used at Pearl Harbor, the Ki 43 and Ki 44 army interceptors, plus the capable Ki 84 Hayate, called "Frank" by the Allies. Bombing by U.S. forces stunted production, however, and the Ki 84 never got a chance to prove itself. Nakajima also built Mitsubishi aircraft under license, including the A6M Zero. It also built countless aero engines, including the Sakae radial that powered the Zero.

When hostilities ceased in August 1945, the Japanese economy was severely crippled. The once-powerful zaibatsu were broken up. Having relied on such firms to keep it in business, Nakajima needed to find another avenue to stay afloat financially.

Renamed Fuji-Sangyo Company Limited, it turned its attention to motor scooters. The quite ingenious Rabbit, which used a lot of aircraft parts (particularly tires), provided the company with a much-needed shot in the arm (revised and updated, the scooter remained in production until 1968). Other projects included rear-engined buses, among them Japan's first double-decker. In 1953, Fuji-Sangyo was broken up into a number of different companies, but these soon merged together to form Fuji Heavy Industries (FHI).

Soon after its formation, FHI started looking at building automobiles. For its new car division FHI president Kenji Kita chose the name Subaru, Japanese for the Pleiades or Seven Sisters star cluster from Greek Mythology. The first car to emerge was a conventional small sedan, dubbed the 1500 or P-1. In many aspects it was a competent car, but production problems meant only 20 examples were ever completed, rendering it little more than a prototype.

By 1958, Subaru was finally in a position to mass-produce automobiles, but instead of taking the conventional route, it found that using aviation technology to build its cars would be a better approach, at least in the short term. It released a 360cc mini car—in some respects a Japanese VW Beetle. It featured a tiny, rear-mounted, two-

The Subaru 360 was offered in a variety of body styles, including a two-door sedan, a wagon and even a convertible. Subaru Global

Given the company's aviation background, it probably wasn't surprising that FHI's first series production car, the Subaru 360, employed an air-cooled, two-cylinder engine. Subaru Global

cylinder, air-cooled engine and offered cheap, no-frills motoring to an increasingly mobile Japanese public. By the early 1960s, and with the availability of different body styles, including a wagon and convertible, production of this little car was quite healthy.

The early 1960s were a time of big change in Japan. Industry and wealth were expanding, and as if to symbolize the country's growing influence, Tokyo was announced as the host city for the 1964 Olympics. The government began a massive public works project, which included a series of high-speed expressways. As a result, Japanese motorists in the future would likely need (and want) to drive something a little faster and more sophisticated than austere, rear-engined mini cars.

FOUR CYLINDERS, FOUR-WHEEL DRIVE

Subaru's answer was the front-drive 1000, launched in 1966. Boasting all-independent suspension and a horizontally opposed,

ORIGINS

Arguably the grandfather of modern Subarus, with its horizontally opposed, front-mounted engine and all-independent suspension, was the Subaru 1000. It was first seen in 1966. Subaru Global

four-cylinder, water-cooled engine up front, it was available as a sedan and two-door coupe. Its basic engineering laid the foundation for virtually all Subarus that followed. It was also hugely popular, with some 237,000 examples of this car and its FF offshoot built over the car's five-year production run.

In late 1971, Subaru launched the 1000's replacement, the considerably more modern Leone (Italian for Lion), which would become a Subaru mainstay for the next 30-plus years. The Leone, powered by a development of the boxer engine, boasted contemporary styling and was initially offered as a fastback coupe, with a sedan, hardtop coupe, and wagon joining the lineup for 1972. Interestingly, the Leone wagon was the first Scoob to feature the company's patented AWD system. Aimed primarily at commercial use, it found a small but loyal niche among private buyers and was largely responsible for initiating Subaru's reputation for building AWD vehicles. Exports to Europe began in the mid-1960s and to the United States (officially) in 1969, after a fledgling deal with Malcolm Bricklin to sell 360s ended. Sales to Europe remained very

WRX vs. EVO

Replacing the 1000/FF during the latter part of 1971 was the Leone, which borrowed much of the earlier car's engineering but featured far more modern styling. The first model to launch was the sporty coupe seen here. Subaru Global

much a trickle, as the company had to deal with import restrictions and a range of cars that, like those offered from Sweden's Svenska Aeroplan Aktiebolag (SAAB), was considered offbeat and quirky by many (UK sales didn't even start until 1977).

The U.S. market, on the other hand, purchased one quarter of all Subarus built by the mid-1970s, as buyers took to the little Leone like cats to milk. The arrival of automatic transmissions and yet more AWD variants only added appeal for American buyers. A more modern, second-generation Leone debuted midway through 1979, powered by 1.6 or 1.8 boxer engines and offered again in sedan, hardtop coupe, and, later, three-door hatchback form (in which guise it appeared in the film *Cannonball Run*, driven by Hong Kong film star Jackie Chan). In 1980, Subaru made its first stab at the World Rally Championship, fielding two hatchbacks in the Safari, with one managing to muster an 18th-place finish.

In 1981, a touring wagon, naturally with AWD, bolstered the lineup. In some markets, notably Australia and North America, a pickup utility was also available. This vehicle is fondly remembered as the BRAT in North America (an acronym for Bi-drive Recreational

ORIGINS

During the 1970s, Leone AWD wagons started gaining a cult following through their simplicity, toughness, and affordable price. It was this car that established Subaru's presence in the North American market. Subaru Global

All-terrain Transporter). In 1982, performance began to creep into the lineup with the introduction of the turbocharged RX Leone sedan and, in some other markets, a turbo pickup and wagon, but all this was a mere warm-up for things to come.

RALLYING THE TROOPS

Although Subaru had forged a well-deserved reputation for building sturdy little AWD cars by the early 1980s, they were still considered by many to be offbeat and quirky. With sales still marginal on the home front especially, FHI figured it was time to change that and looked to the old adage, "competition improves the breed."

Subaru decided to make a return to the World Rally Championship in 1983. Again two works cars were enrolled in the punishing Safari. Yoshio Takaoka drove one to a fifth-place finish, while down in New Zealand, local rally ace Peter Bourne drove another Leone to 14th overall and first in the Group A category.

WRX vs. EVO

In 1984, an updated, third-generation Leone (ultimately called Loyale in some markets) was launched in Japan. Still clearly a Subaru, it was a much more angular design, and it boasted a longer wheelbase and wider track for improved stability. The 1.6- and 1.8-liter boxer engines were also updated with new single overhead-cam cylinder heads. The year 1985 marked a crucial turning point for Subaru The striking XT coupe (Alcyone in Japan) was launched, as was the Leone-based 1.8 RX Turbo, both powered by the same 135-bhp, multiport, fuel-injected engine. Both these cars were significant, as the XT attempted to capture a different slice of the market, while the RX Turbo proved a decent platform for further rally efforts. The RX made its rally debut at the 1985 Safari and one finished tenth overall, but most of the Scoobs running on the rally circuit that year were private entries. Bourne drove an RX to fifth in New Zealand, and another privately sponsored car finished first on the Ivory Coast rally, but Subaru's presence was still very small in WRC circles.

A more concentrated effort for 1986 saw sixth- and seventh-place finishes on the Safari by Mike Kirkland and Frank Tundo, but not

By 1984 Subaru had introduced a second-generation Leone. It formed the basis for the swoopy Alcyone coupe (XT in other markets), sold between 1984-89. Subaru Global

long after, the team suffered a major setback when a member of the Dunlop tire team (which supplied rubber for the Subarus) was killed in an accident, halting rally efforts temporarily. Subaru ended the year 13th in the constructor's cup. In 1987, Peter Bourne scored Subaru's best result up to that point, finishing third in his native New Zealand, again behind the wheel of an RX Turbo. In 1988, FHI formed Subaru Tecnica International (STi), with a budget of ¥250 million, to develop Subaru's motorsports activities (particularly WRC) and a range of performance parts and limited-edition cars.

On the Safari rally that year, local Ian Duncan drove another RX Turbo to sixth overall. Although more money and effort were being poured into WRC competition in 1989, Subaru's highest result was a seventh-place finish from Bourne in a STi-prepped RX on the Safari.

Something clearly needed to be done if Subaru was to be competitive in WRC circles against the likes of Lancia, Toyota, and even Mitsubishi and to capture a bigger slice of the production car market, both at home and overseas. That something was the Legacy.

BIGGER AND BETTER

Launched in February 1989, the Legacy was the biggest Subaru yet, a roomy, three-box sedan and station wagon. True to form, it was powered by four-cylinder boxer engines in 1.8- and 2.0-liter versions, and for the North American market, where it debuted as a 1990 model, there was a 2.2-liter engine with 135 bhp. As with the Leone RX that preceded it, there was also a turbocharged version, the RS type R with a 200-hp 2-liter engine, and by the end of the year, a RS type RA, with further tweaks yielding 220 hp.

Not surprisingly, this was the basis for Subaru's next World Rally Championship car. In conjunction with STi and Prodrive in the United Kingdom, six examples were readied in time for the 1990 Safari Rally. Finnish driver Markku Alen got off to a flying start, but he ran into overheating problems and was forced to retire. The only Legacies that made it to the end were the Group A car of Jim Heather-Hayes (which came in sixth place) and the sole Group N

With the introduction of the Legacy in 1989, Subaru launched its first truly mid-size family car, which would form the basis for its first championship-winning rally machine. Huw Evans

entry, driven by local Patrick Njiru, which finished two spots behind. Nevertheless, the new Legacy had shown its potential, and from here it was onward and upward.

By the end of the season, Subaru had claimed fourth place in the constructor's cup championship, due in part to Alen finishing fourth overall in the 1000 Lakes and Peter "Possum" Bourne coming home fifth in New Zealand. In 1991, things went even better; Alen came in third at the Swedish Rally, followed by a fifth on the Safari and a fourth in New Zealand. In the Lombard RAC Rally of Great Britain that year, Subaru proved a force to be reckoned with. Markku and a young Colin McRae put in some very good times on the early stages before crashing out of contention. A third car piloted by Ari Vatanen came in fifth place overall. McRae won the British Open Championship that year and for 1992 was signed on as an official works driver for the Subaru team.

For the next season, STi and Prodrive worked diligently on some upgrades, including a semiautomatic gearbox. In the Swedish Rally,

McRae proved he was a serious contender by coming in second place—the highest-ever finish for a Subaru driver at the time. On the gravel in Greece, McRae finished fourth overall, but he was blindingly fast and proved stiff competition for Frenchman Didier Auriol, matching the works Lancia driver's number of stage wins. Vatanen managed to pull out another fourth place in the 1000 Lakes, and in the RAC that year he drove his Legacy to a second-place finish. McRae had set the pace for much of the rally but was beset by problems and came in sixth overall. When the final scores were drawn, Team Subaru had finished fourth in the constructor's cup.

For 1993, with a new sponsor on board (British American Tobacco's 555 brand), the Subaru Rally Team adopted the now-familiar overall blue livery for its works cars. By this time, Subaru had decided to phase out the Legacy in favor of the smaller and lighter Impreza, so the works rally team ran both cars during the season. McRae got off to a great start, piloting one of the Legacies to a third-place finish in Sweden, but that was merely a warm-up for muddy New Zealand, where the young Scotsman put in a stellar performance to give the Subaru Rally Team its first WRC victory, much to the delight of rally team head Dave Richards. Colin's win was also significant, since Isamu Kawai, Subaru's president at the time, had stated that he didn't want the new Impreza to replace the Legacy as the company's official WRC platform until it had proven itself as a winning car. With the quick Scotsman's first victory, that time had come.

CHAPTER 2

ARRIVAL

The early 1990s marked a golden age of Japanese performance cars, with hot offerings such as the Nissan Skyline GT-R, Nissan Fairlady Z, Mazda eFini RX-7, and Toyota Supra. Even today, enthusiasts lust after the cars that emerged during this era. Mitsubishi and Subaru, although smaller players at home, also got in the action. Unlike their larger rivals, which relied on sporty coupes, they both decided to base their hot offerings on rather mundane, run-of-the-mill sedans. As we shall see, in terms of performance and fun, they would prove to be anything but ordinary.

1993
MITSUBISHI: THE EVOLUTION BEGINS

On September 7, 1992, although few might have believed it at the time, a new era began at Mitsubishi Motors with the unveiling of the Lancer Evolution, the company's new WRC homologation special. Based on the smooth-looking fourth-generation Lancer sedan, Mitsubishi and Ralliart aimed straight for the WRC crown with this new automobile. Former rally program chief Iwao Kimata (who spearheaded the company's original WRC project in the early 1980s) was brought in to work on the Lancer Evolution, along with winning Mitsu team rally drivers Kenjiro Shinozuka and Kenneth Eriksson. From the very beginning, Kimata was adamant that the new homologation car had to be as "balanced as possible" and make maximum use of existing hardware, rather than relying on technological overkill. The experience gained from rallying with the Galant, Starion, and even previous Lancers would prove invaluable in creating a highly competitive and fun-to-drive car.

The street version of the fourth-generation Lancer made a great starting point for a rally-bred performance car. The unibody structure was light and strong with a considerable amount of attention paid to chassis reinforcements and extensive use of galvanized steel. Another trump card was the car's powerplant. Mitsubishi chose to employ a development of the Galant VR-4's 4G63 2-liter twin-cam four-cylinder motor but made a number of changes for duty in the newer, smaller car. Chief among them was an entirely new reciprocating assembly, including a lightweight crankshaft, special rods, and reduced-friction, lightweight pistons. The slugs bumped up

For Mitsubishi enthusiasts, September 7, 1992 was a red-letter day, marking the introduction of the very first Lancer Evolution. Homologated for the 1993 WRC season, it featured a 250 hp 4G63 engine, five-speed manual gearbox, a version of the Galant VR4's AWD system, and specific suspension pieces. It was offered as a GSR version (pictured) or a stripped-down RS. A total of 2,500 street versions were required to meet WRC rules, but Mitsubishi ended up building 5,000 for the Japanese domestic market.
Mitsubishi Japan

the compression ratio from 7.8 to 8.5:1 and were combined with a new head that featured stouter valves along with revised intake and exhaust ports, plus a more efficient fuel system with new injectors. The chosen turbocharger was a Mitsubishi TD05H with a nickel, chrome, and iron housing. Combined with a low-restriction exhaust system and a standard oil cooler, as well as an air-to-air intercooler, the net result was 250-DIN hp and a fairly healthy 227 lb-ft of torque. A five-speed manual gearbox, with a new, stronger clutch, was employed (no automatic option was offered). Like the engine, the AWD system was pirated from the Galant VR-4, employing front and rear differentials (the latter with a limited-slip setup), plus a centrally mounted third diff to control the torque split from front to rear. Although the system was a bit crude, especially when compared with later Evos, it was mighty effective. When combined with specific suspension tuning, it made the street-going Evo a fun little machine and, for the time, a very quick point-to-point car. The first Lancer Evolution was offered in two flavors—a mainstream GSR variant and the more hard-core RS, aimed at the serious enthusiast.

Although the instrument panel bore a fairly close resemblance to the mainstream fourth-generation Lancer, the driving experience was anything but. All bona fide Lancer Evolution street cars came in right-hand drive form only. Mitsubishi Japan

GSR models boasted standard Recaro front bucket seats, designed to keep the occupants in place during spirited driving. A different design of Recaro seat was offered in the stripped-down RS.
Mitsubishi Japan

Differences on the RS included a mechanical limited slip rear differential (instead of the viscous unit on the GSR), 15-inch steel wheels in place of alloys, an absence of ABS brakes, air conditioning, and power windows, plus no rear washer/wiper, nor Recaro front seats. The RS was offered in only silver or white (GSRs were available in six different hues, including blue, green, black, and red, as well as silver or white). Buyers could order alloy wheels, fog lights, and Recaro seats for the RS as options, but the seats were different from the buckets found in the GSR model.

Not long after the car was introduced, Mitsubishi introduced air conditioning across the Lancer range, along with its patented MIVEC variable valve timing on the 4G63 and other engines.

Initially, Mitsu had planned to build just 2,500 Lancer Evolutions to satisfy WRC Group A requirements, but because of demand, it increased that number to 5,000. Officially, none of these cars were destined for export (despite what contemporary sales literature might have suggested), though a few of them found their way to other countries, especially in the Pacific Rim.

ARRIVAL

SUBARU: IMPREZA LAUNCHES

Although the Legacy had proved itself a championship-winning machine on the WRC circuit, the process hadn't been easy. It was a fairly large car, and even though STi built a street-going version of the Legacy Turbo sedan to satisfy homologation requirements, Subaru needed a car that could better carry the performance mantle on the street and prove more effective in the World Rally Championship.

The Impreza was launched on October 22, 1992, little over a month after rival Mitsubishi first introduced its new Lancer Evolution. Conceived as a replacement for the long-running Leone/Loyale (the two cars were sold side by side for a couple of seasons), the Impreza stayed true to Scoob tradition with its water-cooled, front-mounted boxer four-cylinder engine, fully independent suspension (in this case employing MacPherson struts), and all-wheel drive (a single entry-level front-drive sedan was offered, powered by a 1.5-liter EJ15 boxer engine). For the regular AWD offerings, propulsion came in the shape

Subaru launched the Impreza WRX in October 1992. There were two models, the regular Rex and the Type RA seen here. The latter was a stripped-down version, available only in white, that did without the ground effects and rear spoiler. It proved popular with hardcore enthusiasts. Subaru Global

of 1.6 and 1.8 versions of the flat four motor (coded EJ16 and EJ18, respectively, and based on the units found in the Leone and Legacy). A further powerplant, the 2-liter EJ20 boxer engine, was also built, though it was only found initially between the frame rails of the WRC homologation car, named the Impreza WRX.

Two body styles were offered on the Rex, a four-door sedan and a sport-back wagon. The former was a fairly elegant looking little car, while the wagon was a bit more controversial. Its fairly thick C-pillars and sloping tailgate gave it the look of a fishbowl from the rear, and in North America some drew comparisons with the ill-fated AMC Pacer of the 1970s. As with previous Subarus, both body styles featured the trademark frameless windows. Considerable attention was paid to fit and finish with improved paint and panel gaps, plus better cabin ergonomics and slightly higher-quality upholstery and plastics than found in late Leones.

On the outside, the WRX was distinguished from lesser Imprezas by a deeper front air dam with a massive pair of foglights, perimeter body extensions, a rear deck spoiler, and a mail-slot hood scoop. Its turbocharged EJ20 engine was an all-alloy quad-cam unit with an 8.5:1 compression ratio, four valves per cylinder, and sequential fuel injection. Subaru engineers tuned it to deliver 240 hp (DIN) and 224 lb-ft of torque. Interestingly the turbocharger—a TD04—came from Mitsubishi. However unlike its Lancer rival, the WRX was available with manual and automatic transmissions (the latter debuting six months after the car went on sale in Japan). The stick cars featured a five-speed gearbox—a close-ratio piece with shorter cogs compared with lesser Imprezas—while the auto was a four-speeder with piggyback electronic shift control and a manual option that enabled the driver to hold second gear for better traction on slippery surfaces.

The AWD system fitted to these cars was quite interesting. Stick shift WRX models had front and rear differentials linked by a central viscous coupling that housed a bevel gear. Under regular driving conditions, the torque split was 50/50 front to back, but the coupling would split this depending on which wheels provided more or less traction. On automatic-equipped cars, a slightly different setup employed a 60/40 front-rear torque split under normal driving conditions. A multiplate clutch system not only controlled torque split front to back, but it also sent more or less power to the front or rear wheels depending on whether the driver was accelerating or braking.

WRX models received quicker-ratio rack-and-pinion steering (15:1 versus 16:1 on lesser cars) and unique suspension tuning, with firmer spring and shock rates, special bushings, and thicker anti-roll bars front and back. To save weight, the front lower control arms were made from cast aluminum instead of steel. In addition, the WRX received a more aggressive brake package than regular Imprezas, employing 277mm (10.9-inch) front discs with dual piston calipers instead of 260-mm (10.2-inch) units, while at the back the rear discs were larger in diameter than the fronts but actually narrower. Twin brake boosters were standard, while anti-lock brakes were an option. WRXs rolled on standard 15-inch five-spoke alloy wheels and 205/55/R15 Bridgestone rubber, but buyers could order a set of 16-inch rims and more aggressive tires, if so inclined.

In addition to the regular WRX, a type RA version was offered. Equivalent to Mitsu's Lancer Evo RS, this was a stripped-down special that did without much of the ground effects, had no foglights, very basic interior specs (no power controls, stereo, or automatic climate control), a five-speed gearbox with shorter ratios on speeds 2–5 for more aggressive acceleration, even stiffer suspension settings, and no ABS. Early buff book reviews of the car were favorable. The WRX gained favorable comments for its acceleration, braking, and handling, leading a few to draw comparisons with the Nissan Skyline GT-R, a touring car homologation special and arguably Japan's hottest performance coupe at the time.

EUROPEAN DEBUT

A few months after it went on sale in Japan, the Impreza made its European debut at the Geneva Auto Salon in March 1993. In some countries, such as the United Kingdom, continuing import quotas meant that only a few cars trickled in. Subaru did bring over six of its new WRX models. Three of them went to Prodrive in Banbury for evaluation, as STi made plans to replace the Legacy Group A rally car with the new, smaller sedan, while the others were sold on the used car market. Although Subaru brought these cars over, none of them were official British-spec cars per se.

Back in Japan, the regular WRX and RA sedan were bolstered by wagon counterparts, dubbed the WRX Sport Wagon and WRX SA, respectively. These featured much the same equipment as the sedans, including the chassis and suspension upgrades, body extensions, sport bucket seats, and Nardi steering wheel. The engines were tuned differently, however, with less power—220 hp and 205 lb-ft—but at a much more useable rpm range for daily driving. The SA could be ordered without roof rails or air conditioning but was otherwise better-equipped than the equivalent RA sedan.

MITSUBISHI: RENEWED RALLY EFFORTS

On January 1, 1993, FIA approval for the Lancer's Group A homologation was granted and Ralliart Europe quickly got to work building a new fleet of cars to supplant the bigger and heavier Galants. Two full-time works drivers were signed on for the 1993 season: Kenneth Eriksson, who had been with the team since 1990, and new guy Armin Schwarz, who replaced Timo Salonen, who went to Lancia. The new, lighter Lancer looked like a winner. Eriksson and Schwarz both had trump cards of their own, too—the Swede, like many Nordic drivers, was very quick on loose gravel, while Schwarz had gained a reputation for being highly competitive on tarmac events.

The Group A Lancer made its debut in Monte Carlo. Not surprisingly, because of the road surface, Schwarz made the most progress. The brand new car had teething troubles, however, and Schwarz ultimately retired when the gearbox let go. Teammate Eriksson, although not as fast on this rally and facing mechanical issues of his own, managed to coax the other works car to the finish in fourth place overall.

ARRIVAL

Mitsubishi's Lancer Evolution was formally homologated for the World Rally Championship on January 1, 1993. With a modified version of the Galant driveline in the light and incredibly strong Lancer, the Group A machine looked every inch a winner. The two official works drivers for the season were Kenneth Eriksson and Armin Schwarz. Mitsubishi Japan

Even at this early stage, the decision to use the Lancer Evolution as a WRC platform looked like it would bear fruit. However, Ralliart Europe was still learning the ropes, and the budget for the year only permitted the team to run cars in five events during the season (Group N cars, a mixture of Lancers and Galants, were run in the other rallies to give Mitsu a chance at the constructor's title). In one of the works rallies—Portugal—Eriksson drove a fairly steady pace and brought one of the Lancers home in fifth place. Schwarz, on the other hand, ran into an unlucky streak. On the first day, he damaged the car enough to take out a wheel. After repairs, another crash on the second leg forced him to retire. At the Acropolis, the works team's next foray, things were better. The engineers successfully adjusted the suspension in an effort to improve stability and traction. Schwarz put in a very good drive; he was running as high as second place by the second leg and ultimately finished third, scoring the team's first podium finish in the process. Things didn't go so well for Eriksson. On just the second stage, his car struck a rock, breaking the oil pan and forcing retirement.

New Zealand in 1993 was significant, for with his first win, Colin McRae put archrival Subaru ahead of Mitsubishi for the very first time in the WRC. The best the three-diamond team could muster was a 14th-place finish by Group N driver Yoshio Fujimoto. Australian Ross Dunkerton had been given a Group A car but retired with mechanical problems.

In other races, Eriksson managed a fifth in Finland, and in the Australian rally, Dunkerton put in a good hometown performance to come in fourth overall. Still, by this point Toyota had a comfortable lead in the championship, and Juha Kankkunen had a firm grasp on the driver's crown.

The next works assault came in the last race of the year—the RAC—and despite the mud in dark, damp Wales, the team scored its best results yet. Eriksson drove one of the Lancers to a second-place finish, and Schwarz managed to bring the other entry home in eighth

With a limited budget in 1993, Mitsubishi Ralliart was only able to run cars in five WRC events. In the prestigious Monte Carlo, tarmac specialist Schwarz was doing well until his gearbox broke. Mitsubishi Japan

ARRIVAL

In the 1993 Rally de Portugal, Kenneth Eriksson and co-pilot Staffan Parmander drove a decent rally to finish in fifth place overall—not bad for what was essentially a brand new car on only its second outing. Mitsubishi Japan

place overall. Mitsubishi finished fifth overall in the constructor's championship with 86 points, behind Toyota, Ford, Lancia, and Subaru.

SUBARU: SMALLER AND QUICKER

At Prodrive, engineers got busy putting together a viable rally replacement for the Legacy. Although quite a bit smaller than its predecessor, mechanically the Impreza was rather similar. Thus, making a world-beating rally car out of the Impreza required adaptation and tweaking, versus a clean-sheet approach.

The WRC Group A spec engine was a variant of that used in the Prodrive Legacy, but it featured an air-to-air intercooler in place of the air-to-water unit. Helped in part by valvetrain tweaks and a different turbocharger, sourced from IHI, it made slightly more power and torque at a higher rpm. Prodrive chose to stick with a version of the old STi six-speed semiautomatic gearbox, with the driver being able to change speeds via a console-mounted lever or paddles fixed to the steering wheel. Although tread dimensions were the same as the Legacy, the new Impreza weighed considerably less. Prodrive and STi took advantage of this to improve weight distribution in the smaller car while still staying within then-current WRC guidelines. The final weight bias was about 55/45 percent front/rear. Front and rear diffs with a center hydraulic differential to control torque split were employed on the rally car, as were monster brakes with a special water-cooling system that sprayed water onto the discs to keep temperatures down, reduce warping, and extend brake life for tarmac events.

The Imprezas were homolgated in time for the 1000 Lakes WRC event. One car had been allocated for Ari Vatanen to drive and the other for McRae, but in the Scotsman's absence (he was competing in the Asia-Pacific rounds at the time), Markku Alen was given the driver's chair. With a new car and two Finns competing in their home rally, it would be interesting to see how the new Impreza performed in competition.

Alen's drive was spectacularly short—he crashed out on the first stage, after trying to take a corner too fast. This disastrous result saw him end both his stint as a Subaru driver and also as a major

The very first outing for the Impreza's WRC Group A car was on the 1993 1000 Lakes Rally in Finland. Markku Alen was brought in as a last-minute substitute to drive for Colin McRae, but his outing proved to be a disaster with a crash and retirement on the first stage. Subaru Global

WRC participant, a solemn end to an illustrious rally career. Vatanen, meanwhile, along with co-driver Bruno Berglund, fared a little better. He put in spectacular first-day drive, and it appeared that he was well on his way to victory by the halfway point. However, problems with the heater system caused the windshield to fog up, costing him a lot of time. Still, he managed to take second place overall, and he wasn't that far behind fellow Finn Juha Kankkunen in the Castrol works Toyota Celica.

Because the Legacy was still the primary WRC platform at this time, the next round for the Imprezas was the last event of the year: the RAC in Britain, with one car for Vatanen and the other for Colin McRae. The young Scotsman started off with a scorching drive, clearly liking the new car. After making sound progress on the first two days, Colin was in the lead when disaster struck the following morning. Debris damaged his cooling system, and he was forced to retire. Vatanen and Berglund, meanwhile, set the fastest time on three stages and managed to bring the other Team Subaru car home in fifth overall. Although the Impreza's presence had been small, the 1993 season was Subaru's best ever in the WRC. The Japanese manufacturer finished third in the constructor's cup. Clearly, things were looking up.

1994

MITSUBISHI: IMPROVEMENTS

The competition never stands still, and Mitsubishi knew that if it were to persist with its WRC efforts, its chosen platform needed to keep up. Of course in order to satisfy Group A requirements, that meant that the street Lancer Evolution would also be the recipient of any updates. Thus, the Evo II was born.

Announced in December 1993, the Evo II went on sale in Japan the following January. This time Mitsubishi pegged overall production at 5,000 from day one, and as before, every one of the road-going Evo IIs was accounted for in short order—approximately three months.

The Evo II included a slightly revised front fascia with a bigger air dam and a redesigned rear deck spoiler with a new base section.

WRX vs. EVO

After a somewhat disappointing start in 1993, Ralliart needed an improved Lancer WRC to keep hopes alive in the coming years. In order to satisfy FIA (Federal Internationale d'Automobile) rules, it needed to homologate an updated street version, so the Evolution II was born. Mitsubishi Japan

Although it looked similar to its predecessor on the outside, the Evo II was actually quite different mechanically, with improved steering, a more advanced suspension with a wider track, and a new gearbox with revised ratios. Outwardly the Evo II was distinguished by a new rear deck spoiler design with the words 'Evolution II' embossed on the base. Mitsubishi Japan

ARRIVAL

Inside, the Evo II was similar to the earlier model, though the Recaro seats were redesigned for improved back and thigh support. Mitsubishi Japan

Mechanical changes included tweaks to the suspension to improve handling and stability. These included stronger mounting points and lightweight, forged-aluminum lower control arms at the front, while the steering axis was pushed forward. This increased the wheelbase, and the front and rear track were widened by 15 mm and 10 mm, respectively. The front sway bar was reduced in size, and the rear spring rates were bumped up. Other technical upgrades included a new ceramic-disc clutch, slightly shorter cogs on first and second gears for quicker takeoff, plus a less restrictive exhaust system. Tweaks to the turbo yielded an extra 10 hp from the 2.0-liter 4G63 engine.

As before, two basic trim levels were offered: the GSR and the hard-core RS. The former now featured 205 section tires mounted on five-spoke 15-inch O. Z. alloy wheels, requiring larger inner fenders for clearance, along with a revised pair of Recaro front bucket seats with deeper cushions and improved bolstering. Other changes included a revised in-car entertainment system with better acoustics and a revised air conditioning system that employed CFC-free R134a refrigerant instead of the previous R12. As before, the RS was distinguished by a lack of fancy interior upgrades, including air conditioning and a premium stereo. Although it came with the same tires as the GSR version, those came wrapped around 15-inch steel wheels, not alloys. With the Evo II RS, you could also order it any color you wanted, so long as it was Scotia White. GSRs were offered in Queen's Silver Pearl, Moonlight Blue Pearl, Pyrenees Black metallic, Monaco Red, and, of course, Scotia White. Although the Evo II was up some 22 lbs in curb weight, it was a veritable rocket on wheels. In the right hands, it could blast to 60 mph in under five seconds, which was true supercar territory in the early 1990s. It also offered outstanding grip and handling, not too shabby for a car that was based on a four-door commuter special.

SUBARU: MOVING UP

Spring 1994 saw the Impreza WRX finally available in export markets, notably Australia, but this was actually a slightly different car than the Japanese version. It had a lower-compression engine with less power (208 hp and 201 lb-ft of torque), so it could run on lower-quality fuel. Still, it was a quick little pill all things considered, and the Aussie press on the whole judged it quite favorably. *Wheels* magazine even picked the Rex over the rival Mitsubishi Lancer Evo, despite that car's better performance and perceived greater bang-for-buck value.

As the Aussies were getting their first taste of this little turbocharged AWD wonder, so were the Europeans. Announced at the Geneva Show in March 1994, the turbo Imprezas aimed at Europe were their own unique species. Like the Australian WRX, these cars featured an EJ20 tuned to run on lower-octane fuel and were also rated at 208 hp. They introduced some unique features of their own, however, including different gearing on the five-speed transmission. In the United Kingdom, despite looking virtually identical to the WRX, the car was called the Impreza 2000 Turbo, while in Continental Europe (Switzerland was the first country to receive it), the left-hooker version was badged an Impreza GT. The new car was well priced and well equipped, with a fully loaded interior and standard ABS brakes, among other things. It was also a stellar performer. The British weekly *Autocar* tested one of the new 2000 Turbos and declared "performance is in the Escort Cosworth league." High praise indeed, given that the Escort Cosworth was a rival and highly competitive WRC machine at the time.

The launch of the Impreza 2000 Turbo was significant in Britain, as this car arguably put Subaru on the map in the United Kingdom. Within a few years, these cars and their derivatives would be a common sight, with a very enthusiastic following. Virtually coinciding with the Turbo's launch in the United Kingdom, Prodrive came to market with a selection of go-fast and cosmetic upgrades for the car. These included suspension kits with stouter damping and spring rates, wheel and tire packages, as well as very nice Recaro seats and a few other interior fixtures. The Prodrive upgrades were handled through a select group of approved concessionaires, located in different parts of the country. The tuning revolution was about to begin.

STI GOES IMPREZA

While export markets were getting their first taste of the hot new Scoob, back in Japan Subaru Tecnica International had begun development work on an even hotter version of the home-market WRX. This car was announced a couple of months before Impreza Turbos began reaching Australian and European shores in 1994.

Named after the division that built the car at its own facility in Mitaka (a Tokyo suburb), the very first Impreza WRX STi was a rather special machine. For starters, it had a unique version of the EJ20 boxer engine. It was fully balanced and blueprinted, with special forged pistons, polished exhaust valves, lightweight valvetrain components, tweaks to the Mitsubishi TD05 turbocharger, a modified intercooler with upgraded piping and a water spray system, plus a bigger-bore exhaust and more aggressive engine mapping. Unlike the regular WRX, sedan and wagon versions of the STi featured the same engine in the same state of tune. Advertised power output was 250 hp and 227 lb-ft of torque, which put it on the same footing as Mitsubishi's Lancer Evolution II.

WRX vs. EVO

Subaru Tecnica International built its first Impreza-based car in 1994, the aptly named WRX STi. With a fully balanced and blueprinted engine that cranked out 250 hp, it was built on a dedicated assembly line. Ironically it was never homolgated for the rally series that spawned it. *Subaru Global*

Both Scoob STis featured a nigh-identical version of the five-speed manual gearbox found in the regular WRX, but they did get extra chassis stiffening in the form of a strut tower brace, along with upgraded front brakes. Interior upgrades included special upholstery for the seats and door panels and carbon fiber inserts for the leather Nardi steering wheel and the unique shifter handle. Bridgestone Expedia 205/55R15 tires mounted on 15x6-inch rims were standard, though buyers could upgrade to a 16-inch split-spoke wheel and larger tires. Outside identification included a pink badge on the nose and rear spoiler, itself a rather prominent and heavy piece (unique to sedans). Under the hood there was a tiny "handcrafted by STi" badge on the timing cover and a special plaque indicating the car's serial number and build date as a nod toward exclusivity. Although STi had been conceived to increase Subaru's presence in rallying and other forms of motorsport, the initial 1994 Impreza STi was actually never homologated for rallying and remained very much a prized performance street car among marque aficionados.

In September of the same year, at the Tokyo Motor Show, Subaru announced further changes to its regular WRX lineup. Chief among

ARRIVAL

these were larger 16-inch wheels and 205/50/R16 performance tires and tweaks to the engine and the turbo (slightly more boost), along with revised engine mapping. Power now stood at 260 bhp, while torque was pegged at a 227 lb-ft. Incidentally, the hard-core RA version of the regular WRX received further upgrades, including a new, stronger engine block and stouter valvetrain pieces—enabling it to scream all the way up to 7,500 revs—plus slight tweaks to the exhaust, turbo, and ECU. As if perhaps to signify a slightly more hard-core direction for the WRX line, the automatic transmission and SA wagon were dropped.

MITSUBISHI: PROGRESS MADE

The new Lancer Evolution II appeared in Group A form during the 1994 WRC season. However, the new works cars weren't quite ready for the series opener in Monte Carlo, so Schwarz and Eriksson ran that event behind the wheel of updated 1993 models. Both drivers appeared to be getting quite comfortable with the Lancer and set a torrid pace, taking 11 of the 22 stages. But disaster struck during a controversial incident with a bunch of rowdy spectators—Schwarz was unable to avoid them without driving off the course. This slowed him down considerably, and by the end of the event, he was down to seventh overall. Eriksson did somewhat better, rounding off the Monte in fourth place.

The FIA had altered the rules for the 1994 season, requiring the works teams to run at least 9 of the 10 events, and this proved highly challenging for Mitsubishi. The team ultimately decided that this wasn't the year to field a full works effort, so Ralliart's results would not count toward the constructor's cup. Still, that didn't stop progress from being made. The next works assault was the 1994 Acropolis Rally, where Ralliart Europe brought out the latest Evo II Group A spec cars for both Eriksson and Schwarz to drive (Group N entries having been fielded in Portugal and on the Tour de Corse). Eriksson's drive in Greece was a bit of a rocky one and rear suspension problems brought his retirement early. Schwarz, on the other hand, with co-

WRX vs. EVO

The 1994 Rally season proved a bit tough for Mitsubishi. Ralliart Europe introduced the Group A Evo IIs in the tough and rocky Acropolis Rally in Greece, with Schwarz putting in an excellent drive to finish second. Mitsubishi Japan

In the 1994 Rally of New Zealand, both works Mitsubishi entries managed to finish, with Schwarz (seen here) coming in third place. Teammate Eriksson came in fourth place. Mitsubishi Japan

driver Klaus Wicha, put in a very impressive drive. The hot and dusty conditions took their toll on a number of drivers and cars, but by the third day Schwarz was hot on the heels of eventual winner Carlos Sainz and finished second overall—Mitsubishi Rally Europe's (MRE) best result yet.

New Zealand—where Ralliart fielded a full works effort—was the third event of the 1994 season, but it proved to be a difficult one. The works drivers had difficulty getting a decent amount of grip, but the Schwarz/Wicha machine managed to bring home a third-place finish, with Eriksson and co-driver Staffan Parmander right behind.

As if to signify Mitsubishi's determination to make its mark on the WRC, the Ralliart Europe crew was back, this time in uncharted territory as it put a two-car Evo II team in action for the San Remo in October. Schwarz was given one car for the tarmac event, while Eriksson sat this one out, the other mount being given to Finn Tommi Makinen. The rally didn't go too well for Tommi; he was out on the first day when his rear suspension broke on Special Stage 5. Things appeared to be going much better for Schwarz; he charged hard, claiming two stage wins, but it all came apart on the final leg, first with two rear tire punctures. Then on a transit stage a fuel line ruptured, burning the car to a crisp—not the best end to his career with Mitsubishi!

The RAC was a Group N deal all the way, with Isolde Holderied and Tina Thorner driving a German-prepped car to 16th overall and second in class. In the Asia-Pacific championship, Eriksson won both the Rally of Thailand and Rally of Indonesia, landing him second in the driver's points chase of that six event series, behind Subaru and Peter "Possum" Bourne.

SUBARU: CHANGES IN RALLYING

The 1993 season had been a year of transition for SWRT, but the new Impreza had showed a lot of promise. For 1994, the Legacy was finally retired as an official works car, leaving the team running an all-Impreza field. The cars themselves got a new, hydraulic front diff that could be controlled via cockpit-mounted controls, and the tire supplier switched from Michelin to Pirelli for the year. Colin McRae's contract was renewed for another season, but Ari Vatanen left the team to go to Ford. In his place, Spaniard Carlos Sainz was signed up as the other full-time works driver. Sainz was already a veteran on the WRC circuit, having won the 1990 and 1992 WRC driver's titles with Toyota. After a disappointing 1993 season spent struggling with the increasingly outmoded Lancia Delta Integrale, he looked forward to trying his luck with the 555 crew. A third car was also prepped for Brit newbie Richard Burns to run at select events. Burns also drove in the Asia-Pacific Championship (APC), along with veteran Subaru stalwart Peter "Possum" Bourne.

The 1994 WRC season didn't get off to the greatest start. The Monte Carlo Rally—the first on the calendar—was plagued by incidents with aggressive and foolhardy spectators. McRae made good time until he hit a patch of snow while entering a blind corner. The resulting crash nixed any chances for a good finish as he and co-driver Derek Ringer could only manage 10th place overall. Sainz and his co-driver Luis Moya, however, fared quite a bit better, coming in third place on their first outing.

In Portugal, the next round on the calendar, Sainz put in a fairly steady drive to finish in fourth place overall. McRae continued with problems; his engine caught fire, and he was forced to retire.

Subaru chose to sit out the Safari rally in official capacity and instead fielded Group N cars. Although Toyota, the only team with a works presence, took first with Ian Duncan driving, Subaru secured a decent fourth-place finish with local driver Patrick Njiru. Along with a fine fifth from Richard Burns, this result helped Subaru cement its position in the constructor's cup.

On the Tour de Corse in April, the works cars were given larger 18-inch wheels and tires, along with new active center differentials to better exploit the tarmac conditions of this event. Sainz was driving very well, closing on leader Didier Auriol by the last day as Auriol started developing clutch problems. However, Sainz's luck ran out when a tire blowout cost him valuable time. The damage was repaired

ARRIVAL

and Sainz and Moya continued on, but there was no catching Auriol and thus they had to settle for second. McRae and Ringer continued their string of bad luck and crashed out of contention on the first day.

The Acropolis Rally was surrounded with quite a bit of controversy in 1994, at least as far as the Subaru team was concerned. McRae blasted off like a rocket from the beginning and set the fastest time on the first six stages. His pace was so quick that team manager Dave Richards asked him to calm it down a bit. On day two, during a road section between stages, a scrutineer failed to secure the hood latches and the hood flew open, smashing the car's windshield. Repairs were performed at the next checkpoint, and Colin was allowed to start at the front for the next stage with a fresh windshield. By the middle of night, however, race officials decided to exclude him for the event because of issues surrounding the repairs.

Sainz, meanwhile, enjoyed a spectacular drive amid the dust and rocks. He took the lead on day three and gave the Impreza its first WRC victory, finishing ahead of Armin Schwarz in the new Mitsubishi Evolution. As a result of his win, Sainz was now neck-and-neck with Frenchman Didier Auriol for the driver's championship.

In Argentina, Sainz was on form again, pushing hard from the start and giving Didier Auriol a real run for his money, playing a game of cat and mouse with the Toyota driver right until the end. In a spectacular finish, Sainz and Moya were just six seconds behind the winner. While Sainz was hot on the heels of the Toyota, McRae and Ringer weren't having the best of times. They were leading the rally come the start of day two, but an apparent tire puncture resulted in a major crash, sending the Impreza rolling off the road and down an embankment. Luckily, neither McRae nor Ringer was seriously injured.

New Zealand proved to be a turning point in the Scotsman's fortunes, and it came in just the nick of time, amid growing concern that he might not be all that competitive in the WRC. Because the New Zealand Rally was part of both the APC and WRC circuits, two Subaru works cars were entered for Sainz and McRae, plus two more

WRX vs. EVO

The Imprezas took over from the Legacies as the Group A Subaru works entries in the 1994 WRC. Veteran rally driver Carlos Sainz signed up, as did quick Scotsman Colin McRae. McRae had mixed fortunes in the 1994 Rally of Argentina. He was leading by the start of the second leg, though a spectacular crash brought about early retirement. Subaru Global

for Richard Burns and Peter "Possum" Bourne. Reliability played havoc with the Subarus, and three of the four cars were out by mid-point of the rally—only this time, McRae and Ringer weren't among them. McRae, seemingly comfortable at last with the smaller Impreza, put in an excellent drive and proved to be a master on the gravel course, beating out the Toyotas of Juha Kankkunen and Armin Schwarz to finish first overall.

Round eight in the championship took the teams to Finland for the 1000 Lakes. Among the trickiest of rally courses to master for non-Nordic drivers, it proved no less challenging in 1994. Despite his win in New Zealand, McRae sat this one out; consequently, only one Subaru works car was prepped, for Sainz and Moya. Considering the difficulty of the course and the fast pace, Sainz put in a very canny drive to preserve his championship hopes. Two of the most experienced drivers

ARRIVAL

Seen here in the 1000 Lakes Rally in Finland, Sainz put in a solid drive to finish third.
Subaru Global

on this course, Toyota's Juha Kankkunen and Ford's Ari Vatanen, crashed out early on, paving the way for fellow Finn and Mitsubishi pilot Tommi Makinen, who was followed by Didier Auriol and then Sainz. Carlos battled Auriol for as long as he could, but in an effort to save his car, he wisely backed off and accepted third overall.

A sizeable chunk of the San Remo in October was run on gravel instead of tarmac. Team Subaru was back with a two-car effort, one for McRae and Ringer and the other for Sainz and Moya. On the first day, Sainz set the pace, with Malcolm Wilson in a Ford Escort being the closest to him. That meant the Spaniard started first on the second day—a distinct disadvantage when competing on gravel, where the roads get faster as each car passes. He still made good time, despite spinning his car and lightly touching an Armco barrier. But during the last few stages, where the drivers had to contend with tarmac roads, things started to unravel. Didier Auriol proved to be quicker on the hard stuff and started reeling in Sainz. Still, a second place overall was a far from shabby result, and with McRae and Ringer coming in fifth,

Subaru was still very much in contention, even as the WRC headed into the final round.

At the RAC that year, three works cars were prepped—for McRae, Sainz, and Richard Burns and co-driver Robert Reid. Sainz had a bit of a tricky drive in the dark and wet RAC. On the first day, he entered a water crossing too fast and drenched his engine, but after repairs he was back in contention. However, on the last day on the infamous Welsh gravel roads, he misjudged a turn and ended up in a ditch, his championship hopes dashed. Burns had retired earlier, but McRae was on form. By Stage 3 and with no team orders in force, he'd taken the lead and maintained it right until the last day. His first win in front of a British crowd was definitely one to savor; he'd proven beyond a doubt that he was a serious championship contender in the pinnacle of rally racing. Subaru ended up finishing second overall in the constructor's cup championship, behind Toyota—a very good result all things considered. The APC was another matter, as Subaru and Peter Bourne took the respective titles that year.

ANOTHER STI SPECIAL

About the time the 1994 WRC season was wrapping up, back in Japan STi released another hot rod Impreza. This was the WRX Type RA STi, based on the bare-bones, all-business WRX RA model. It featured the most powerful EJ20 engine to date with turbo and intercooler changes and a specially calibrated ECU that netted a sizeable 275 hp and a fairly meaty 235 lb-ft of torque. There were also stronger engine mounts and twin electric cooling fans to help keep this gnarly engine running at its best.

More power and torque meant changes to the AWD system were in order. Thus the STi Type RA cars received stronger rear axle shafts, a special two-way mechanical limited-slip differential, and a special parking brake (designed for sharper sliding turns) that featured a five-step button, allowing the driver to control the amount of power being transmitted to the front and rear wheels, from a 50/50 split to a 65/35 rear bias. There was also a new shift linkage, replete with a new leather-wrapped handle and sturdier bushings, though internal gear ratios on the five-speed remained the same as on the garden-variety WRX Type RA model. Buyers could order quicker ratio steering (with a larger reservoir and oil cooler).

Outwardly there were a few differences between this and the first STi, namely special covers for the massive front foglights and special WRC-inspired touches, including a unique hood scoop and roof vent, plus a prominent rear deck spoiler. As a nod toward the Group A cars, each STi RA came with gold-colored, 6.5x16-inch, five-spoke aluminum wheels and Bridgestone Potenza P205/50-section rubber at all four corners. There was STi badging on the trunk lid, and most (but not all cars) featured the pink grille emblem. Just in case that wasn't enough, a STi logo was featured on the top of the engine, and a special FHI Aerospace division engraving appeared on the strut tower brace that FHI supplied for the car.

Interior specs were very similar to the first STi with carbon steering wheel inserts and specially trimmed bucket seats and door panels. Unlike its predecessor, this version came exclusively in one color—Feather White—complete with black mirrors and moldings like the RA from which it was derived.

Almost as soon as it went on sale, the STi Type RA became a cult classic. Performance was impressive with contemporary magazine road tests clocking the car at 5.3 seconds for the 0–60 mph dash and 13.5 in the quarter-mile, which put it almost on equal footing with the Lancer Evolution II. STi had initially set production at just 50 cars per month, but demand was such that this car ended up being built for nearly two full seasons. This STi Type RA was also significant in that it was the last of the Imprezas to be hand-built at Mitaka. When the last one rolled out the door, it marked the end of a brief but exciting era.

1995

MITSUBISHI: ENTER THE III

Outwardly, the Lancer Evolution III, which debuted in January 1995 and went on sale the following month in GSR and RS trim,

WRX vs. EVO

Ever-changing rally regulations meant that it wasn't long before an updated street going Lancer Evolution III arrived. It was more garish in the looks department, with a bigger front airdam, rocker panel extensions and new rear spoiler. Although heavier than the I or II, it had a more powerful 270 hp engine, and was actually quicker. Mitsubishi Japan

looked quite a bit different than preceding iterations. However, from a mechanical standpoint, it was very similar to the II. The most noticeable changes on the III were a larger, restyled front air dam with bigger scoops for the brake cooling ducts and front-mounted intercooler, plus a completely new three-post rear deck wing with the third brake light incorporated into the spoiler base instead of at the top. Rocker panel

Capable of running from 0-60 mph in 4.8 seconds and covering the standing quarter mile in 12.8, the Evo III was an absolute hoot to drive. As before, all 5,000 cars were destined for Japanese-market consumption.

extensions and a revised rear bumper cover rounded out the exterior mods. As before, Mitsubishi planned for 5,000 Evo IIIs to be sold, again on the Japanese market only, though a few did slip away to foreign shores (the vast majority of the 220 exported cars were RS models). Under the hood, the 4G63 got new pistons for Lancer Evo III duty, bumping up compression from 8.5 to 9.0:1. Tweaks to the exhaust system, turbocharger, and intercooler yielded another 10 bhp, bumping the overall power rating to 270 bhp (DIN) at 6,250 rpm. The five-speed manual gearbox (still the only transmission available) received a slightly taller fifth gear in an attempt to boost fuel economy.

The Evo III also received a revamped interior with new upholstery patterns and shifter handle. The GSR model also got a new, three-spoke Momo steering wheel. In addition, on the GSR, the color palette shifted slightly and a new, not-so-subtle hue called Dandelion Yellow replaced the more somber Moonlight Blue Pearl offered on the Evo II.

Although this latest Evo was again some 20 lbs heavier than its immediate predecessors, performance was every bit as good as the II. Official runs clocked 4.8 seconds for the 0–60 mph test, while the standing quarter-mile came in at 12.8 seconds. For an AWD machine with a peaky engine, that was simply amazing stuff. Few cars for the same price could compete against it—although the Subaru Impreza STi was catching up, something that didn't go unnoticed by the folks at Mitsubishi and Ralliart.

SUBARU: THE STI VERSION II

In many respects, the first two STi models were very special cars, but demand for both of them, in particular the Type RA version, had shown that it would be wise for Subaru to consider higher volumes for these cars. That meant that another facility other than the STi works at Mitaka needed to be utilized in order to cope with greater production levels. It was decided that from 1995 on, future STi variants would be built alongside regular WRXs and Imprezas at Subaru's massive Yajima facility in Ota City. In order to differentiate these cars from previous editions, Subaru referred to the 1995 STi model as the "Version II" car.

As if to signify the "going mainstream" aspect of the STi, the Version II cars were offered in sedan or wagon form, as Pure Sports, a 555 Edition, or a type RA. Like with previous regular WRX cars, the sedans and wagons had engines with slightly different states of tune. The STi Version II sedans featured an EJ20 engine rated at 275 bhp and 235 lb-ft of torque, at 6,000 and 4,000 revs, respectively, while the wagons got a version of the then-regular WRX powerplant rated at 260 hp and 227 lb-ft of torque.

Although these cars were somewhat less special, the hard-core RA version in particular was still aimed squarely at die-hard rally homologation enthusiasts and was virtually built to order. Like the car it superseded, it came only in white. The 555 cars were a little less radical but sported WRC-inspired touches, such as a roof vent for the sedans, rally mud flaps, special Sports Blue paint with gold accents, 555 decals (installed at the buyer's request), and Speedline 16-inch wheels, naturally finished in gold. These cars were pretty scarce, as only 600 were built, with only a token of those being wagons. Not surprisingly, that made them rare and ultimately quite collectible, but if you wanted to feel like Colin McRae or Carlos Sainz on the open road, at the time there was no better substitute.

The Version II cars went on sale in August 1995 and were quickly snapped up. By this point, the WRX and its derivatives were already accounting for a hefty chunk of overall Impreza sales. And while Japan was getting its taste of a rally-inspired street STi, in Banbury, England, Prodrive was already testing the waters with a limited-edition, turn-key car alongside its tuning parts catalog: the Series McRae. Launched in mid-1995, its timing could not have been better, as the 1995 WRC was shaping up to be a memorable one for Subaru.

MITSUBISHI: TURNING UP THE HEAT

For 1995, rule changes required teams to field cars in each and every WRC round (eight were listed for the season). To get around budget issues, MRE decided to field Group N cars, courtesy of Ralliart Germany, entering them as works machines. Because the Evo III wasn't

ARRIVAL

For the 1995 season, Mitsubishi was able to get around the obstacle of having to field cars in every round by running Group N cars in some events as works entries. The team dominated in Sweden, with Eriksson winning on his home turf.
Mitsubishi Japan

homologated in time for the start of the season, MRE continued to run IIs with a few updates, among them new differentials. Signing up as drivers for the '95 season were Kenneth Eriksson; Tommi Makinen (replacing Armin Schwarz, who went to Toyota); and, for select rounds, Italian driver Andrea Aghini.

The season opener in Monte Carlo saw Makinen charge hard from the opening stage. It looked like he was set to finish third overall, but a diff on his car went during the final day, knocking him out of contention. Still, his times on each of the stages up to that point allowed him to finish fourth overall. Aghini, in the other Group A works entry, after a canny drive, came in sixth place.

From here, the WRC moved north to Sweden—the first time this rally had been included in the WRC for a number of years. It proved to be a Mitsubishi race all the way. Eriksson and Makinen, clearly in their element, dominated from start to finish. They delivered a stunning works 1-2 overall, despite the onset of snow squalls during the latter part of the event. With this result, MRE had clearly shown that given the right conditions it would be a force to be reckoned with.

WRX vs. EVO

Group N cars were chosen to run in Portugal. The top-finishing Mitsubishi, driven by locals Rui Madeira and Nuno Silva, came in ninth, while the female crew of Holderied and Thorner finished 11th. As the teams headed to Corsica, Ralliart Europe finally had the newly homologated Evo III Group A machines ready. Aghini and Makinen were given the new cars, but on the tarmac roads it was Aghini's turn to shine. Although Celica driver Didier Auriol (on home turf) and rival Frenchman and Escort pilot Francois Delecour set the pace, Aghini managed an impressive third overall.

Although fifth was the best place a Lancer could muster in New Zealand, Australia was another matter. Amid the heat and dust, Eriksson (in one of his favorite events) was on form once again, putting in a steady, progressive performance and showing his dirt and gravel skills. He even out-drove Colin McRae to come home in first place, giving Mitsubishi its second win of the season. In Catalunya, a race fraught with controversy, it was a mixed bag. Makinen made steady progress until the last day when he misjudged a corner and slid off the road, ending his chances. Aghini, meanwhile, started off in very good form, and he secured a fifth-place finish by the end of day four.

Finn Tommi Makinen, whose name became synonymous with the team in later years, signed up as the official number two works driver in 1995. He's seen here plugging thorough the Welsh mud in the RAC. Mitsubishi Japan

ARRIVAL

The RAC, the last race of the year, proved to be heartbreaker. Going into it, Mitsubishi and Eriksson were leading the championship. On the first day, things appeared to be going well, but then Makinen damaged his suspension on the second day, forcing him into retirement. Eriksson, on his last outing as a MRE works driver, was doing well until he lost control and plowed his car into a marsh. This paved the way for archrival Subaru to take top honors for 1995.

Mitsubishi wasn't about to let that one slip stop them. For 1996, the battle for WRC supremacy between these two automakers would prove to be more intense than ever.

SUBARU: YEAR OF THE SCOTSMAN

As always, a new WRC season brought with it some changes to the rules. For the Group A cars, FIA regulations required new tire specs for tarmac, gravel, and snow. Smaller-diameter inlet tubes to the turbochargers were also required in an effort to level the playing field among the top teams. Prodrive and Subaru sought to make maximum use of this new restriction. New, more aggressive camshafts were specified, along with changes to the ECU and tweaks to the turbocharger wastegate to offset the loss in power output. An electronic front differential was also employed at the start of the 1995 season. As per the previous year, SWRT and Prodrive built three Group A spec works cars to run—one for Carlos Sainz and one for Colin McRae, both of whom renewed their contracts for a full season, plus a third that was split between Richard Burns and team newcomer, tarmac specialist Piero Liatti.

The season kicked off once again in Monte Carlo, and the Subarus got off to a great start, setting the pace on the first day. McRae shot off like a rocket, making good time, but conditions got increasingly slippery. During the second special stage, he skidded off into a snowbank, setting him back and putting teammate Sainz in the lead by the end of the first day. Day two saw a hotly contested battle for the lead between Sainz and a reinvigorated Francois Delecour in his Ford Escort Cosworth, but by the end of the day, Sainz was still ahead. Both McRae and Liatti slid off the road the following morning in almost the exact same spot, and although McRae was forced to retire, Liatti managed to get his car back on the road and complete the rally in eighth place. Sainz and co-driver Luis Moya managed to just stave off the Delecour assault and secured the overall win for the season opener.

Snowy Sweden marked a crucial change in the WRC series. It didn't prove to be Subaru's event because all three of the works entries—Sainz, McRae, and local Mats Jonsson—retired with mechanical troubles. As if to signify things to come, the Mitsubishi team had a spectacular run, with both Kenneth Eriksson and Tommi Makinen clearly at home with both the Lancer Evolution II rally car and the snowy conditions, even with reduced visibility in some spots.

The tables turned in Portugal. Sainz was off to a good start, and although he had a battle on his hands with Juha Kankkunen in the brand new works Celica, the Scoob's Pirelli tires handled the gravel conditions much better. When a rock damaged Juha's suspension, Carlos got a much-needed breather to start the second day. Ultimately, Portugal proved a good rally for SWRT. Sainz and Moya crossed the line first overall, McRae and Ringer came in third, and Richard Burns and Robert Reid managed to come in eighth.

The Tour de Corse was a mixed bag, as the Subaru team struggled to keep pace with the Escorts, Evos, and Auriol's Celica. Evidently,

Without doubt the biggest news of the 1995 season was Subaru winning both the manufacturer's and driver's championships in the WRC, with Colin McRae (seen here at speed in the Swedish Rally) becoming the youngest driver ever to do so. Subaru Global

the 18-inch Pirelli tarmac tires just weren't helping, and the best finish the team could obtain was a fourth, fifth, and six from Sainz, McRae, and Liatti, respectively (though these points were invaluable in the championship race).

Down in New Zealand, McRae was looking forward to another good event; with two victories under his belt there, he was aiming for a third. It all came together for him on day three as the drivers attempted the tough Motu stage. The Impreza proved well suited to the twisty, narrow roads, and McRae's driving style put him far ahead of his nearest challenger, Didier Auriol. His performance here was enough to keep him in the lead, and he scored his third New Zealand win in three years. Peter Bourne finished seventh, and Richard Burns was making good progress until his engine got a soaking while crossing a creek.

As the teams moved to Australia, Carlos Sainz was back in the saddle, a shoulder injury having forced him to sit out the New Zealand rally. However, luck didn't go his way, and a damaged radiator brought retirement early on. Bourne didn't fare much better, and only McRae lasted until the end. As usual, he proved exceedingly quick, but he was not quite fast enough overall to match Kenneth Eriksson in his Mitsubishi, who just seemed to have the edge in the dirt and mud. Still, a second-place finish for SWRT was better than nothing.

A new fixture on the WRC calendar, the Rally Catalunya in Spain, proved controversial. The Toyota team was banned for a whole year because of its use of illegal air intake restrictors, and all its accumulated points were reneged for the 1995 season. As a result, that put Mitsubishi and Subaru in joint first place heading to Spain. Team orders meant that despite a fine drive from McRae and Ringer, Carlos Sainz was declared the winner. Shortly afterwards, the Spaniard announced, of all things, he would be leaving the team come the end of the year. Still, winning the top three spots (Liatti came in third) helped bolster the team's championship points total.

There was still one more round to go, and although the constructor's cup was almost a given for Subaru, Sainz and McRae were neck-and-

WRX vs. EVO

1995 proved to be a banner year for the Subaru World Rally Team, as its cars were very competitive. A new event this year was the Rally de Catalunya in Spain, which was won, perhaps quite fittingly, by Spaniard Carlos Sainz, though the final results were surrounded by controversy over team orders. Subaru Global

neck in the points race. In order for either of these guys to win, one of them had to at least finish the next event, the RAC.

At the start, it looked like the twin Mitsubishis of Eriksson and Makinen would cause some real problems, but Makinen went out with a broken suspension and then Eriksson slid off the road. With the main threat gone, the Subaru team plowed on. Sainz took the lead by the end of the second day of his last drive for the team (he signed on to drive for Ford in 1996 after his Toyota deal fell through), but he was eclipsed by McRae, who rocketed through almost every special stage, setting the fastest time on all but a handful. It was enough to secure the championship, and, at 27 years old, McRae was the youngest driver in history to win it. With Sainz coming in second and Burns third overall, the RAC was a fine finish to an interesting and sometimes challenging rally season. Despite capturing both driver's and manufacturer's championships for the first time, SWRT knew that that it couldn't rest on its laurels. The 1995 season had proven that Mitsubishi Ralliart was becoming a force to be reckoned with in WRC circles, and Subaru needed to be more prepared than ever.

CHAPTER 3

THE ROAD TO STARDOM

As the cult of Japanese performance cars continued to grow during the 1990s, Mitsubishi and Subaru found themselves locking horns in a battle for supremacy, both on the street and in the World Rally Championship, asserting their dominance against long-established players such as Ford and Toyota.

1996

MITSUBISHI: LANCER'S NEW GENERATION

On October 17, 1995, Mitsubishi took the wraps off its latest small family car—the fifth-generation Lancer. Styling was evolutionary, though slightly sharper contours and a new door handle treatment gave it a more modern look. Besides this, a standard high-mounted stoplight and a redesigned tail treatment were the most noticeable touches. The last was important because trunk room was increased quite a bit when compared with its predecessor. Refinements included better interior ergonomics, improved sound deadening, and minor tweaks to the chassis and suspension. Model choices ranged from the thrifty 1.3-liter T sedan up to the 1.8-liter turbocharged, all-wheel drive GSX. The Evolution variant was still a year away, however.

As the latest Lancer hit the showrooms, chief engineer Chiaki Tsujimura and his team were busy readying Ralliart's next homologation special—the Evolution IV, a car that would emerge to become the most radical of this species yet. Mitsubishi's top brass were determined to see their rally car get its first tarmac win, but there was still work to be done both on the street and the WRC circuit.

SUBARU: V-LIMITED ANNOUNCED

Winning the 1995 World Rally Championship in both driver and constructor categories was no small feat for the Subaru World Rally team. Back at headquarters in Japan, that meant celebrations were in order. To that end, a special-edition WRX V-Limited was announced in January 1996 (covered in greater detail in Appendix B).

MITSUBISHI: WORLD RALLY ASCENSION

It would be fair to say that, as far as Mitsubishi Ralliart was concerned, the 1996 season marked a turning point. Having already showed tremendous promise, Finn Tommi Makinen got a renewed contract (as the only full-time MRE works driver for 1996), though Richard Burns, having switched from Subaru, took the driver's seat in a second car for a select number of rounds. The team employed the Evolution III for much of the year, as the homologated IV was not ready until much later.

With the somewhat controversial rotation system still in effect, there was no season opener in Monte Carlo; instead the first round began in snowy Sweden. Having had to let teammate Kenneth Eriksson win the 1995 event, Makinen got down to business almost immediately. He blasted off on the first day and set the fastest times on 10 special stages. His torrid charge continued, and, as if to prove a point, he kept up this pace all the way to the end, earning a placing ahead of Carlos Sainz and the Subaru of reigning world champion Colin McRae. A pair of Group N cars finished 14th and 16th overall.

THE ROAD TO STARDOM

The 1996 WRC season began in Sweden. Tommi Makinen put in a sterling performance to win the event, setting the fastest time on 10 separate stages! Mitsubishi Japan

The classic Safari was back on the WRC calendar for 1996. Makinen faced some rather interesting weather conditions and a broken driveshaft on day one, but took it all in his stride. With the car repaired he pressed on, making good enough time to start off in first place by day three. From there, he just kept going, taking first overall and becoming the first driver in two decades to win this challenging event on his first attempt.

Japanese rally ace and Safari veteran Kenjiro Shinozuka, along with his Finnish co-driver, Pentti Kuukkala, in a second Group A car came home sixth overall. Clearly, this Lancer Evolution was becoming a car to beat. Indonesia was on the WRC calendar this year, and for some reason the works team found it rather tough going. Engine troubles following a pair of accidents plagued both Makinen and Burns, with neither driver managing to finish (Burns crashed into a tree). Instead, the victory went to Carlos Sainz and Ford. The Group N entries fared much better with one, driven by Chandra Alim, finishing ninth overall and a second car, piloted by Bambang Hartono, coming in right behind.

Back in Europe for the Acropolis, the dust and rocks once again proved to be a challenge for all except Colin McRae. With but a single works car entered, MRE piled on the pressure as best as it could; Makinen, although not quite able to match the Scotsman's pace, managed to keep going despite suffering from steering problems early on day two. He took second overall, sufficient to keep the Finn ahead of the Subaru driver in the championship race.

Just over a month later, the WRC circus traveled to the other side of the world once again, this time to Argentina. Mitsubishi dominated, with Makinen and co-driver Seppo Harjanne thriving on the loose surface. Tommi was in a class of his own and led this one from start to finish. Burns and Robert Reid in the other Group A car also did well and came home in fifth place overall.

The 1000 Lakes in Finland was next and, as in years past, it proved to be a rally dominated by Finns. Tommi Makinen was naturally in his element here, but he faced stiff competition from Juha Kankkunen in the Toyota Celica, who kept the pressure on right until the last stage. A second Group A car was entered in this race, driven by Lasse Lampi, and he did pretty well, too, finishing in eighth place overall, ahead of another Celica piloted by Rui Madeira.

By Australia, Makinen had extended his lead in the driver's championship to the point that a victory would secure the championship over nearest rival Carlos Sainz. Despite the wettest Rally Australia most could remember, he pulled it off. His victory marked the first for a champion driving a Mitsubishi, but with two rounds still to go, the constructor's race between Ralliart and Subaru was a dead heat.

On the San Remo in mid-October, former world champion Didier Auriol took a seat behind the wheel of one of the MRE Group A cars. Despite being a tarmac specialist driving a tarmac event, he failed to finish, as did Makinen, who suffered a spectacular crash that injured his co-driver Seppo Harjanne, who remained out of action for the last round in Spain.

After a very strong season, the Rallye de Catalunya proved to be a bit of an anticlimax for the Mitsubishi works team. Burns failed to finish.

THE ROAD TO STARDOM

Although Makinen was the only official MRE works driver for the 1996 season, Richard Burns and Didier Auriol drove at select events. In the San Remo, conditions were slippery and neither Didier (shown), nor Makinen finished. Mitsubishi Japan

With fellow Finn (but unfamiliar co-driver) Juha Repo navigating, Makinen wasn't able to match his usual pace. He just couldn't catch the Subaru of McRae and Ringer and finished a disappointing fifth. Despite Makinen's driver's championship, Subaru took home a second consecutive constructor's cup. Still, the Mitsubishi team had proved itself as being at the top of the pack, and the other teams, especially Subaru and Ford, found it tough at times to keep pace. Ralliart and Mitsubishi desperately wanted to get that constructor's crown for 1997, and as the season ended, it looked like they would finally have the car to do it.

SUBARU: FACING TOUGHER COMPETITION

Just as the last of Subaru's V-Limited cars were finding owners, plans were already in place for SWRT's next assault on the World Rally Championship. As the incumbent champions, Subaru and McRae had a lot to lose. With the Mitsubishi threat appearing larger with each passing event, it looked as if tough times were ahead.

Italian tarmac king Piero Liatti, after some impressive driving in 1995, was signed on as a full-time works driver. Former Mitsubishi stalwart and 1986 world champion Kenneth Eriksson replaced Sainz. On paper, it looked like SWRT was ready to take on all comers.

The first rally on the 1996 WRC calendar was Sweden. Although a three-car team was fielded, the last was a guest entry, as teamless Didier Auriol was offered a one-off drive. Some bizarre conditions and a lack of ice and snow in several spots wreaked havoc with the studded tires for many teams on the first day. Subaru was no exception, as both McRae and Eriksson suffered with poor traction. However, a heavy snowfall arrived for the following day, and both drivers, armed with much better bite, began making progress. Although he couldn't catch Tommi Makinen or former teammate Carlos Sainz, McRae started making strides, passing Ari Vatanen and then getting by Juha Kankkunen as the latter struggled to get to grips with his big, wide, and heavy Toyota Celica. McRae finished the rally in third overall, the only non-Nordic driver in the top 10. Teammate Eriksson came home in fifth, behind Kankkunen.

The second event on the 1996 calendar was the grueling Safari, which featured some of the longest special stages in the world, searing temperatures, and numerous hazards (the stages weren't closed to traffic). Shock absorber problems hobbled all the Subaru works cars. Despite this, Eriksson and co-driver Staffan Parmander managed to finish second overall, with McRae coming in fourth (despite a rock taking out his rear suspension) and Liatti finishing fifth in the other works entry.

Indonesia brought with it some challenging conditions. The combination of heat, humidity, and some sections that were exceedingly slippery made it quite treacherous for nearly all drivers, causing a spate of accidents and breakdowns. Eriksson's car developed mechanical issues, forcing him to retire, but McRae appeared to be on his way to victory, especially once a hard landing put rival Tommi Makinen and Mitsubishi out of contention. However, on Special Stage 10, Colin misjudged a turn, and the Subaru barrel rolled for some 80 meters

THE ROAD TO STARDOM

Three works Subaru entries were fielded for the 1996 season for McRae, Piero Liatti, and Kenneth Eriksson. In the grueling Safari rally, where attrition often takes a major toll, all three cars managed to finish, in second (Eriksson), fourth (McRae) and fifth (Liatti). Subaru Global

before coming to a rest on its roof. The car was utterly destroyed, but again McRae and Ringer walked away. With both Eriksson and the champ now out, that left Liatti in the third works car to keep the end up for Subaru. Liatti, with great instruction from co-driver Fabrizia Pons, managed to avoid just about every obstacle in his path, bringing the car home in a magnificent second place behind the Escort of Sainz and Moya.

As the teams exchanged muggy Sumatra for the dust and rocks of Greece, the three-car team of McRae, Eriksson, and Liatti was back in action. Colin had a battle on his hands almost from the beginning, facing off against the sole MRE works entry of Makinen and co-driver Seppo Harjanne. To add further drama, mischievous spectators put obstacles in the way on Special Stage 6, altering the route, and a huge rock caused both McRae and Eriksson to take evasive action and go off course. On day two, the Scotsman extended his lead as Makinen suffered steering problems, and a careful drive on day three netted first place. The other works cars came in fourth (Liatti/Pons) and fifth (Eriksson/Parmander).

The Subaru team didn't have a great rally in Argentina. In an unfortunate incident, McRae first hit a wandering spectator and then a nasty rock that damaged his rear suspension. Although repairs were carried out at the next service interval, problems persisted and the Scotsman retired. Eriksson made steady progress throughout the rally and was lying in second come the last day, but a punctured tire allowed Carlos Sainz to slip by. Still, he and Parmander managed a solid third, while Liatti brought the other remaining works car home in seventh place.

New Zealand wasn't on the calendar in 1996 because of the rotation system, so the next WRC event was the 1000 Lakes in Finland. The rally didn't get off to the greatest start, thanks to a severe accident that injured more than 20 spectators and killed one on the first stage. With a locally entered Celica (Toyota Team Europe still being banned for the use of illegal air restrictors at this point), former world champion

Another surprise during the 1996 WRC season was Greece, where once again all three cars finished, this time with McRae winning the event. Both he and Eriksson (shown) did have minor off-course excursions en route, however. Subaru Global

THE ROAD TO STARDOM

Juha Kankkunen set the stage. Of Subaru's two cars, reigning champ McRae crashed on Stage 6, where he rolled another car into retirement. Eriksson, clearly more at home with the conditions, managed to keep a steady pace and proved the quickest non-Finnish driver in the event, coming in sixth overall.

A very wet Australia saw many drivers struggling in the mud and having to cope with vast puddles of water and deep crossings. McRae struggled with traction problems throughout the event but kept his cool and plodded on to an honest fourth-place finish. Eriksson put in another excellent drive in one of his favorite events. Apart from Tommi Makinen, he was far and away the quickest through nearly all stages, as he battled a very determined Carlos Sainz. He managed to fend off the Spaniard and bring his Subaru home in second place, four seconds ahead of the Ford driver. Makinen's scorching pace had sealed his first world championship driver's title, but with two more events still on the calendar, the constructor's cup remained very much undecided.

In the 1996 Rally San Remo, McRae was back on form after disappointing performances in Argentina, Finland, and Australia. On the early, long gravel stages, the Scotsman proved to be in his element, setting the fastest time. Piero Liatti, on home turf, almost kept pace. As the drivers entered the Italian Riviera, Carlos Sainz began another charge. When Liatti couldn't get his car started on the last day, Sainz moved up to the number two spot and started catching McRae. Still, Colin reached the finish line 11 seconds ahead. Thanks to his win and a fifth-place finish by Kenneth Eriksson behind the Belgians Bruno Thiry (Ford) and Freddy Loix (Toyota), the 1996 constructor's championship was within reach for Subaru.

Traditionally, the last round of the year was the RAC in Britain, but with the rotation system in effect, Catalunya was the final event of the 1996 season. Liatti, a tarmac specialist, clearly loved the conditions in Spain and set the pace on the first day. Hot on his heels were the two Belgians, Thiry and Loix, with McRae in fourth. As the rally progressed, Colin started reeling in the others. With no official team orders, McRae took second by day three, battling it out with Liatti, who was on fine form. Ultimately, the Scotsman took a slim lead, but with it he beat out Carlos Sainz to finish second in the driver's championship, also giving Subaru the constructor's championship for the second year in a row.

1997

MITSUBISHI: HAIL THE IV

Introduced in September 1996 as the WRC season raced toward its conclusion, the street-going version of the Lancer Evolution IV caused quite a stir. Like its predecessors, this latest offering came in GSR and RS forms. Outwardly, when compared with the III, this new car looked all business, with busy, boy-racer touches, though thankfully they were functional. The front was particularly aggressive, with a massive air dam that housed a big scoop to feed the intercooler, flanked by equally massive PIAA driving lights. The aluminum hood gained a larger scoop, and the rear spoiler featured a center pedestal and a base that curved away on each side. Perimeter extensions were

Based upon the fifth generation Lancer sedan, Mitsubishi unveiled the Evolution IV in September 1996. Looking more businesslike than previous incarnations, it boasted a 4G63 engine with numerous improvements, boosting power and torque to 280 bhp and 260 lb-ft. As before, two models were offered, the GSR (shown) and the stripped-down RS. Mitsubishi Japan

carried around the car, from the front bumper to the side rocker panels and wraparound rear valance. Engineers paid considerable attention to making this the best-performing Evolution yet. Although the regular sixth-generation Lancer boasted increased torsional rigidity, on the Evo IV extra bracing was employed around the cowl, upper frame rails, and shock towers, plus RS models added a strut tower brace.

And while the new Evo might have been 40 percent stiffer than the base Lancer, that extra bracing translated into more weight. Thus, in order to maintain performance quite a few changes were made to the 4G63 engine. For starters, the engineers chose to mount it in completely the opposite direction (though still transverse). A new red cam cover hinted at big internal changes, including new, lighter, lower-compression pistons (8.0:1 instead of 9.5:1), a thinner and lighter block casting, and also a new, thinner cylinder head that housed a pair of new-profile camshafts and sturdier valvetrain pieces. Plumbing was quite a bit different, too, with a manifold that featured new, straight-through intake runners and an air injection system upstream of the turbocharger, which now was a different Mitsubishi TD05HR unit.

The intercooler was enlarged by some 15 percent, and the exhaust system was revised, becoming a larger, single system, instead of the twin-pipe setup employed on the III. This bigger bore setup helped reduce backpressure, improving mid- and top-end throttle response. Maximum power output was now quoted as 280 hp (the maximum permitted by Japanese legislation at the time), while torque stood at an impressive 260 lb-ft. A new five-speed gearbox with shorter ratios was also employed to aid in quicker takeoffs.

The IV also featured a more sophisticated independent rear suspension with four links and was the first of these cars to introduce the now legendary active yaw control (AYC). This was an electronically controlled rear differential that would automatically increase or reduce torque to the left or right wheels in cornering conditions to maximize grip. Combined with the 16-inch wheels and tires and bigger 11.6-inch front and 11.2-inch brakes, the Evo IV was quite a different car to pilot. Contemporary road tests were very favorable, with many

WRX vs. EVO

Improved interior ergonomics were a hallmark of the IV, as was a quicker-shifting five-speed gearbox with shorter ratios. This was the first Evo model to employ the hallowed Active Yaw Control as standard fitment on the GSR and optional on the RS.
Mitsubishi Japan

testers commenting on the car's greater refinement, stability, and surefootedness at high speeds, somewhat contrary to the car's more aggressive looks. The mainstream GSR variant, as with previous editions, came fully loaded with air conditioning, power windows, locks, and mirrors, and standard Recaro seats with specific stitching. The palette of exterior colors it was offered in included Parma Red, Icella Blue Pearl, Pyrenees Black Pearl, Steel Silver metallic, or Scotia White. The RS version, as ever, was aimed at the more serious enthusiast. Besides extra stiffening, it featured shorter third through fifth gears for even better acceleration.

In addition, RS buyers could choose between two final drive ratios: 4.529:1, which was the tall option and the same as on the GSR, or a short 4.875:1. The RS model kept the Evo III's smaller brakes, but the larger GSR units were optional, as was the active yaw control rear diff, a helical limited-slip front differential, and a 16-inch alloy wheel and larger tire package.

As with previous Evos, demand was red-hot for the IV. The first batch of 6,000 cars sold out in just three days—hardly surprising considering that the latest Evo was the closest thing to a full-blown WRC car one could buy for street use.

Although more refined than previous versions, the Evo IV was still very much a hooligan. Road testers and enthusiasts alike adored the car for its raucous personality, crazy acceleration, and simply amazing handling attributes. Simply put, very few cars were as quick in point-to-point driving. By 1996, word was spreading worldwide about this incredible machine. Mitsubishi built another 3,000 Evo IVs to satisfy home-market demand, but now it was clearly time to look at selling this car in overseas markets as a viable proposition.

SUBARU: MAJOR UPDATES

In September 1996, just prior to the WRC season's end, Subaru took the wraps off an updated Impreza. Outwardly, it looked very similar to the 1993 to 1996 cars, but there were a number of technological improvements, enough to categorize it as a virtually new car in many respects. The styling, although very similar, was slightly more grown up with a nose and tail that were smoother and more contemporary (clear turn signal lenses at the back of Japanese-market cars eventually spread to export models). WRX and STi models also received a revised hood scoop with new vents and a modified front splitter. Refinement was emphasized, and each of the boxer engines offered in the latest Impreza were reworked considerably, with new, molybdenum-coated pistons designed to reduce friction, along with a new intake manifold, revised cylinder heads with improved cooling passages and new valvetrain pieces, recalibrated electronics, and an intercooler that was now mounted flat (instead of at an angle) underneath the hood scoop. The EJ20 four, as fitted to the latest WRX, also featured a more efficient, Mitsubishi-sourced TD04L turbocharger that boosted

WRX vs. EVO

Subaru launched an updated line of GC chassis Imprezas in the latter half of 1996. Outwardly they looked very similar, but a number of engineering improvements made them more powerful and fun to drive. This is a Japanese domestic market 1997 WRX sedan. Subaru Global

power to 280 DIN bhp (the maximum power rating then permitted by Japanese law). Perhaps more impressive was the torque figure, which swelled to 242 lb-ft. Wagons featured a differently tuned version of this engine, but it still got a bump in power—up to 240 bhp and 224 lb-ft. Although a five-speed manual gearbox was still standard, revised forward ratios were specified along with a new, shorter-throw shifter and revised synchros to improve not only overall acceleration, but also shifting feel as well. This helped answer the longstanding criticism of ropey gear changing on Subaru manual gearboxes.

Other technical changes included improved chassis stiffening, revised shock valving, and tauter steering, though the wheel was actually lighter to the touch than before. In addition, the WRX wagon also got a new AP Suretrac rear differential for improved tire grip. The wheels were enlarged to 7x16-inchers with Bridgestone P205/50VR16 Potenza tires. As before, the WRX Type RA remained the more hardcore, bare-bones offering—it had no side extensions nor a rear deck spoiler, and it came with utilitarian black exterior mirrors and door handles (the standard WRX had them in body color). The RA was offered only in Feather White for 1997, while the regular WRX could be had in five different hues, including silver, red, blue, and black.

On the home market, the Version III WRX debuted to rave reviews from the local automotive press, though the RA was still considered to be the hard-core driver's car, requiring considerably more concentration and effort to drive than the regular WRX. It was quite an accomplishment for Subaru to still offer such a pure performance vehicle, especially in an age where automobiles were becoming increasingly docile and easy to drive.

Along with the standard updated WRX models, a new Version III STi and STi Type RA were also unveiled. Outwardly, these were distinguished from their lesser brethren by STi-branded front foglight covers, light pink grille badging, prominent WRX logos on the trunk lid (plus a roof vent and rear spoiler on the STi RA sedan), and more visible spoilers on STi wagons. These cars also boasted unique interior upgrades, including STi-specific seats with embroidered logos, an

Besides the "regular" WRX, STi also released a batch of new cars, dubbed Version III. These were the quickest up to that time thanks to a very torquey EJ20 engine that made 253 lb-ft. They were also the first to adopt the trademark STi foglight covers.
Subaru Global

optional Nardi three-spoke steering wheel with a carbon fiber hub, a carbon fiber center stack (regular STi only), and special red stitching on the steering wheel and shifter. As before, the Type RA featured fewer creature comforts and less interior sound deadening.

Mechanically, these cars received similar changes to the standard WRX. The EJ20K engine in the STi versions featured new, lighter, and higher compression pistons good for an 8.0:1 squeeze, plus an ECU with revised throttle mapping and more boost from the turbocharger. Other upgrades included a bigger, STi-specific intercooler, a revised cooling system with a bigger-capacity radiator, and a unique, low-restriction exhaust with a single tailpipe. So although power remained at 280 bhp, torque jumped to a meaty 253 lb-ft. Thus, the 1997 STis were the quickest ones yet.

In addition, the hard-core Type RA also received standard automatic water spray for the intercooler, plus the now-trademark red intake manifold and a special carbon fiber/aluminum strut brace. In order to handle the extra torque, the standard five-speed manual gearbox was strengthened for STi use and a stouter clutch was installed. Type RAs also featured up-rated differentials including a new driver-controlled center unit, though the rear diff was still mechanical (a viscous on the regular STi). The RA also offered an optional and quicker 13:1 steering ratio (15:1 was standard) and a specific brake package with larger rear discs, though the fronts on both models featured 277mm (10.9-inch) front discs gripped by four-piston calipers. Wheel and tire fitments mirrored those on the regular WRX, although the STi could be fitted with a handsome set of dealer-installed multispoke BBS wheels.

On the export front, Subaru began making a few waves for the 1997 model year—especially with its blown Imprezas and particularly in two of the hottest markets, Australia and the United Kingdom. The Aussies were among the first to receive the original WRX, which had debuted to favorable public reaction, but there hadn't been a major update for some time. Along with the more grown-up fascia, the Australians finally got an automatic version of the WRX sedan, which was joined a few months later by a slushbox-equipped WRX wagon. Although slightly slower, the automatic cars proved rather popular with their target buyers. Interestingly enough, five-speed WRXs sold in Oz featured a nice three-spoke Momo steering wheel, while the automatic cars got a somewhat dull-looking four spoker with an airbag housed in the hub.

In addition, Subaru Australia actually lowered the price of a new Rex, another good strategy, especially in light of the fact that new cars in Australia were—and still are—rather pricey on the whole. The Aussie cars also got similar engine tweaks to the home-market offerings, but in this case the result was 214 hp and 211 lb-ft of torque at a lower, more useable rev range (5,600 and 4,000 rpm, respectively). One major difference between these and the Japanese cars concerned the wheels and tires. While the home-market models got a 16-inch combo, the Aussie cars strangely stuck with the 15-inch setup from 1995 and 1996. Australia also received the first Club Spec edition WRX, a limited-production version aimed at enthusiasts/amateur racers (see the appendix on special edition cars).

On the other side of the world, in the other important RHD export market, Subaru chose the 1996 Motor Show at the National Exhibition Centre just outside in Birmingham in November to showcase its newest offerings. The British-market equivalent to the WRX was still called the Impreza 2000 Turbo, and like the Japanese and Australian cars, it received updates for 1997. With a higher compression ratio, along with freer-flowing heads, the new Mitsu TD04L hairdryer, and changes to the ignition and ECU, it was rated at 208 bhp and 214 lb-ft of torque. Again, the new car was more tractable, with peak power and torque coming in at lower rpm. Like the Aussie cars, the British Turbo retained a 15-inch tire and wheel package, but it received the same new car facelift, including a revised front fascia, rear bumper, and side extensions. Most Impreza 2000 Turbos were loaded to the gills, with options such as air conditioning (still a relative novelty in a mid-priced car in the United Kingdom), leather seats, a sunroof, and power locks and mirrors. The British motoring press, traditionally some of the harshest when it comes to judging foreign cars, praised the car's performance and handling, despite criticizing the interior as being "bland and rather dated." In March 1997, Subaru dealers in the United Kingdom also got the opportunity to sell the limited edition Catalunya (see special edition cars).

A NEW BREED OF STI

The updated WRX and Turbo, despite receiving good reviews, were perhaps merely a warm-up, at least as far as enthusiasts and rally homologation were concerned. In January 1997, STi took off the wraps of its latest WRC homologation special, the WRX STi Type R. Although technically part of the Version III STi series, the Type R differed substantially in the fact that it was a two-door coupe, using the body of the Impreza-based Retna (introduced in 1995). For Type R duty, the look was beefed up with a STi-spec front air dam, rocker panel extensions, rear bumper, and prominent decklid spoiler. The Type R was offered in Sonic Blue, Feather White, and rather shocking Chase Yellow exterior colors. Rolling stock was also STi-spec, with the same 16-inch, five-spoke wheels and the same P205/50VR16 Potenza tires, although the rims were finished in gold for the blue cars and black for the white and yellow ones, giving them a rather menacing appearance.

Mechanically, the Type R was like the STi Type RA with an EJ20 engine rated at 280 hp and 253 lb-ft of torque, a close-ratio five-speed manual gearbox, and that car's differential and braking setup. However, unlike the RA, the new performance coupe came as a fully loaded car, with power windows, locks, and mirrors (that also folded electrically); automatic climate control; height-adjustable front bucket seats; and some unique interior features of its own, including blue-faced gauges and special SWRT 555 logos on the seat backs. Each of the Type R cars also carried a special 1996 rally victory badge on the decklid, along with Type R graphics on the trunk and rear doors. These Japanese-market-only coupes also received tinted quarter and rear window privacy glass.

THE ROAD TO STARDOM

MITSUBISHI: PUTTING IT TO WORK

One of the primary reasons for the creation of the Evolution IV was that Mitsubishi's Motorsports manager, Shouuke Ingnaki, desperately wanted "his baby" to win a WRC tarmac event. But, as always, there were more than a few difficulties to contend with. The FIA finally ditched the controversial rotation system for rally events in 1997 (whereby certain events would alternate every other year). Instead, each season would have the same fixed number of rally venues moving forward, but manufacturers were required to enter each of the 14 rounds in order to compete. In addition, the old homologation regulations bit the dust as the previous Group A gave way to the World Rally Car format. The new rules meant that a manufacturer no longer had to build 2,500 street-going examples of its rally car to qualify, so more dedicated rally machines could be fielded, even if they were contracted out to specialist companies. Still, the basic car itself had to be based on a road-going production machine.

Although rivals Ford and Subaru embraced the new WRC regulations wholeheartedly, Mitsubishi stuck with machines that followed the old, but still legal, Group A regulations. However, unlike previous years, the new Evo IV was ready to go right from the first round. Tommi Makinen signed on for a full season with the team as the number one driver, partnering once again with Seppo Harjanne. German driver Uwe Nittel, who teamed up with veteran Group N co-driver Tina Thorner, also signed on to drive (mainly in the old Evo III), while a third car—dubbed the Carisma GT, but in reality little more than a Group A spec Evo IV with different graphics and badging—was fielded for Richard Burns and co-driver Robert Reid.

After a two-year absence, the classic Monte Carlo rally was back on the WRC calendar for 1997, and it proved as eventful as ever, thanks to a tremendous range of weather and road conditions. The leaderboard amounted to musical chairs, with different drivers vying for the lead on each day. Makinen got off to a bit of slow start, coming in eighth on the first day, far behind the leader—young Belgian Freddy Loix in a Toyota Celica. Things began to improve on day two,

WRX vs. EVO

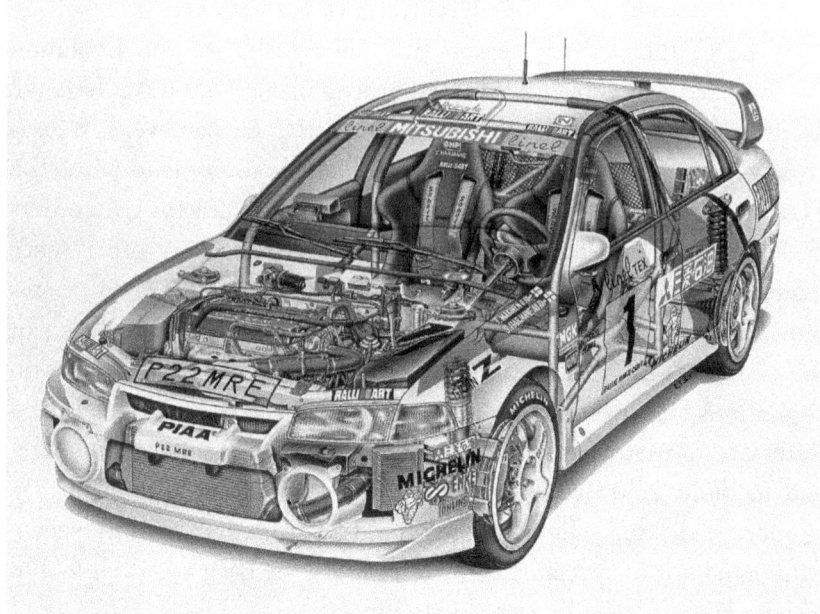

New rules were instigated for the 1997 World Rally Championship, allowing the top teams to field more radical cars. Interestingly Mitsubishi stuck with the old Group A regulations. As a result it developed the Evo IV and later V and VI into world-beating rally machines. Mitsubishi Japan

as Tommi locked horns with Carlos Sainz, finishing just a whisker behind him and second overall come the end of the day. It appeared Mitsubishi would have a great chance at winning this one, but a wrong tire selection on the second-to-last day dashed any hope of a win as Subaru's Piero Liatti and Carlos Sainz passed the Ralliart works driver. Still, despite some minor damage, Makinen managed to nurse his car to third overall while Nittel finished in fifth place.

Moving to Sweden, Makinen set the fastest times on the first day, but problems arose when he lost all his tire studs on day two after encountering some sections where there was little or no ice. A transmission service that took longer than normal set the Finn back even more. As a result, Tommi found himself in fifth place, behind Thomas Radstrom and far behind the Subarus of Eriksson and McRae.

THE ROAD TO STARDOM

He started chipping away, however, and got past both Radstrom and then McRae to finish third overall behind Erikson and Carlos Sainz, despite a spectacular spin on Special Stage 23. Nittel crashed out on the last day.

The Safari, compressed into a shorter, three-day format, still proved as grueling as ever. Makinen made steady progress in his Mitsubishi and by stage two had taken the lead, but this was short-lived. Like many other drivers, he suffered from tire punctures on day two (three almost at once), and although he elected to keep on going, he finally had to call it quits when the rear diff let go. Burns fared a lot better. He was in third when Makinen went out and piled the pressure on leader Colin McRae. Although minor suspension and clutch problems slowed his progress a bit, Burns brought home the Carisma GT in second overall—his best-ever result up to that point.

In Portugal, it finally came together for MRE and Makinen. Although Richard Burns retired with driveline issues, Tommi and the Evo IV were in top form, and the Finn was able to use the car's fast-shifting sequential gearbox to maximum advantage. The very first stage saw controversy rear its ugly head when Makinen's brake system was damaged following a weight inspection. The officials recognized their error and cancelled the stage, declaring a fresh start on Monday morning. By Stage 6, Makinen was coming on strong. With McRae out, Tommi caught and then passed a slowing Kenneth Eriksson, putting in a seamless drive to win his first rally since Australia in 1996. It was enough to put him in first place in the driver's championship race.

A milestone was reached in Catalunya. Although all eyes were on the F2 front-drive Peugeots of Francois Delecour and Gilles Panizzi, which proved very nimble through the tight corners, this tarmac event witnessed a three-car battle for the lead, with the Subarus of Liatti and McRae fending off a hard-charging Makinen. When McRae spun out, Tommi began closing in on the remaining Scoob. On the last day, he took the lead in the second stage and stayed there until the end. His second win of the season gave the Evo IV its first on asphalt—Ingaki

San was overjoyed that day. Meanwhile, Nittel and Thorner managed to bring the old Evo III home in eighth place overall.

Proving how unpredictable World Championship Rallying can be, the next tarmac event, the twisty Tour De Corse, didn't go so well for the Ralliart team. Uwe Nittel brought the old Group A Evo III machine home to finish in eighth place, but for Makinen things went pear-shaped on day two. Barreling along at well over 70 mph, he came across a cow standing right in the middle of the road. With nowhere to go, he slammed into the hapless creature, and the car went off the road, sliding down into a ravine. It was a horrendous crash and the car was completely totaled, but neither Makinen nor Harjanne was seriously hurt.

In Argentina, things really went Tommi's way. Although the Escorts of Juha Kankkunen and Carlos Sainz were quickest on the first stage, by the start of day two Makinen was in the lead and he stayed there, despite a valiant effort from McRae. Burns also made excellent progress, until a pounding on Special Stage 16 damaged his rear suspension, forcing him to retire.

Greece always proved to be a challenging event: The hot and rocky conditions often wreaked havoc with tires, suspension, and cooling. The Mitsubishis of Makinen and Burns managed to stay ahead of all but Juha Kankkunen on the first day, but the rocky surface caused numerous tire problems for Makinen. He ultimately couldn't contend with hard-charging Carlos Sainz, and he finished third overall. Burns, meanwhile, made very good progress, with only a minor overheating issue getting in his way. He finished right behind Makinen, having incurred a penalty stop under team orders to let the incumbent champ past. Nittel, in the third Mitsubishi, scored his best result to date, coming in sixth.

Next up was New Zealand. If things were bad for Makinen in Greece, they proved worse here. Tommi and Seppo went off the road in spectacular fashion, essentially slicing off the rear of their car. Burns and Reid pushed on despite ongoing transmission problems, and the Brit managed to nurse the Carisma GT to fourth overall.

THE ROAD TO STARDOM

By the mid 1990s, Evolutions were also becoming highly competitive in the Group N class. One of the most competitive drivers of these cars was Uruguayan Gustavo Trelles, pictured here in the 1997 Acropolis Rally behind the wheel of an Evo III.
Mitsubishi Japan

Back in Europe for his home event—the Neste Rally Finland (formerly 1000 Lakes)—Makinen needed a good result to have a fighting chance at the 1997 driver's title. The Toyota works team was back in action with its new Corolla WRC car, and it proved a bit of a thorn in the side of Mitsubishi, Subaru, and Ford. Two works MRE cars were entered, one for Tommi and Seppo and a veteran Evo III for Nittel and Thorner. As in the last four years, Finland proved to be Makinen's rally. Although fellow Finn Marcus Gronholm and the brand new Corolla were leading by the first day, by day two, Makinen was on a charge. Juha Kankkunen desperately tried to catch him, but it was to no avail. On the last day, Tommi lessened his pace a little but still finished seven seconds ahead of Kankkunen, his nearest rival. In the other works-entered car, Nittel also put in an amazing drive. Battling an outmoded machine and slippery conditions, he was the top finishing non-Nordic driver, coming in seventh ahead of Didier Auriol.

WRX vs. EVO

In the 1997 "Gravel Grand Prix," also known as the Neste Rally Finland, Makinen put in another scorcher of a drive, finishing seven seconds ahead of second-placed finisher, fellow Finn Juha Kankkunen. Mitsubishi Japan

In the hot and sticky Rally Indonesia, it was Burns' turn to shine. As in 1996, this event formed part of both the WRC and Asia-Pacific championships. Burns got off to a decent start, ultimately coming in fourth, but Makinen's car suffered from myriad problems right from day one. First it was the fuel injection system, and then a minor excursion off-road damaged the turbocharger. On day two he was ready to go, but a cooling fan worked its way loose and pierced the radiator and the engine overheated. With no service available at the end of the stage, the reigning champ had little alternative but to retire.

At San Remo, Makinen saw his luck improve, yet crowd control issues cancelled one stage and spectators continued to be a problem during the event. Although it proved to be a Subaru-dominated race, Makinen still managed to hold his ground in a tenacious battle with Carlos Sainz and his Ford Escort. Driving with his foot to the boards on the last day, the reigning champ managed to come in third, just enough to maintain his lead in the championship. Teammate Nittel, on the other hand, wasn't having much luck and a spate of accidents brought about his retirement.

In Australia, two works cars were entered, one for Makinen and Harjanne and a Carisma GT for Burns and Reid. During the first super special stage at Langley Park in western Australia, Makinen got airborne, and the resulting landing caused quite a bit of damage to the car; he was unable to start the first leg the following morning. His pit crew had to push the car back to the service area, resulting in a 30-second penalty. Makinen did get back on track, but he hit a tree on Special Stage 4 that caused further damage. By the end of the day, he was in sixth place. With a championship at stake, he knew he had to make up for lost time and put in another amazing drive. An engine failure put rival Carlos Sainz out of contention for the crown, but Colin McRae was another matter. Although the Scotsman beat Tommi to the finish, Makinen finished a fine second. Burns brought the other works Ralliart car home in fourth, while a privateer entry driven by Aussie Ed Ordynski came in sixth place.

Going into the RAC, Makinen required just one point to secure his second-straight WRC driver's championship. Burns, on his home turf, did well in the wet and dark conditions and brought the Carisma GT home in fourth place. Although suffering from flu symptoms and thus somewhat off his usual torrid pace, Makinen, with his eyes firmly fixed on acquiring that single point, managed to drive consistently enough to finish sixth overall, and that was all he needed. At the end, Tommi and Seppo celebrated in style, though this marked Harjanne's last time as Makinen's co-driver.

SUBARU: BIG CHANGES AT THE TOP

For the 1997 World Rally Championship, Group A regulations were supplanted by the new WRC (World Rally Car) format. Unlike rival Mitsubishi, SWRT was one team that embraced the new regulations wholeheartedly. In fact, as early as the beginning of 1996, development work had already begun on Subaru's new WRC car. As the street counterpart was the Japanese-market STi Type R coupe, the new rally car naturally adopted the Retna two-door body. Ex-Lotus designer Peter Stevens beefed up the contours with an aggressive, slightly forward-jutting air dam with a vee'd opening; massive, bulging fenders; an aluminum hood with special extractors; and a large rear deck spoiler designed to increase downforce at speed.

Mechanically, the new WRC offering was still based around an EJ20 powerplant, but special attention was paid to the turbocharger and wastegate. Exhaust plumbing (the system now exited from the right side of the car instead of the left) and an increased-capacity intercooler were installed. The result of all this was a substantial increase in torque—up to 347 lb-ft, at a very useable 4,000 rpm. Horsepower

With the launch of the Type R, the 1997 Subaru World Rally Cars sported two-door coupe bodies with pronounced, bulging fenders. These were the most radical machines yet from the brand. Tarmac specialist Piero Liatti and co-driver Fabriza Pons stole the show during that year's San Remo. Subaru Global

was 300 at 5,500. Despite being one of the first manufacturers to pioneer sequential gearboxes in rally cars, SWRT reverted to a traditional Prodrive-sourced six-speed manual for the 1997 season, even as the other teams (including Mitsubishi) turned their attention to sequential units.

The 1997 WRC Impreza also employed active front and center differentials with a mechanical unit employed for the rear wheels. Inside, a more modern dash did away with analog instruments, instead using a centrally mounted screen to display speed, rpm, and other functions. The team stuck with Pirelli as its official supplier of tires.

An extensive test program was employed for the new car, and with homologation certified on January 1, 1997, the car was ready to do battle in the first round of the championship—the famous Rally Monte Carlo. As before, SWRT elected to field a three-car team for the season, with McRae as lead driver, though Welshman Nicky Grist replaced Derek Ringer as the Scotsman's co-driver. A second car was entered for Kenneth Eriksson and Staffan Parmander, while Piero Liatti and Fabrizia Pons ran a third car mainly on the tarmac events.

The Monte opened with plenty of drama; aside from the snow and ice on the mountain stages, the lead position seemed to change as much as the conditions. Freddy Loix and his Toyota Celica were first by the end of day one, but on day two, as the streets gave way to mountain stages, Carlos Sainz and his Escort took over the lead. Then Tommi Makinen, after a somewhat shaky start, took the lead by the end leg three. On the final day of competition, however, it was Liatti's turn to shine. The Italian had been making steady progress throughout the rally and put in a superb drive. Makinen was having tire problems by then, and Sainz just couldn't match the pace of the Subaru driver. Liatti's first win was a magnificent one, and he couldn't have picked a better event to do it. Not only did Piero win his first WRC rally, but he did it in a brand new car that four days earlier had been unproven in competition! McRae wasn't so lucky; he hit a patch of ice on the first stage on the third day, causing extensive suspension damage and forcing retirement.

Sweden proved to be a hotly contested ordeal, with multiple leaders and very close stage times. McRae briefly took the lead, but then a hard-charging Carlos Sainz started chipping away and pulled ahead. On the last day, Eriksson found new momentum, putting in a spectacular performance to outdrive Sainz and an exceedingly quick Tommi Makinen. His Scottish teammate, meanwhile, struggled somewhat because of tire issues, but McRae managed to bring the other works car home to a fourth place overall.

Next, the teams headed for East Africa and the Safari, which was finally compressed into a three-day format for 1997. The conditions were also fairly dry this year, but that didn't mean the event was without problems. Eriksson was out early on when a huge rock took out his right rear wheel and caused extensive damage to the car. He managed to nurse it to the end of the stage, but lengthy repairs cost him the rally. Speaking of rocks, some reckless spectactors decided to have a bit of fun and plant big stones on one of the stages. The first car to come in contact with them was the other Impreza of McRae and Grist, which went straight through the blockade; luckily, there was minimal damage. Although electrical problems threatened to end their rally early, McRae and his co-driver managed to keep it together and took a well-deserved victory.

Both McRae and Eriksson were back in action for Portugal, but it wasn't to prove a successful event for SWRT as both cars went out with engine problems—McRae at the end of the first day when his engine started misfiring and Eriksson the following afternoon when his car developed similar problems.

Things were better in Catalunya, Spain. McRae and Liatti, in a second works car, started the event. The paved conditions suited the Italian's driving style. Both Subarus proved highly competitive on the first day, but they had a battle on their hands with a resilient Tommi Makinen in the Mitsubishi. Ultimately, the flying Finn won out, with Liatti finishing second and McRae fourth.

The Tour De Corse, another tarmac event, was next on the calendar, so Liatti and Pons were again allocated the second works drive. A very quick Carlos Sainz proved a tour de force in the early stages, but McRae countered with what was perhaps one of his most memorable drives. Determined to catch his former teammate, McRae drove his little Impreza to the absolute limit. He snatched away the lead on the last stage of the day and bagged another win, putting him firmly in the lead for the driver's championship. Liatti, meanwhile, battled the somewhat slippery roads to come home in fifth, giving SWRT another solid result.

Kenneth Eriksson was back for Argentina, ready to prove his mettle. Although a gravel specialist, he wasn't too familiar with the Argentine event, but he made the most of the situation and drove a steady rally to wind up third overall. McRae was determined to hold on to his championship lead and battled incumbent Makinen from start to finish. Ultimately, it was the Finn who took the honors. Colin had to deal with a steering issue that set him back, but a 2–3 for the Subaru team wasn't half bad.

The Acropolis rally in Greece always brings plenty of drama, and the 1997 event proved to be no exception. Tire punctures and accidents abounded. Freddy Loix rolled and destroyed his Toyota Celica on the first day, and after suffering from steering problems, the same thing happened to Eriksson. The service crew managed to patch the car up, however, and he brought the battered Impreza home to finish the last stage on the first day. However, problems persisted, and the Swede was out of the event by the following morning. McRae had retired on the second stage during the first day of rallying when a rocky section of road severely damaged his steering linkage.

New Zealand (traditionally a McRae favorite) ended up a disappointment for the Scotsman this time, as a blown engine forced retirement. Meanwhile, Eriksson and co-driver Staffan Parmander took on the Sainz/Ford challenge and held their ground; they were aided when Sainz crashed into a sheep that was standing in the middle of the road. Eriksson took the win for the team (not only strengthening SWRT's standings in the constructor's cup, but also his chances at bagging another Asia-Pacific driver's crown). Speaking of that, regular A-P contender Peter "Possum" Bourne brought a second Subaru Australia-entered car home in fifth place.

In Finland, both McRae and Eriksson again suffered from mechanical setbacks. On the second day, in a seemingly spooky fashion, both drivers had their boxer engines go south because of cam failure—McRae on the first leg of the day and then Eriksson on Special Stage 12 that afternoon.

After this string of bad luck, the Rally of Indonesia proved at least a partial change in fortune for the Subaru team. McRae got off to an excellent start, setting the pace early, but unfortunately his luck took a turn for the worse on day two when he hit a tree that severely damaged the cooling system, resulting in retirement. Eriksson, meanwhile, contending with the mud and humidity, started gaining momentum after a somewhat sluggish start. He brought the remaining works Scoob home in third, behind the Ford Escorts of Sainz and Juha Kankkunen.

For the San Remo, Piero Liatti was called in again to show off his exceptional skills on tarmac events in front of a home crowd. Unruly spectators disrupted the planned first and second special stages, so it wasn't until Special Stage 3 that the competition really began. Freddy Loix and the new Toyota Corolla set the pace on the first day, but sure enough, Liatti emerged overall leader by the end of the last stage. From there, the San Remo became a Subaru-dominated event, as McRae mounted an assault, eventually catching and passing Liatti. A game of cat and mouse then ensued. To have any chance of winning the championship, Colin needed to win this one, so Liatti followed team orders and relented, though the San Remo in many respects was the Italian's event.

There were just two rounds left on the calendar: Australia and Britain. Down under, it was an all-out race for the WRC driver's championship between Colin McRae, Tommi Makinen, and Carlos Sainz. The Scotsman took a little off-course excursion during the infamous Langley Park stage, but it wasn't enough to cause any serious problems. McRae and co-driver Grist then started a hard charge,

THE ROAD TO STARDOM

In the dark damp Welsh forests, Colin McRae was on form during the RAC. He won the event, but Makinen and Mitsubishi garnered enough points to win the championship that year. Subaru Global

setting the fastest times for the day and ending up first overall. Sainz ultimately retired with engine failure. After a number of setbacks, Makinen started catching the leader, but ultimately it wasn't enough. McRae drove a superb rally and clinched another win, giving him a fighting chance to win the championship, but only if Makinen didn't garner any points in the RAC. Eriksson, meanwhile, had a rough Australia, rolling his car out of action.

In Britain, McRae and Grist (on home turf) were once again a force to be reckoned with. From start to finish, the Scotsman was on fire even in the tricky Welsh gravel stages, despite an off-course excursion during a bout of thick fog. It was a spectacular win to end an exciting season, but a sixth-place finish by a tired and ill Makinen robbed Colin of a second driver's crown. Still, Subaru had secured its third manufacturer's title in three years and also bagged the A-P, European, and African series constructor's championships.

1998

MITSUBISHI: SILVER LINING

Aside from Makinen's driver's championship in the WRC, Subaru was still the dominant manufacturer in the series. To make matters worse, at this time, rumors of financial scandal rocked Mitsubishi Motors right to the highest corporate level in Japan. The response was to come clean, regroup, and launch a redirected product and marketing focus. It also resulted in a new ad slogan in Japan, "Innovation in motion," which in many respects perfectly described the company's halo car, the Lancer Evolution.

Come the fall of 1997, Mitsubishi took the wraps off its latest incarnation of the famed Lancer homologation hot rod, the Evolution V. Incorporating styling touches that were adopted for the rest of the Lancer line, including a slightly smoother nose, it was the baddest and most aggressive-looking Evo yet seen. The aluminum hood featured pronounced twin scoops, and the bulging front fenders were also aluminum pieces, designed to save weight. The front fascia/air dam assembly was restyled and looked even more aggressive than the

Before the 1997 rally season had even drawn to a close, Mitsubishi took the wraps off its next contender, the Evolution V. A huge front air dam with massive foglights, bulging fender flares, and a prominent, four way-adjustable rear deck spoiler lent a menacing look on the street. Satin Silver was a popular exterior color. Mitsubishi Japan

IV's. The openings for the intercooler and brake cooling ducts were huge and, combined with foglights that were now recessed into the bumper cover, resulted in a more exaggerated boy-racer appearance. A revised (and four-way adjustable) rear deck spoiler, more aggressive rocker panel skirts, and rear fender extensions added menace to the new look.

The Evo V delivered a number of mechanical upgrades, the most noticeable being the adoption of massive 12.6-inch Brembo brakes with four-piston calipers (GSR only). In order to clear these huge discs, the new car ran on a set of gorgeous OZ multispoke 17-inch wheels (necessitating the more pronounced fender lips—required to meet Japanese tire/bodywork clearance standards). The tires were Bridgestone Potenzas, sized at a meaty 225/45ZR17. Other mechanical changes included a stiffer chassis, thinner glass (to save weight), plus a wider front and rear track (59.4 and 59.2 inches, respectively) to

More a driver's car than ever before, changes to the steering and suspension, plus the presence of new Brembo brakes on the GSR model, made the Evo IV a delight on both the street and track. Mitsubishi Japan

improve stability. Changes to the suspension included longer control arms at the front, shocks retuned for greater travel, modified spindles, altered steering rack positioning, and a brand new power steering pump that eliminated the need for an externally mounted cooler. At the back, engineers moved the suspension attachment points, resulting in a lower roll center.

Driveline upgrades mainly revolved around the 4G63 engine's exhaust plumbing (though the four-banger received twin camshafts with slightly different duration and new, lightweight 8.8:1 compression pistons). Both the radiator and intercooler were increased in size (hence the larger front air dam opening), and a new Mitsubishi TD05 turbocharger was used: a twin-scroll HR-16G6. With minor tweaks to the ECU, the engine was rated at the same 280 bhp, but that was purely to satisfy Japanese requirements. The true impact of these updates was in the torque figure, which now officially stood at 274 lb-ft coming in at a very useable 3,000 rpm. As a result, the five-speed manual gearbox was strengthened with stouter gears and syncros, though the actual ratios were unchanged from the IV.

Without a doubt, the Evolution V was one bad machine. Nearly everybody who tested one came away impressed. *Autocar* magazine managed to its its hands on a Japanese-spec example, even pitching it against the rival Impreza STi. To give an idea of how mind-bending the Evo V was at the time, the magazine summed up the car's performance by saying, "The Evolution V is the quickest car we've tested across country, bar none." In Japan, veteran Belgian auto journalist and racer Paul Frère also sampled one of the new cars (a stripped-down RS— the car was available in GSR and RS configurations as before), and even he waxed lyrical about it, noting its "razor-sharp handling, superb efficiency, and balance" for a four-door sedan. Coming from a true racer, that was high praise indeed.

The Evolution V finally went on sale in January 1998 in Japan. As before, the lighter (and cheaper) RS models were available only in a single color—Scotia White—and featured less standard equipment, 15-inch steel wheels, and the IV's braking system. GSR models,

THE ROAD TO STARDOM

So popular and fast was the Evo V that today, more than a decade after the car's introduction, examples are still popular for amateur track racing and rallying. This Evo V RS was photographed at Fuji Speedway in January 2008. Note the absence of front fog lights and black door mirror housings. **Huw Evans**

meanwhile, could be purchased in six different colors: Scotia White, Pyrenees Black, Palma Red, Satin Silver, or an interesting color called Dandelion.

For those who wanted to stand out from the crowd, Ralliart dished up a plethora of accessories for the Evo V, including more aggressive shocks and struts, a performance-tuned exhaust system, strut braces, mud flaps, Recaro front seats, and, for RS buyers, a narrow body (without all the add-on aero extensions), plus the GSR's 17-inch OZ wheel and Potenza tire package, which resulted in a few very unusual combinations. By the time the Evo V's production run had ended, approximately 6,000 cars had found buyers, with 777 being sent abroad, though all the cars were essentially Japanese market-specification models and all were right-hand drive.

Today, despite having been superseded by newer variants, the Evo V remains an enthusiast favorite. The car's outlandish styling, firm ride, race car–like handling, torquey engine, and balls-out persona endeared it to drivers the world over. Today, the surviving examples remain among the most desirable of all Evos.

SUBARU: MORE GRUNT UP FRONT

While Mitsubishi released its hottest-ever Evo for 1998, at the Subaru camp, refinement and power were the buzzwords heading into the 1998 model year. After having tweaked the exterior the year before, Subaru now refreshed the cabin. New white-faced gauges, along with a redesigned center console stack, new seats, and better-quality materials answered criticisms about chintzy interiors. Furthermore, automatic-equipped WRXs also received a Mercedes-esque shifter gate with staggered settings for the "PRND" sequence. Regular WRX models got a standard Sure-Trac rear differential, and on the wagon, engineers bumped up power from EJ20 engine to 250 bhp and 225 lb-ft, though the wagon still lagged behind its sedan counterpart in the performance stakes.

STi also unveiled its lineup of Version IV cars for 1998. Under the hood, the EJ20 engine received valvetrain and cam timing adjustments, along with changes to the IHI turbocharger, wastegate, and plumbing. The result was improved throttle response, particularly in the low and mid range. Although power was unchanged at 280 bhp (in order to satisfy Japanese legislative requirements), torque now stood at 260 lb-ft. Three different body styles were offered on the Version IV cars: sedan, wagon, and coupe, in either standard, hard-core type RA, or, in the case of the coupe, Type R. These last two models also received more powerful rear brakes with larger rotors to improve overall stopping power. As with previous incarnations, the Type RA was only available in white and the R coupe in three different hues, now blue, silver, and black (the standard STi sedan and wagon had options for five and four exterior colors, respectively).

On the export side of things, changes somewhat mirrored those of the Japanese-market cars, although these markets saw a few unique items, too. In Australia, perhaps the biggest announcement was a drop

THE ROAD TO STARDOM

For 1998, there were a number of tweaks to the EJ20 boxer engine. Japanese market cars were rated at 280 bhp and 260 lb-ft of torque, thanks primarily to changes in cam timing and exhaust plumbing. Subaru Global

in the sticker price of all Imprezas to help boost sales appeal and, finally, on the WRX models, the adoption of a 16-inch wheel and tire package. Combined with the a revised range of standard equipment, including power controls and standard air conditioning, the 1998 Australian spec Rex was the most tantalizing yet.

WRX vs. EVO

On the other side of the world meanwhile, the Aussies' British cousins also got an updated Impreza Turbo, which featured similar engine tweaks and interior refinements to those found in the Japanese-market WRX. The UK-spec versions also got 16-inch wheels and tires, a slightly altered front air dam, and perimeter body extensions. The additional torque was welcomed by the British automotive press, and during an instrumented test, *Autocar* flogged a 1998 Turbo to a 14.2 second run in the standing quarter-mile.

In January 1998, Subaru took the wraps off another spate of limited-edition STi V-Limited models to celebrate yet another WRC manufacturer's title (see special edition cars).

A couple months later, STi stole Mitsubishi's thunder somewhat, introducing a car that still has enthusiasts talking. That car was the legendary STi 22B. Actually, this car had first been seen a few months earlier at the 1997 Tokyo Motor Show, where it had been dubbed the WRCar-STi. On March 16, 1998, Subaru Tecnica International revealed it as the STi 22B. The designation was significant, as 22B

Arguably the most special of all GC Imprezas was the formidable STi 22B, first seen in the spring of 1998. Although it looked every inch a rally homologation special, the car never actually qualified because of its enlarged engine. Huw Evans

referred to the car's engine displacement. So, although it looked every inch the next homologation special for the WRC, the 22B never actually qualified, because the rally cars still relied on modified EJ20 engines for power.

No matter, the STi 22B was a pure performance machine. The engine was a closed-deck design with a larger 96.9-mm bore (but the same stroke as the EJ20). Contained within the block were four 8.0:1 compression-forged alloy pistons. Sodium-filled valves and metal head gaskets, plus a water spray system for the intercooler, were the icing on the cake. Featuring a variation of the same turbocharger used on the 1997 regular STi, the EJ22 was rated at the same 280 bhp as its cousin, but the extra displacement resulted in 267 lb-ft of torque. With maximum grunt arriving at just 3,200 rpm, the 22B was perhaps the closest thing yet to a Japanese muscle car.

Combined with a variant of the STi Type RA's close-ratio five-speed manual gearbox, but with stronger cogs to cope with the swell in torque, this AWD monster could scoot from rest to 60 mph in just 4.3

The heart of the STi 22B was its 2.2 liter flat-four engine. Based on the EJ20 but with a larger bore, it was a very torquey unit with a maximum of 267 lb-ft arriving at just 3200 rpm. Huw Evans

seconds. It could also pull more than .92 lateral g on the skidpad, due in part to a seriously upgraded suspension that included special Eibach springs, specially designed premium Bilstein shocks (inverted for use in this application), lightweight aluminum control arms, stouter bushings, and rose joints on the front and rear sway bar links. In addition, the 22B boasted a track that was 0.39 inches wider up front and stretched 1.57 out back, for a menacing, road-hugging stance. Special 17x8.5-inch BBS spoke rims were shod in premium Pirelli P-Zero rubber (P235/40ZR17s all-around). The 22B stopped pretty well too, thanks to massive vented discs at all four corners (11.6-inch front, 11.4-inch rear—among the largest seen on an Impreza up to that time).

Other nifty features included a carbon fiber strut tower brace and a driver-adjustable torque split, from 35:65 to 50:50 front/rear. Inside, the cabin received a standard three-spoke Nardi steering wheel, special dash treatment with antiglare material, and a limited-edition 22B plaque on the center console.

As befitting its image as a true competition-bred machine, there was no stereo system, nor ABS, but strangely power locks, windows,

Only 425 STi 22Bs were built, of which just 25 went overseas. Today they remain among the most desirable and sought-after of all Imprezas. Huw Evans

and air conditioning were fitted. On the outside, you could get your STi 22B in any color you wanted so long as it was Sonic Blue Mica. Besides special badging, the 22B also boasted unique ground effects, including a different-style front air dam and a massive rear spoiler. With bulging front and rear fenders (just like the WRC machines) and gold-painted, multispoke rims, it looked every inch a street-going rally machine. The 400 cars allocated for the home market were quickly snapped up; in fact, all of them had been spoken for within a day of the car's announcement.

Subaru built a further 25 examples of the 22B as export cars, 16 of which went to the United Kingdom. These were official UK-spec cars, featuring mph speedos, different lighting (including standard rear foglights), improved rust protection to cope with salted winter roads, and other touches designed for the inclement British climate. Although each one of these cars stickered at just under £40,000 (which was nearly enough to buy two regular Impreza Turbos at the time), they were eagerly snapped up and today remain highly prized among enthusiasts.

Launched on the heels of the 22B in the United Kingdom was another limited edition, the four-door Impreza Turbo Terzo (see Appendix B: Special Edition Cars for more on this model).

MITSUBISHI: NEW SEASON, NEW CHALLENGES

With the latest homologation special making waves on the performance front, Ralliart appeared more ready than ever to tackle the WRC season for 1998. Testing with the Evo V had begun in the latter half of 1997, and although homologation was approved in January 1998, the new rally cars weren't ready until Catalunya. So for the first four rounds of the season, MRE fielded updated Evo IVs. Makinen was once again lead driver, but the seat beside him was now filled with fellow Finn Risto Mannisenmaki. A second car, again dubbed a Carisma GT, was offered up for Richard Burns and Robert Reid, while German driver Uwe Nittel was given a second Carisma GT for select WRC rounds.

WRX vs. EVO

Monte Carlo was again the season opener, and Mitsubishi got off to a seemingly fine start with Makinen setting the pace—clearly the pairing between him and Mannisenmaki appeared to be working. That is, until he slid off the road, damaging the car to the point that he was forced to retire. Burns, meanwhile, put in a solid and steady performance to come in fifth overall, behind the Subarus of McRae and Liatti.

The cold, snowy conditions in Sweden proved better for Makinen. Although he had to battle a determined Thomas Radstrom in the Toyota Corolla for much of the event, Tommi's perseverance paid off and he drove around the Swede to clinch his first victory of the year. Burns went off course, and the delays in getting the car back in action dashed any chances of a points finish—still, he and Reid made the most of a bad situation, and Richard's driving was hard to fault.

The Safari, however, was an entirely different affair. As usual, it lived up to its grueling reputation, with less than half of the 48 entries lasting through the three-day event. The Mitsubishi team was on good form, but this time fortune smiled on Richard Burns. Reliability issues ultimately got the best of Makinen, when broken engine mounts forced him to retire on the second day. Meanwhile, Burns seemingly dodged all the obstacles to secure his first-ever WRC win—and what an event in which to do it! After Burns' three years with the team, his hard work and growing experience had finally paid off.

Portugal proved to very much be a Subaru versus Toyota affair, and the best the Mitsubishis could muster was a fourth by Burns and Reid in the Carisma GT, with Makinen crashing out of contention fairly early on.

For the next round, it was back to the other side of the Iberian Peninsula and the tarmac roads of Rally Catalunya; this time, MRE had its latest weapon ready for battle, the Evolution V rally car. Although the new car had been in testing since 1997, most of that had been conducted by Lasse Lampi and Burns, with incumbent world champion Makinen having very little seat time. In Catalunya, it showed, particularly in the early stages. Still, after a bit of a rough start,

THE ROAD TO STARDOM

Makinen and Mannisenmaki picked up the pace and battled their way, stage after stage, to come in third place overall, with Burns and Reid finishing right behind. Nittel and co-driver Tina Thorner came in ninth, ahead of the third Corolla. With four rounds already run, MRE was in very good shape for the constructor's championship.

The tight roads of the Tour de Corse proved tough for the Ralliart team, as neither of the works cars finished. Makinen's race was run when his car's ECU went on the fritz, and Burns went out when his front suspension collapsed. With no result in the top category (Mitsubishi did bag a 1–2 in Group N with Manfred Stohl and Gustavo Trelles), things needed to improve for the next round in Argentina if both MRE and Makinen were to have a chance against Subaru in the championship.

Luckily, they did. Argentina proved another chance for the flying Finn to shine, and he put in a very memorable drive. He battled McRae for much of the event, but he came out on top to secure his second win of the season. Burns and Reid managed to dodge the obstacles thrown at them to take fourth place overall.

As always, the Acropolis rally had plenty of punishment to dish out; however, in Makinen's case, it was neither tires nor suspension. The electrical gremlins that plagued him in Corsica returned, and after losing much time on the first special stage, he took the decision to retire early on. Burns, meanwhile, made steady progress, running within the top five up until Stage 16. After a few too many poundings on the rocky surface, he was forced to retire with damaged rear suspension components. This was the second time in three events in which neither of the regular works Mitsubishis finished.

As teams moved across the globe to New Zealand, accumulating points was clearly on the mind of MRE, but that wouldn't prove to be easy. Tommi and Risto managed to survive this one, but Makinen seemed strangely off the pace and was way behind the Toyotas of Carlos Sainz and Didier Auriol. He did manage to bring the car home for a podium finish, however. Burns, after an impressive charge, took a corner too hard and rolled his car on the last day. However, the damage wasn't enough to keep him from continuing. After 15 minutes, the car was back on the course. It was too late for any chance of a points finish, but coming in ninth overall wasn't bad considering the circumstances.

The Gravel Grand Prix, a.k.a. Neste Rally Finland (previously 1000 Lakes), is usually pretty hard for non-Nordic drivers, but Burns and Reid, on their first outing in Finland, managed to drive a steady race to bring the Carisma GT home in fifth place (Carlos Sainz was the only other non-Nordic driver to finish in the top six). Makinen, without winning that many special stages, drove quickly enough to be crowned the undisputed victor. By winning in front of a home crowd, he also set another record as the first WRC driver in history to win the same event five times in a row.

The works cars received a bit of a shot in the arm in San Remo. Ralliart Europe fitted new electromagnetic clutches to the rear

Richard Burns became a full-time MRE works driver for the 1998 season. Although his car wore Carisma badging, it was an Evo V; the actual Carisma was an entirely different vehicle. He's seen here in action during the 1998 San Remo. Mitsubishi Japan

THE ROAD TO STARDOM

In the Telstra-sponsored Rally Australia, Makinen faced a fierce challenge from Carlos Sainz, but he took the lead and eventually won the event. Makinen's victory also proved instrumental in securing the 1998 WRC driver's championship. Mitsubishi Japan

differentials on both Makinen's and Burns' machines. Along with tweaks to the ECU, the result was that torque sensing ability and traction were vastly improved on all road surfaces. In practice, the new system delivered on its promise when Makinen scored yet another victory. Richard Burns couldn't quite keep the same pace as his teammate and ended up seventh.

In Australia, the penultimate round of the season, Burns got off to a blinding start, leading the rally right up through the first leg, but it all went downhill from there. Carlos Sainz gained momentum on the second day, and then along came Makinen to regain the lead for Mitsubishi after a tenacious battle with the Spaniard Didier Auriol and briefly Colin McRae. Tommi won this one—finishing ahead of Sainz—but after his impressive start, Burns's Rally Australia ended on a sour note when he crashed the Carisma GT on the final special stage at Langley Park.

Similar to the previous season, the driver's title was still hanging in the balance as the teams headed to Britain, with two points separating

Makinen and Sainz. It seemed that any hopes of a championship victory would be dashed for Makinen after he lost a wheel early on. But then, in an unusual and truly gut-wrenching situation, the engine in Sainz' Corolla let go just 500 meters from the finish line on the last stage of the event. Up to that point, the 1998 driver's title looked to be firmly within the Spaniard's grasp. With Sainz a DNF, Tommi Makinen was declared champion because of his two-point lead going into the RAC.

The Finn had now won three driver's crowns in a row, and with a spectacular win by Burns in front of his home crowd, Ralliart had, for the first time, also won the WRC constructor's cup—talk about a fine end to the season!

SUBARU: MIXED RESULTS

With the announcement of the 22B, Subaru enthusiasts had plenty to salivate over, along with the STi V-Limited models released to commemorate SWRT's 1997 rally success. For most of 1998, the WRX and STi marked time, save for the introduction of some special editions in various markets. For the 1998 WRC season, Prodrive dished up 11 new World Rally–spec cars, still powered by 300-bhp EJ20s, utilizing the Prodrive six-speed manual gearbox and weighing in at a lithe 1,230 kg (2,706 lbs), as per FIA rules.

The driver lineup consisted again of McRae as number one, but Piero Liatti was now listed as the secondary works driver, which meant he would compete on tarmac, snow, and gravel events. In addition, former team head Dave Richards left SWRT to pursue a career in Formula 1, his place taken by David Lapworth.

Monte Carlo was the season opener once again in 1998. Liatti got off to a blinding start on the opening tarmac stages, but the mountain switchbacks and inclement weather slowed his progress somewhat. Still, a fourth overall was hardly shabby. McRae, meanwhile, more at home on the slippery winding roads, put in a steady performance to finish one place ahead of his teammate. He scored the best result for a British driver on the Monte since Vic Elford in 1968.

THE ROAD TO STARDOM

Kenneth Eriksson's last official drive for the works Subaru team came in the 1998 Swedish Rally. Driving a car with specially tuned suspension, he set the pace for much of the event. Subaru Global

In Sweden, Lapworth made a choice to bring in Kenneth Eriksson and Staffan Parmander one last time in a third works car, and it proved to be a wise move. While Liatti struggled with the conditions in a special WRC98 fitted with electronic shock valving, Eriksson made seemingly light work of them—it was only when his car developed gearbox problems that he lost time. Still, a fourth-place finish in his last outing for the team was decent enough. McRae and Grist developed electrical problems and were out by the second leg.

Once again, the Safari proved to be hard on drivers and even harder on cars, with just 18 of the 40-plus starters making it to the end. Unfortunately, none of the remaining works cars were Subarus. Liatti was out on Special Stage 10 with engine failure, and then, in the following round, McRae's EJ20 croaked after suffering cooling issues.

Rally Portugal proved to be a change of fortunes for the team. McRae maintained a brisk pace, but on the final stages he faced some stiff opposition from Carlos Sainz, who was closing the gap for the lead. The Scotsman held him off to give SWRT its first win of the season. Liatti and co-driver Fabrizia Pons came in sixth.

In contrast, things just didn't seem to gel on the 1998 Rally Catalunya. The Subarus struggled to match the pace of the Toyotas and Mitsubishis, seemingly due to a lack of traction, but it didn't help matters when McRae broke a rear driveshaft on the final morning of competition, forcing retirement. Liatti hit a marker on Stage 12, taking out a front wheel and part of his suspension, also ending his rally early.

With even tighter tarmac roads on the horizon for the Tour de Corse, Subaru looked for a better result. The manufacturer got it when McRae and Grist scored their second victory of the season, leading virtually from start to finish. Liatti, at home on the narrow paved roads, also put in an excellent drive, but a puncture slowed his progress. By the final stages, he couldn't quite match the front-drive Peugeot 306 of Francois Delecour. Still, a first and third captured valuable points for the team.

McRae was leading in Argentina until an altercation with a huge rock caused a healthy amount of damage to the car. Still, the crew patched the damage up enough for the Scotsman to keep going; the two Subarus came in fifth and sixth, respectively, with Liatti and Pons putting in a steady performance throughout the three-day event.

In Greece, there was plenty of drama, but Subaru's works cars proved reliable throughout the event. McRae had to battle a very determined Richard Burns—until the latter went out with suspension issues—and then Didier Auriol, but he and Grist remained cool and set the fastest times on the last three stages to snatch victory from the Frenchman. Liatti, meanwhile, was driving a good, steady rally and looked set to come in fourth until a mishap on the second-to-last stage saw him careen off the road and into a ditch. He recovered but could only manage to finish sixth overall.

New Zealand didn't go as many expected. While running third, McRae suffered a tire blowout on Special Stage 20; with no spare he

THE ROAD TO STARDOM

had to limp on for 30 km, costing him two places at the finish. Liatti brought the other works car home right behind in sixth.

Liatti sat out the very tough Rally Finland. Instead, SWRT brought in local driver Jarmo Kytolehto to run the second car. He and co-driver Arto Kapanen came in eighth, the best result for Subaru. McRae crashed his car into a tree, severely damaging the suspension and forcing retirement.

The San Remo proved a mixed bag. A puncture slowed McRae early on, but he managed to claw back enough time to battle Carlos Sainz and ultimately snatch third place from the Spaniard. Liatti put in a spectacular drive and outpaced everybody but Tommi Makinen to take an excellent second place overall.

Australia was a gut-wrenching event for Colin McRae. Still in contention for the driver's championship, he had his hopes dashed when his turbocharger gave up, leaving a fourth-place finish as the best he could muster. With Makinen winning and Sainz coming in second, the championship was decided. Liatti had even worse luck; he

Colin McRae had a fighting chance of winning the world championship by Australia, but when his turbocharger let go all bets were off. Subaru Global

crashed out quite spectacularly on Special Stage 5 to bring an end to his 1998 WRC season (it was his last drive for the Subaru team before going to SEAT).

The final round, at the RAC in Britain, saw three works Subaru entries, with Colin's younger brother, Alistair McRae, and Ari Vatanen piloting the second and third Imprezas. The McRae brothers were doing well, Colin leading and Alistair in second, when piston failure brought retirement for Colin's car. For Alistair, a thick fog proved his undoing; he misjudged a corner and rolled the car, damaging it enough to make continuing the rally unwise. Vatanen also retired when his engine gave up the ghost.

Overall, the 1998 season was mixed for Subaru, with extreme highs and lows. Having lost the constructor's championship to archrival Mitsubishi, Subaru needed a renewed effort for 1999. As we shall see, big changes were in store.

1999

MITSUBISHI: STREET HEAT

The Lancer Evolution V had set the performance car market on its ear with its outstanding performance and agility, but in the never-ending quest to stay ahead of the competition in the WRC homologation game, it was only a matter of time before it was superseded. In January 1999, Mitsubishi took the wraps off the Evo VI, which in various guises would become the last of the fourth-generation Lancer-based Evolutions. Outwardly, it looked very similar to the V, but changes included a smoother, more integrated one-piece front fascia assembly. This had smaller foglights and a license plate bracket offset to the left to help clear the flow of air for the massive radiator and intercooler assembly. In addition, there was an oil cooler duct on the right side only. Further exterior changes included clear front turn-signal lenses, a slightly simpler taillight treatment, and a smaller rear spoiler (to comply with the latest FIA homologation regulations).

As before, the Evo VI came in either GSR or RS trim. The former wore 17x7.5-inch OZ alloy wheels wrapped around the same P225/45/

In January 1999, Mitsubishi took the wraps off the Lancer Evolution VI. Outwardly it looked similar to the V, but there were numerous changes, mainly to the intercooler and suspension. This was also the first variant designed officially for export with left-hand drive. Mitsubishi Japan

ZR17 tires as the Evo V, though the rim design was slightly different with a greater number of (and more evenly spaced) spokes. The Evo VI also boasted better structural rigidity thanks to improved spot welding and the use of more advanced adhesives during assembly. Suspension tuning was revised with a lower roll center and stiffer upper mounts for the front shock towers, greater suspension travel, and more extensive use of aluminum for the rear, including the control arms and links.

The driveline was mostly carried over from the Evolution V. The active yaw control–equipped rear diff was revised to improve cornering response, while the two-liter 4G63 engine also got a number of revisions, mainly in the interest of durability. There was a new oil pan design, a bigger oil cooler, and new pistons with special oil passages to help improve oil circulation and cooling. The actual cooling system was also improved with revised hoses and improved ducting. There was also a larger-diameter cold air intake assembly to improve breathing.

In addition, RS models received a revised turbocharger (a TD05 HRA G-16; the Evo V's HR G-16 was carried over for the GSR) with a turbine that sported new titanium-aluminum alloy blades for quicker spool up and thus improved throttle response. In addition, RS models could also be ordered with a twin-disc racing style clutch and the firmer Evo V suspension. As before, the RS model rode on steel 15-inch wheels and tires, though upgrading to the Brembo brakes required the adoption of the OZ 17-inch wheel and tire package (the Brembos, standard fitment on the GSR, got revised calipers to reduce fade and improve clamping force).

On the inside, there were only minor changes, mainly to the upholstery, steering wheel, and gearshift stitching. The instrument cluster featured blue backlit gauges, which gave it a somewhat calming appearance at night. As before, the GSR version could be spec'd in a variety of different exterior colors, including Satellite Silver, Lancer Blue, Pyrennees Black, and Scotia White. The all-business RS model

Thanks to changes in the suspension and chassis, and a revised Active Yaw Control system, the Evo VI was the most capable yet. To this day it is often regarded as the most fun and involving-to-drive of all Evolution models—high praise indeed. Mitsubishi Japan

came without the front foglights, featured less interior content, and was finished in Scotia White.

The Evo VI was, and still is, considered by many to be the most involving to pilot of all Evos. It was smoother to drive than the V, but the performance was every bit as good, if not better. The combination of the 4G63's willing and infinitely useable power, coupled with outstanding grip and even better agility through corners, made it an enthusiast's dream. Stab the throttle, row the gears, point, and go. No matter the obstacle thrown at it, the VI gobbled up miles and miles of twisty tarmac with ruthless efficiency. It was a huge adrenalin rush on wheels and inspired confidence in a way few cars ever do, blazing its way into the history books in the process.

Mitsubishi built some 7,000 Evo VIs, and this car was significant in that it was the first of its breed designed with export in mind. As a result, it was offered in both right- and left-hand-drive versions, and total export sales were more than double those of the V—1,869 units versus 777.

In Britain, the Evolution VI was brought over to supplant the 3000GT coupe as Mitsubishi's top-of-the-line, UK-spec performance model (prior to that Evos had entered the country only as unofficial

To clear the massive Brembo front brakes on the GSR model, 17-inch OZ wheels and meaty 225-section Yokohama tires were required. Lancer Blue paint was only offered on the GSR during the production run. Mitsubishi Japan

"gray market" imports, mostly from Japan). The United Kingdom responded well to the Evo VI, and in testing, the British motoring press was enthralled, including *Autocar* magazine and the BBC's *Top Gear*. A select few British constabularies adopted the VI for high-speed chase work, to which it proved highly suited. In Continental Europe, Evo enthusiasts were elated that they could finally get their hands on a true left-hand-drive example, with most orders coming from Germany.

The one major market that had still yet to sample the Evo was North America, but thanks to growing global interest and the arrival of a video game called Gran Turismo, a growing, pent-up demand would, eventually, need satisfying.

SUBARU: FURTHER FORWARD

While SWRT was still pushing hard in the 1998 World Rally Championship, in September of that year Subaru introduced an updated line of Impreza WRXs in Japan (Australia actually received its 1999 models first, in August). Most of the changes centered around a new generation of boxer engine, dubbed the Phase II. Refinement and throttle response were the focus here, with the motor tuned to give more low- and-mid range torque, as well as smoother delivery, thanks to a revised crankshaft design. As before, manual and automatic WRXs got engines in different states of tune. Interestingly, the WRX Sports Wagon lost 10 hp, going back down to 240 bhp, despite having the highest compression ratio of all the new turbocharged EJ20s (9.0:1 versus 8.0:1 on the 280-hp version of the WRX five-speed sedan). The shifter on manual gearbox cars was also improved, with better feel and smoother action, while the transmission mounts were strengthened and a greater number of bolts were used on the bell housing to secure it to the engine—a response to complaints that the gearbox was still a weak link on turbocharged Imprezas.

Other technical changes included the adoption of a 22B-style suspension with inverted struts and stouter bushings. It added weight, but the tradeoff was further improved handling and cornering ability.

THE ROAD TO STARDOM

Externally, WRX models got a new grille with a honeycomb inserts and multidiamond reflector head and foglight assemblies for a slightly more modern look. Changes to the interior included a new door panel design, Momo steering wheel, and upholstery patterns.

The hard-core RA model returned alongside the mainstream WRX. It came with a factory WRC-style roof vent and Pure White paint. It could be optioned with automatic climate control, ABS brakes, and dual airbags. However, in reality few buyers did, as these options added weight and cost, and they compromised performance (ordering the air option mandated deletion of the intercooler water sprayer).

Regular WRXs were offered in a choice of Pure White, Artic Silver, Black Mica, and Cool Grey metallic. Interestingly, there wasn't a blue exterior hue offered this year, but the wagon could be specified in a red shade called Rose Mica.

Alongside the mainstream WRX offerings, Subaru announced a new batch of STi Version V cars as well, consisting of two sedans, a wagon, and a two-door coupe. These adopted the same styling tweaks as their WRX counterparts, but they sported a new design of STi

Subaru launched a spate of updated models for 1999, including a new Impreza STi "Version V." This was distinguished from previous models by a revised front air dam and fog light housings. Internally, there were updates to the EJ20 engine, a stronger gearbox, and more compact center differential. Subaru Global

foglight covers. Also employing variations of the Phase II EJ20 engine, the STis received improvements to the cooling system with a revised water jacket, better plumbing, and new pistons with thinner rings, plus a more efficient cold air intake system. Like the standard Rex, the five-speed manual gearbox on these cars received a stronger casing with greater reinforcements. A new smaller, lighter, and more efficient center-mounted differential was installed, while stouter shocks—some 10 percent stiffer than those on other WRX models—were specified for the STi type RA, which also got a quicker 13:1 steering box. Improved brakes with a more intelligent ABS system were standard across the board.

Exterior colors on the STi Version V models mirrored those on regular WRX models, and there were minor interior changes, including a slightly revised steering wheel and STi embroidery on the front seats that incorporated a slightly different pattern. An interesting option was the sports edition interior, which added bright red trim on the center console, instrument cluster, door handles, dash vents, and the steering wheel and shifter knob.

RIGHT HOOKIN' EXPATS

As already mentioned briefly, the first market to receive the 1999 model year Imprezas was actually Australia. As in previous years, the Aussie-spec WRX differed from the JDM version with a differently tuned engine. It got a bit of boost, up to 218 hp and 214 lb-ft of torque, with notably improved throttle response, particularly through the mid-range. It also received an improved braking system with new rotors (vented both front and back) and improved four-piston calipers. Cosmetic upgrades ran to the mesh-style front grille, revised front bumper with new turn-signal treatment, and a new, taller rear spoiler. Soon the Aussies enjoyed the appearance of the STi Type R coupe. Subaru shipped an example over from Japan, and it did the rounds with various press publications. Response was so favorable that Subaru Australia soon started bringing STis from the motherland, though initially in very small numbers. However, for Australian Subaru enthusiasts an important milestone had been reached, and there'd be no going back.

On the other side of the globe, in the other major right-hand-drive export market, 1999 UK-spec Scoobs adopted similar changes to their Australian counterparts. Power on the UK Turbo models was increased to the same 218 bhp and 224 lb-ft of torque, the improved braking system was added, and styling updates were nigh identical to the Aussie cars, including the new front fascia, grille, and bigger rear spoiler. Inside, the UK cars also got the new-style Momo steering wheel (with standard airbag) and standard antitheft system, including an engine immobilizer. With car theft remaining a huge problem in Britain, the last feature was particularly welcome. In an effort to curb such activities, approximately half a dozen police forces in the country ordered a number of specially built Prodrive Impreza Turbo patrol cars, which proved excellent mounts for police work because of their manageable size, rapid acceleration, outstanding handling, and excellent wet-weather traction.

By this point, the Impreza Turbo had become somewhat of a cult car in Britain. With Subaru also topping the J. D. Power and Associates customer satisfaction surveys, things were looking remarkably good for FHI's car division in a market where, two decades prior, the brand had barely existed.

MITSUBISHI: CHANGES AT THE TOP

Unlike previous years, Mitsubishi Ralliart Europe, with new sponsorship from Marlboro, had its latest WRC contender ready to go for the start of the 1999 season. Lead driver Tommi Makinen spent more time testing the Evo VI rally car this time around, and he lauded the improvements, particularly chassis and suspension tweaks that gave it rock-solid stability in virtually any conditions.

As before, MRE had an official two-car works team, and for marketing reasons the second car was still dubbed a Carisma GT, despite being an Evo VI in all but name (the true Carisma being an entirely different machine and cousin to the Volvo S40). Risto Mannisenmaki signed up to co-drive with Makinen, while the number two works entry was taken over by the young Belgian Freddy Loix (Richard Burns having gone back to Subaru to supplant Colin McRae, who'd gone to Ford). In the seat next to Loix was fellow Belgian Sven Smeets.

The first two events of the year saw the reigning world champion assert his dominance once more. In the Monte Carlo, an event that saw very tricky weather conditions, including rain, snow, and particularly ice, Makinen dodged the obstacles, proving his versatility with fast times when tackling a tarmac street course or winding mounting road. By the end of the first day, he was in the lead, and there he stayed, right until the end. Loix, on the other hand, got off to a rocky start with his new team. He hit a patch of ice and crashed the Carisma GT on the first day, damage to the radiator bringing about retirement.

Sweden, despite a distinct lack of snow, again saw Makinen on top form. Despite a brave effort by Carlos Sainz in the Toyota Corolla, the reigning champ gained a comfortable lead by the final day, claiming his third Swedish Rally victory in the process. In the meantime, Loix, still struggling to get to grips with his new mount, managed to bring the second MRE car home in ninth place. With a driving style very different to Makinen, the young Belgian would need a few changes to the car to maximize his potential.

Punctures were rife during the 1999 Safari, and sure enough, Makinen ruptured a tire, an incident that became surrounded in controversy. Stopping in a village to change it, both he and Risto were surrounded by locals who offered assistance. A TV crew was filming the entire incident and, although the two-man team tried to usher the villagers away, the FIA rulebook stated that outside help was forbidden during an event and Makinen and Mannisenmaki were disqualified. Loix didn't have much luck either. Coming over a crest, he hit a huge pothole and rolled the car. His Carisma GT was written off, and Freddy was taken to the hospital.

Loix's injuries forced him to sit out the next event in Portugal, so Ralliart brought in Finn Marcus Gronholm to pilot the second works car. The young Finn did well, making steady progress—particularly impressive considering the Mitsubishi was a far cry from the Peugeot he was used to driving. However, at half distance he developed brake problems. Then the clutch blew, and he had to call it a day. Makinen got off to a slow start because of driveline issues, but he picked up the pace. Still, the cancellation of two stages on the second day meant a fifth place was the best he could muster. In Group N, Miguel Campos managed to bring a Lancer home in the top spot, so that at least was something to savor.

Loix was back for Catalunya, an event that saw the front-drive F2 cars dominate. Still, he drove his most impressive event yet for the Ralliart team and got into quite a scrap with Carlos Sainz before finishing fourth overall. Makinen, dealing with electrical gremlins related to the brake and transmission setup, was handicapped on the early stages. As the rally progressed, the problems were progressively ironed out. However, a misjudged tire choice and then a controversial jump start on Special Stage 10—in which he, former teammate Richard Burns, and SEAT's Harri Rovanpera were all given a one-minute penalty for leaving the start line too soon—didn't help matters. Tommi ended up finishing third after passing his teammate on the third day.

On the Tour de Corse, brake issues plagued Makinen's car throughout the event. With Loix suffering from similar maladies, the best results they could manage were a sixth and eighth, with the Subaru of archrival Burns sandwiched between them.

His chances for the championship now hanging in the balance, Makinen needed to pull out all the stops in Argentina. Once again, his progress was hampered by reliability issues; this time, it was transmission woes. Still, he and Risto made the best of a bad situation and brought the car home in fourth place overall. Loix, on his first outing in Argentina, hit a rock on Special Stage 5, spinning the car. After also having to contend with a wandering horse, Loix and Smeets recovered. But on the third day, after making steady progress, Freddy lost control and crashed out.

WRX vs. EVO

Joining the Mitsubishi works team in 1999 was young Belgian driver Freddy Loix. His performance in Argentina wasn't memorable, but as time went by and he got more comfortable with his new mount, Loix became a real contender. Mitsubishi Japan

As always, attrition was high at the Acropolis rally, but Mitsubishi was the only one of the top concerns to have both its works cars finish the event. Makinen was off to a fine start, but the punishing conditions resulted in suspension problems. Although repairs were made, he wasn't able to catch Burns or Sainz this time. Still, with a third-place finish he held on to the lead for the driver's championship. Loix drove a decent rally, dodging the obstacles to finish fourth.

The next round was in New Zealand just over a month later. Makinen and co-driver Mannisenmaki made this one look like a breeze. A strong start translated into a healthy lead, especially once electrical problems put an end to a challenge by Colin McRae in the Ford Focus. Makinen was able to cruise casually through the last few stages and secured his first New Zealand victory ahead of Juha Kankkunen in the Subaru. Loix, struggling a bit on the loose gravel and mud, kept it going and brought the second works car home in eighth place.

Back in Europe for the Neste Rally Finland (1000 Lakes), and on home ground, Tommi Makinen looked set to win once again, setting the pace on the opening day. However, a gearbox problem on Stage

THE ROAD TO STARDOM

14 robbed Tommi and Risto any chance of a meaningful finish. On the same stage, Loix rolled the Carisma GT, though the car was soon back in action and he and Smeets eventually finished in tenth place. Mitsubishi's dominance continued in the production car class as Jouko Puhakka upheld Group N honors driving an Evo V.

The next round was a new one for WRC: China, which doubled as the 11th rally in the Asia-Pacific championship. The MRE works team had a fairly tough ordeal, being plagued by accidents. Makinen was making good time when he hit a tree on Special Stage 5, and although the car was repaired, he hit a rock on the last stage of day two, damaging the suspension; he had little choice but to retire. Loix, while trying to get past Colin McRae and in a valiant effort to make up for lost time, slid off the road during Special Stage 7, ending his rally early on the first day. However, Gustavo Trelles battled his way to a second in Group N, and Japanese driver Katsuhiko Taguchi clinched both the APC driver's crown and Group N championships, making for a silver lining to this Chinese thundercloud.

Although Makinen still had a fair shot at the championship, he needed to score big in the San Remo to keep his hopes alive. Fairly traumatic weather conditions (thanks to plenty of rain) made many stages dicey to say the least, but Makinen eventually pulled ahead of Gilles Panizzi and his Peugeot 206 on the last stage to snatch the victory. Loix, with the Carisma GT now set up for his own driving style, was superb and finished a strong fourth overall.

There were now just two rounds left to go for the year, Australia and Britain. In the former, Makinen's old teammate Richard Burns blazed ahead for Subaru. Although Tommi couldn't match Burns nor Carlos Sainz for speed, a third-place finish was more than enough to secure his fourth driver's title. Loix put in another strong performance, finishing right behind his teammate. In Group N, Gustavo Trelles, after crashing out in San Remo, bagged enough points to win the class championship ahead of Hamed al-Wahaibi.

The last round of the year, as always, had the WRC teams contending with plenty of mud and poor visibility in the Network

WRX vs. EVO

Nineteen-ninety nine proved to be the year of Tommi Makinen. The Finn once again exercised his dominance and took his fourth world championship. Mitsubishi Japan

Q RAC Rally. Makinen retired with engine troubles; Loix, by now seemingly comfortable with the car, finished fifth.

Although, Makinen had scored yet another driver's crown, the team had finished third in the constructor's race, behind Toyota and archrival Subaru. On the positive side, in both in Group N and the Asia-Pacific Championship, there was absolutely no doubt that the Mitsubishi Evolution was the car to beat.

SUBARU: BURNS RETURNS

In terms of production cars, 1999 was shaping up to be quite the year for Subaru, especially as the enthusiast market was concerned. With STi models now starting to reach foreign shores and the 22B having been launched to critical claim, it seemed that it was onward and upward for FHI's car division.

However, the one arena in which all things were measured, at least as far as the Impreza WRX and STi were concerned, was the

THE ROAD TO STARDOM

FIA's World Rally Championship. For the 1999 season, there were big changes, not in the least being an entirely new driver lineup for the SWRT works team. Both McRae and Liatti had departed, the Scotsman to Ford and the Italian to SEAT. Richard Burns signed up to drive for his old team again, partnering with longstanding co-driver Robert Reid. The second car was given to veteran Finnish driver and four-time WRC champion Juha Kankkunen, who'd spent much of his career with Lancia, Toyota, and lately Ford. Riding with him was fellow Finn Juha Repo. A third car was allocated to another former Ford driver, Belgian Bruno Thiry, who entered it in a few events.

Technical changes included a new roof vent design that was said to add an extra two mph at speed, while the Prodrive six-speed manual gearbox received a new automated shift feature that, via oil pressure, allowed the driver to change gears sequentially without using a clutch, either by the lever itself or a button by the steering wheel. A total of 10 WRC 1999-spec cars, again based on the Retna/Stevens two-door body, were built by Prodrive for the season, spec'd with Bilstein shocks and Pirelli tires. Also, with no more sponsorship from British American Tobacco, the gold 555 logos were replaced by fluorescent yellow Subaru decals.

Cars were fielded in the Monte Carlo for Burns and Kankkunen, but one of the biggest surprises was Gilles Panizzi, who did a cracking job as a privateer in an old 1998 spec car; he helped earn himself a works Peugeot drive later at the Tour de Corse. The Frenchman led three special special stages on the first day and was still running well until leg three, when he hit a patch of black ice and spun the car into a wall, causing it flip and slide on its roof for close to 300 feet. Despite not being able to catch Tommi Makinen, Kankkunen clearly appeared to be more at home with the car than the other works drivers, in both the street sections and slushy mountain switchbacks; he came in second overall. Burns, on the other hand, was a rather disappointing eighth.

In Sweden, the drivers had to contend with a serious amount of ice; despite the cold conditions, snowfall wasn't what it had been in years past. The Subaru drivers found it tough going, their Pirelli tires proving highly unsuited to the conditions. With no chance of catching Makinen, Sainz, or even Didier Auriol, Burns and Kankkunen waged their own battle. The Brit finished fifth, Kankkunen was sixth, and Thiry, who was in a third car, came home 10th behind the second Mitsubishi of Freddy Loix.

The Safari was next on the calendar, and although it was dry this year, it was no less challenging than usual. Kankkunen's rally ended when his Scoob developed electrical problems, but Burns, the 1998 winner, made steady progress and was in the lead by the end of leg one. Punctures started taking their toll on the second day, but Richard saw his race come to an end when a suspension bolt sheared off. Thiry had also retired, out on the first day with electrical maladies similar to Kankkunen's.

Three cars were again entered in the Rally de Portugal. Although the rally itself went more smoothly than in the past—thanks to better marshalling and crowd control—for the Subaru team, it wasn't

Juha Kankkunen signed up with the Subaru team for 1999 along with Richard Burns, who'd previously been with Mitsubishi. Kankkunen's fortunes during the season were mixed; in Portugal he retired when his car suffered a mysterious engine failure.
Subaru Global

THE ROAD TO STARDOM

particularly memorable. Kankkunen was making progress until the second leg, when his engine mysteriously decided to self-destruct. Burns, struggling again with traction problems, managed to reach the end in this one, albeit in a distant fourth behind McRae, Sainz, and Didier Auriol, though he did finish ahead of the formidable Tommi Makinen, with Thiry rounding out the top six.

In Spain, things went from bad to worse for SWRT. The F2 front-drive cars dominated this one, with the Citroen of Philippe Bugalski taking the flag. The works Subarus were well off the pace, but they did at least finish in fifth, sixth, and seventh overall, the order being Burns, Kankkunen, and Thiry. The fact that the rival Mitsubishis also didn't fare well was at least some consolation.

The Tour de Corse, with similar conditions, turned out to be a lot like Catalunya, only worse. The Citroens and the new Peugeot 206s of Francois Delecour and Gilles Panizzi proved the cars to beat. Burns, again struggling with the Pirelli tires, came in seventh despite spinning his car several times during the last leg. Thiry, in the only other works entry (Kankkunen chose to skip this one and hone his gravel skills), retired after his mount suffered accident damage.

Argentina marked a change in luck, but not without controversy. The relationship between Burns and Kankkunen was proving to be testy at best. Both drivers performed well, taking the lead on the first leg, first Richard and then Juha, seemingly in a game of cat and mouse. On day two, despite a slight delay thanks to a penalty and gearbox trouble, Burns came roaring back into the lead, passing Auriol in the Toyota, until his teammate, making a late charge, caught and passed him on day three. With no team orders in force, Kankkunen scored his first WRC win in five years, which also brought his total to 22, matching Carlos Sainz for the greatest number of championship victories at the time. Burns came in second but wasn't particularly happy about the result and believed the win had been partly engineered. Still, the rally had shown that the Subarus were highly competitive once again.

The next round saw the teams battling in Greece at the Acropolis Rally. As always, reliability played a key part in this tough event.

WRX vs. EVO

Among the casualties was Kankkunen, when, on the second day, his front suspension collapsed. Burns dodged nearly every obstacle the rocky rally could throw at him and beat the odds to take his first ever win for Subaru.

A fairly wet New Zealand saw Kankkunen score an impressive second overall, thanks to a very canny and consistent drive, though he couldn't quite match the pace of fellow Finn Tommi Makinen. Burns dodged gearbox problems, eventually succumbing to them on Special Stage 8.

In the Rally Finland, Kankkunen, on home turf, look set to do well, having practiced his skills with the Subaru on gravel during numerous occasions. He didn't disappoint, proving he was still the master when it came to this blindingly fast, loose-surface event. Although Burns was the quickest on day one, Juha maintained a strong and steady pace, ending the day behind Richard. On the second leg, the veteran Finn started to show his experience. He passed Gronholm on the second

Burns is seen here in the 1999 Rally Finland, where he finished second behind teammate Kankkunen. Burns started gaining momentum as the season progressed, taking the checkered flag on home turf at the RAC in November. Subaru Global

stage of the day, and from there he kept the lead all the way to the end. Burns, despite a puncture, started pushing hard as the final day wore on and was catching his teammate, but not rapidly enough to stand any chance of winning. Still, a 1–2 for Subaru and a DNF for rival Tommi Makinen and Mitsubishi put SWRT in a strong position for the constructor's championship.

The China rally proved a fairly good one for SWRT, despite monsoon-like weather conditions with plenty of mud. The works WRC Subarus were competitive; Burns managed to finish second behind Didier Auriol (after having led for a good portion), while Kankkunen, having suffered from a malfunctioning front differential, came home in fourth. In Group N, Toshihiro Arai brought home an Impreza to win the class, ahead of Gustavo Trelles in a Mitsubishi Evo V.

At San Remo, the teams once again found themselves running on tarmac. Both works cars suffered from driveline issues, with a faulty clutch costing Kankkunen valuable time (he ultimately came in sixth) and a broken gearbox ending Burns' rally, though Arai once again took top Group N honors.

Despite the driver's championship being clinched by Makinen, Australia ultimately proved to go Burns' way. Richard had taken the lead from Carlos Sainz by day two and, although the Spaniard pressed hard in the opening stages on the final day of competition, Burns ultimately won by 11.6 seconds. Kankkunen's rally ended early when he hit a tree stump on Special Stage 5, damaging the suspension. Although Sainz had clinched the manufacturer's title for Toyota by finishing second, the Subaru team had come roaring back in the second half of the season and there was still one more round to go.

The 1999 Rally of Great Britain again saw the Subarus dominant. Kankkunen took the lead on Special Stage 2, but then Burns came on in the second leg, proving the master of the dark and damp Welsh forest stages. He extended his lead to over 25 seconds by day's end, despite the cancellation of Special Stage 15 caused by an overflow of spectators. The Subarus were the only ones to enjoy a relatively trouble-free final leg as accidents and mechanical troubles took their toll on most of the entrants. With a 1–2 to round out the season and a second place in the constructor's championship, SWRT looked good for 2000.

MITSUBISHI: TOMMI MAKINEN COMMEMORATED

Celebrating Tommi Makinen's fourth consecutive WRC driver's crown, Ralliart pulled out all the stops and revealed the Mitsubishi Lancer Evolution VI Tommi Makinen Edition (TME) at the 1999 Tokyo Motor Show in September. The production version of this car went on sale in January 2000 and became an instant collectible. In many respects, this car was its own beast, bridging the gap between the last of the fifth-generation Lancer Evos and the larger, more angular, sixth-generation Cedia based cars that would follow it. As a result, the TME is often referred to as an Evolution 6 1/2 or 6.5.

The TME, like previous Evolution models, was offered in both GSR and RS trim, with the latter again being the more hard-core, competition-oriented version. The two-liter 4G63 twin-cam four-cylinder engine was similar to that of the regular Evo VI, but Mitsubishi's engineers had tinkered with the turbocharger and plumbing. As a

Built to celebrate the flying Finn's dominance in the WRC, the Lancer Evolution VI Tommi Makinen edition was a very special machine and became an instant collectible. Available in team MRE colors, it wasn't for the faint of heart. Milsport UK

THE ROAD TO STARDOM

It's not well known that the Makinen edition was also offered in more subdued exterior hues. The car is often called an Evo VI 1/2 model because it introduced some unique features of its own, namely a revised turbocharger and bigger-bore exhaust system. The front air dam was also different from "regular" Evo VI models. Mitsubishi Japan

result, the GSR version of the production TME featured a new turbo with lighter and stronger titanium-aluminum turbine blades, plus a smaller-diameter compressor disc, which enabled the turbo to spool up even quicker than before. Combined with a new, less restrictive and bigger bore exhaust system, the result was improved throttle response, particularly in the low- and mid-rpm ranges, helping answer criticism that the Evo was still a peaky, thrashy, hot-rod hooligan that needed to be flogged within an inch of its life to deliver its world-beating performance.

Interestingly enough, RS buyers had to request the improved engine and turbo system, as it was listed as an option on this model, not standard as on the GSR. Thus, if you ordered the RS version of the TME, it came standard with the Evo VI engine in regular tune. The five-speed manual gearbox on both models was the same as on the Evo VI, utilizing the same gear ratios on all five speeds. Still, with the extra torque, the Tommi Makinen Edition felt notably quicker under acceleration on both the street and racetrack.

Other engineering improvements on the TME included a redesigned fuel tank designed to prevent fuel starvation during hard cornering, a standard strut tower brace to stiffen up the front end, and a revised steering box with a quicker 13:1 ratio for sharper response, plus standard 17-inch Enkei multispoke wheels, nigh identical to those on the WRC cars and finished in a dazzling shade of white. These chassis improvements were designed to give the car improved stability and handling on rally tarmac stages. In street trim, they made a noticeable difference to the Evolution's balance and controllability—quicker reflexes and a more surefooted feel were evident. Further helping was a drop in ride height over the regular Evo VI by 10 mm overall, combined with changes to the suspension geometry to further improve handling. As ever, the ride remained on the firm side, with references to a buckboard being made more than once.

Cosmetically, the biggest difference between the Makinen Edition and the earlier Evo VI was the front fascia. The front foglights were binned, replaced by a small cylindrical opening on the left side and a squared up hole on the right side to feed the externally mounted engine oil cooler. The air dam itself was also more prominent, jutting further forward with a pronounced lip that curved up to the fenders on

Inside, the Makinen edition featured a unique upholstery pattern with special red stitching on both the front and rear seats. Mitsubishi Japan

either side. The rest of the aero package, including the side extensions, rear bumper, and decklid spoiler, was carried over from the regular Evo VI. The cabin, familiar to anybody who'd spent time behind the wheel of a VI, was also jazzed up a little with red instead of white numbers on the black gauge faces. Red stitching was featured on the steering wheel rim, shifter boot, and seats. GSR models got special red inserts and a special T. Makinen emblem embroidered into the seat backs. The RS version made do with regular Evo VI chairs, unusually finished in blue.

The Tommi Makinen Edition was available in several exterior colors: Satellite Silver, Pyrennees Black, Scotia White, Canal Blue, or Passion Red for the GSR and just Scotia White for the RS version.

Buyers who opted for the Passion Red GSR could, at additional cost, add the Special Color Package, which dressed up the car to look like Tommi's winning Group A machine. This included special silver, black, and white graphics that ran along the flanks on each side, a small Ralliart emblem on the corners of the front fascia, and a Mitusbishi diamond logo on each side plate of the rear spoiler. Those who purchased one of the 2,500 Tommi Makinen Edition cars built also received a signed, commemorative scale model mounted on a wooden stand.

The GSR version was priced at ¥3,278,000 in its home country, with the RS quite a bit cheaper at just over ¥2,500,000. Both were quite a bargain, especially considering the level of performance on offer. Although primarily aimed at the Japanese domestic market, a select few of these cars went overseas (the majority, 286 of them, to Germany), and in 2001 (almost a year after the car was launched), Ralliart UK offered up a few for sale in the Britain, alongside the nutty 340-bhp Extreme (see Appendix B: Special Edition Cars). To this day, the Tommi Makinen Edition is one of the most, if not *the* most, sought-after of all Mitsubishi Lancer Evolutions. To many enthusiasts, it represents the pinnacle of the car's raw performance in the purest sense, a complete, purely race-bred driver's machine. With the launch of the larger and heavier Evolution VII on a new platform, things wouldn't be quite the same again.

SUBARU: THE GC BOWS OUT

As Mitsubishi was winding down production of the Evolution VI, Subaru was finishing up with the GC chassis Impreza. By early 2000, with the new GD platform car almost ready to hit the showrooms, the last of the old models were introduced. Australia saw a couple more special editions, the first being called just that, the WRX Special Edition, launched at the end of 1999. Very similar to the WRX Classic, it was followed up in January 2000 by the not-so-subtle Club Spec Evo 4, which, unlike previous versions, came as a sedan or wagon in a shocking yellow hue with contrasting gunmetal-finished 16-inch wheels.

However, one car that outdid even this for sheer garishness was the Japanese-market STi S201 (see Appendix B: Special Edition Cars). Save for these, it was otherwise business as usual. The final GC chassis Imprezas rolled off the line during the summer, though in North America (Subaru's biggest export market and ironically the only major one where turbocharged Imprezas were not available), the outgoing car would be categorized as a 2001 model for its final season.

CHAPTER 4

GLOBAL SUPREMACY

It was a new decade and the dawn of a new century and millennium. By this stage, both the Lancer Evolution and Subaru WRX had proven themselves among the elite of the world's performance cars, yet they were still within reach of the common man (or woman). As we shall see, both cars developed into even quicker and more refined machines as the decade wore on, though in world championship rallying, circumstances and competition proved tougher than ever.

2000

MITSUBISHI: NEW DECADE, GREATER CHALLENGES

As far as Mitsubishi Ralliart Europe and its WRC program was concerned, 2000 was a year to mark time. The team continued to field the Group A spec Evolution VI models, and once again, Makinen was named lead driver with Loix returning for his second season in the number two works car that again ran with Carisma GT badging. Both drivers paired up with the same partners, Risto Mannisenmaki and Sven Smeets, respectively.

Mechanically, the cars were little changed from the 1999 season, though power was rated slightly less—at 290 bhp instead of 300. Torque was unchanged, still a healthy 375 lb-ft at 3,500 revs.

WRX vs. EVO

The season got off to a good start, with Makinen exerting his dominance in Monte Carlo. Although Gilles Panizzi and his Peugeot 206 won the first stage, Makinen made steady progress, and by stage four he was in the lead and began setting an electrifying pace that he kept despite entering the difficult mountain stages, including the tricky Sisteron Pass. He slowed the pace a little bit toward the end, but he still finished comfortably ahead of a determined Carlos Sainz. Loix, having struggled somewhat during the 15-stage event, brought the Carisma GT home in sixth place.

More snow was in the cards for Sweden, but this one belonged to the front-drive Peugeot of Marcus Gronholm, not Makinen, who ended up playing cat and mouse with Ford's Colin McRae for good deal of the event, eventually finishing ahead of the Scotsman in third place. Loix, however, was not having much luck. Fairly sluggish stage times aside, he kept plugging away, ultimately finishing 11th behind the SEAT Cupras of Toni Gardemeister and Francois Delecour.

As in 1999, the third event of the season was the Safari in Kenya, a far cry from snowy Sweden. Makinen's car took a severe pounding;

Makinen and Loix signed up for the 2000 season with Mitsubishi, and in the opening round in Monte Carlo, Tommi proved he hadn't lost any of his touch, setting the pace and winning the event by a healthy margin over Carlos Sainz. Mitsubishi Japan

he had three punctures on stage two and damaged the suspension, and the car finally conked out with electrical problems brought on by a dead battery. Loix kept the surviving Mitsubishi works entry going a little while longer and was driving a steady pace when, on leg two, his car finally gave up the ghost, bowing out with suspension maladies.

In Group N, there was greater success with Italian driver Claudio Menzi behind the wheel of an old Evo V. He finished in ninth place, winning the Group N class in the process behind Luis Clement in the Skoda Octavia.

Portugal didn't prove to be much better for Makinen; he was way off his usual pace, running down in eighth place when he crashed out. The car was patched up, but problems persisted and the Finn was out before half distance with a broken suspension. Loix, who on previous occasions had done well here, was a bit off form, too, but he maintained enough momentum to hold onto sixth place.

With Subaru's Richard Burns having taken the lead in the driver's championship, Makinen needed to make a comeback in Catalunya to stay in the running. Things improved somewhat, though the

Spain proved to be a tough event for the MRE works drivers. Loix and co-driver Sven Smeets came in eighth place overall, though Makinen did somewhat better, finishing in fourth. Mitsubishi Japan

competition was fierce, with McRae, Burns, and Sainz all vying for the lead over much of the event. Brake issues hampered Makinen's progress, but he did manage to stay the course and finish fourth overall, though the championship points gap between him and Burns, who finished second, was starting to widen. Loix and Smeets drove a fairly steady rally but only managed to finish eighth, behind the third Peugeot of Francois Delecour. German driver Uwe Nittel, running a Group N car with Carisma GT logos, held up the end for Mitsubishi, winning the class and finishing 17th overall.

After three disappointing races, the works MRE team scored a podium finish in Argentina, with Makinen coming in third. Although he couldn't catch Burns or Gronholm, he elected to just bring the car home, rather than trying to push it, as any points MRE could get were beneficial by this stage. Loix bolstered the tally by coming fifth on only his second outing in Argentina. Group N Lancers once again dominated their class, with Gustavo Trelles winning and Gabriel Pozzo coming in second place.

Greece was a bit of a disaster, with both works entries going out early. Loix retired on the very first special stage where he crashed and damaged the suspension, and then Makinen was out two stages later when he went off the course and broke his rear end links. Richard Burns also retired, much to the relief of Makinen.

In New Zealand, things got off to a cold but dry start. Makinen was well off the pace, finishing the first leg in a distant ninth place as he struggled with handling and torque transfer issues. During the first stage of leg three, he spun the car, hitting an embankment and causing extensive damage to the Evo. Although he limped back to the service area, the suspension was severely bent; having struggled for two days already, Tommi felt it best to retire. Loix had also gone out, leaving the rally in the hands of the Group N cars for Mitsubishi. This time it was Manfred Stohl who took top honors, finishing an impressive seventh overall behind the Subaru of Peter "Possum" Bourne.

In the notoriously fast and difficult Rally Finland, MRE had updated Group A cars, prepared to Evo 6.5 specifications and incorporating the revised front end also seen on the street-going Tommi Makinen Edition. For co-driver Risto Mannisenmaki, suffering from back injuries, the second leg in particular, with its numerous jumps was tough going. Makinen brought the car home in fourth place and secured valuable championship points in the process, although the season was looking like it would favor Marcus Gronholm by this juncture. Loix was barreling along until, on the first stage of leg two, he went off course, ruptured his radiator, and blew the engine.

Next on the calendar was the Rally Cyprus, a new event on the WRC calendar that took place on the dusty, rocky hills surrounding the port city of Limassol. On the opening leg, things didn't go to well; Tommi's car suffered from gearbox problems, hampering any chance to make good stage times. However, as the rally progressed, things improved for Makinen. By leg three, he was back on form, setting the fastest time on the first stage of the day and then passing Estonian Markko Martin in the Toyota Corolla on the following one. He kept up a healthy pace, setting another fastest time on Stage 21, but it was too late. The delays from day one meant the best result he could get was a fifth overall, but he wasn't too far behind fourth-place finishers Richard Burns and Robert Reid.

Freddy Loix and Sven Smeets drove an excellent rally overall, setting the fastest stage times on two occasions and staying right in the thick of action among McRae, Burns, and Delecour. However, like Makinen, Loix had got off to a sluggish start and that first leg would come back to haunt him. He ran out of time (and road) to catch up and came in eighth. Still, the young Belgian was happy with his progress. "We got our speed back," he later recalled. In Group N, Gustavo Trelles drove another outstanding rally in his Evo VI, bringing the black and white car home in first place once again, ahead of Gabriel Pozzo. In fact, Mitsubishis finished in the top seven places in Group N.

On the tight, twisty tarmac roads of the Tour de Corse, the Ralliart works team looked for better progress than last year, but once again success seemed to elude them. Loix was out on the very first stage after an accident. and although Makinen was still in contention by leg two, it went pear shaped the following morning when he misjudged a turn and the car went sideways, sliding off the road. With no chance of scoring any points, he had no hope of winning a driver championship for the season. The same couldn't be said for Austrian Manfred Stohl, however, who won yet another rally in Group N and extended his championship lead in the class over Gustavo Trelles.

The last tarmac rally of the year, San Remo, saw the front-drive Peugeots dominate, but things went better for the works Mitsubishi gang than on previous tarmac rallies. Three cars were entered, and Makinen maintained enough speed to stay comfortably in third place. By the last day, he was really starting to make progress. Despite a fairly major accident involving Markko Martin's Toyota Corolla that caused organizers to render the last stage of the event noncompetitive, Makinen still managed to bag a podium finish and was the first of the AWD cars to come home. Loix also made it to the end in 8th, and Andrea Aghini, given a drive in a third works car, came home 12th. In Group N, Mitsubishis were yet again the dominant force, only this time it was local lad Gianluigi Galli who took top honors.

Australia proved hot, dusty, and grueling, but it appeared that things were really going Makinen's way. He picked up the pace considerably and led much of leg three to finish first, albeit just 5.5 seconds ahead of then WRC leader Marcus Gronholm. However, the jubilation was short-lived. FIA stewards deemed that Makinen's car had been equipped with a nonregulation turbocharger prior to the event. Although it was believed to be a genuine mistake and not the team's fault, in the interests of sportsmanship Ralliart would not attempt to overturn the FIA's decision. It was a bitter blow, though there was some consolation in Group N, where Trelles won the class and Stohl came in third to maintain his class championship lead.

The RAC, run in Wales, decided the driver's championship for 2000. Although Makinen was out of the running, he decided to go out with a bang as best he could. After a shaky start, including a minor shunt, he went as fast as he could, tearing after Burns and Gronholm to finish on the podium once again. It was an emotional moment when

GLOBAL SUPREMACY

Tommi had to hand over the championship cup to Marcus Gronholm after so many years of winning it, but the Peugeot driver's title was justly deserved.

Loix didn't have a good rally, rolling the Carisma GT on a muddy stage two and damaging the car enough to warrant retirement. Austrian Manfred Stohl clinched the Group N title, however, after an excellent drive that saw his archrival Trelles suffer from punctures that slowed his progress.

Despite the Group N success, the 2000 season had been a disappointing one for MRE. Tommi Makinen came in 5th in the driver's points chase; Loix was a lowly 15th. The Group A spec cars simply struggled to keep pace with their rivals for much of the season, particularly Subaru, Ford, and Peugeot. Furthermore, the FIA was starting to pressure Ralliart to join the World Rally Car program, and the long development time needed for such a change would mean that improvements to the existing package needed to come first if the works Mitsubishi gang were to stand any chance of remaining in the running for 2001.

SUBARU: TRANSITION ON THE RALLY SCENE

With a heavily revised, second-generation Impreza just months away by the start of 2000, SWRT trundled out merely updated 1999 rally machines as the WRC season began. As before, Richard Burns signed on as lead driver, partnering up with longtime companion Robert Reid. The second works car again went to Juha Kankkunen, but as the season developed, Simon Jean-Joseph, the team's main test driver, made select appearances on the tarmac rounds and Markko Martin and young Norwegian Petter Solberg saw time behind the wheel.

The season kicked off with the Monte Carlo Rally, where Burns made a good go of things. Despite spinning his car early on, he grabbed the lead on stage two. He proved highly competitive until, amid bitterly cold morning conditions at the start of the second leg, his car's engine refused to start (along with all three of the Peugeots), which brought about retirement. Kankkunen had somewhat better luck, picking up the pace on the second leg after having intermittent brake problems. He set the fastest time on Stage 7, and by Stage 13 on the final day, which took place on the multiple switchbacks of the infamous Sisteron pass, he set the fastest time once again, maintaining a healthy fourth place in the overall standings, nudging up to third by the last few miles when McRae and the Focus retired with a blown engine.

Sweden proved unusually warm. The normally snowy conditions had every chance of turning into a mixture of gravel and mud, prompting some stages to be shortened or cancelled entirely. The conditions naturally resulted in grip problems for many drivers, and Kankkunen struggled on the first day, losing a lot of time. Burns couldn't quite keep up with the pace of Gronholm's Peugeot, and by the end, the SWRT drivers only managed to come in fifth and sixth.

The Safari went Subaru's way, and a lot of that had to do with the tires. While many other teams, including Ford, Mitsubishi, and

On the Subaru front, the team stuck with the old 1999 cars for just two events, Sweden and the Safari. In the former, both Kankkunen (shown) and Burns suffered from traction issues brought on by exceedingly mild weather conditions. *Subaru Global*

Peugeot, struggled with punctures and mishaps, the Pirellis specified for the SWRT cars proved their worth. Burns led almost from start to finish (taking the lead on stage two and not looking back), while Kankkunen drove a superb rally to finish right behind his teammate. Japanese driver Toshihiro Arai brought a third works car home in sixth.

The TAP-sponsored Rallye de Portugal saw the team debut its latest WRC machines. Although they looked outwardly similar, these cars boasted a whole host of improvements. In many respects, these were 2001 season cars wearing the old two-door Retna bodies.

Revisions included a new engine with an improved and better-balanced reciprocating assembly, along with new pistons, an updated turbocharger and exhaust, and improved cooling. The driveline also benefited from a new, heavier flywheel and a more intelligent six-speed sequential gearbox. This sent power to three active differentials that powered all four wheels. With 300 bhp and 347 lb-ft of torque on tap, along with improved weight distribution, the new car proved to be a veritable tour de force in Portugal. Burns, despite developing steering problems on the latter half of the first leg, came roaring back to give SWRT its first win with the new mount on its debut event. Kankkunen wasn't so lucky, hitting a tree on the first day and retiring shortly afterward.

Reliability problems cropped up in Catalunya. Burns' car developed gearbox problems with the shifting mechanism, while Kankkunen's engine couldn't maintain an electrical charge thanks to a broken alternator pulley. This slowed his progress so much that an off during the early part of leg two was the final nail in the coffin, and he decided to call it a day. Burns pressed on and made excellent progress, finishing second behind Colin McRae in the Ford Focus.

Argentina seemed to be void of the controversy that surrounded the Subaru team in 1999. Burns, despite damaging his radiator early on, blazed a trail through much of the event to finish first, withstanding desperate efforts to catch him from Marcus Gronholm and Carlos Sainz. Kankkunen—although facing problems of his own, especially on stage three when he hit a tree stump—still managed to come in fourth. Subaru was now edging ahead of Ford in the constructor's championship.

The Acropolis dished out plenty of punishment for both Burns and Kankkunen. The Brit's turbo blew on unlucky Special Stage 13, and while he made it to the next service, the engine refused to start after repairs and Richard was out. Despite a faulty gearbox and a suspension that had taken a tremendous pounding on the rock-strewn stages, Kankkunen kept his end up and delivered another podium finish for the team. Toshihiro Arai, in a third works car, came in an excellent fourth place.

Fortune did not favor the Subaru camp in New Zealand. Both works drivers got off to a good start and Burns looked likely to bag at least third overall, but on the final leg's Stage 20, both cars mysteriously developed steering issues. On the following stage, the engines in both cars died, and Burns and Kankkunen were out.

By Finland the team was campaigning extensively updated cars, though they still used the old two-door bodywork. Richard Burns did exceptionally well during the early stages, but an accident forced him to retire. Subaru Global

GLOBAL SUPREMACY

Heading to the Neste Rally Finland, Burns and Subaru were still leading their respective championships, though Gronholm was catching up. Burns got off to a decent start in Finland, setting the pace on four of the early stages and fending off a hard-charging Gronholm, but an accident put him out early on. Kankkunen was not enjoying his home event; a nasty puncture cost him valuable time and put him out of the points chase for this one, his final result being eighth place. With another disappointing result and a Gronholm win, the Peugeot driver was now leading the driver's points cup.

The Cyprus Rally offered similar conditions to Greece, and Kankkunen, celebrating his 150th WRC event, maintained a steady pace and came home seventh. Burns was doing well until a faulty ECU caused him to lose power, which cost him time. However, the problem was resolved, and on the last two stages of the rally, he set the fastest overall time to secure a fourth-place finish, behind Francois Delecour.

Switching from rocks to tarmac in Corsica, SWRT test driver Simon Jean-Joseph was brought in to run in place of Kankkunen, while Norwegian Petter Solberg was given his first works Subaru drive. However, it proved to be a difficult one as mechanical problems brought about the Norwegian's retirement. Jean-Joseph's car caught fire, but the damage was repaired and he stayed in contention, coming home in seventh. Burns, facing stiff competition from the Peugeots and Carlos Sainz, set the pace on the opening stage but then found it tough going. He began charging on the final stages of leg three, but couldn't catch the leaders and had to settle for a fourth-place finish.

San Remo proved disappointing for Burns and Reid, for although they were fastest on the opening stages, the Peugeots once again asserted their dominance, pushing the Subaru driver back to third by the end of leg one. After damaging his oil pump, Burns had his engine overheat, and he was forced to retire. Two more works cars, driven by Jean-Joseph and Solberg, came in seventh and ninth, respectively.

Juha Kankkunen was back for Australia and made good progress on the opening leg, finishing on top of the heap by the opening day. Teammate Burns assumed the mantle for leg two, while Juha's day ended badly when he hit a tree stump on Special Stage 16 and damaged the car enough to cause retirement. Burns, getting into a major battle with Makinen and Gronholm on the last day, had to ultimately settle for third. But with one rally to go, he could still win the championship.

The last race of the year saw the SWRT team end the 2000 season in good form. Despite suffering a rear suspension failure early on, Burns came back to drive a superb rally and won in front of a home crowd. Kankkunen finished fifth, and Solberg was running well until he went off the road toward the end of leg one. Still, with Gronholm coming in second, Burns had to settle for runner-up in the driver's championship, while the team had to contend with third in the constructor's race, behind Peugeot and Ford but ahead of Mitsubishi.

Over in the Asia-Pacific championship, however, Subaru had a much better go, proving dominant for much of the season. Peter "Possum" Bourne won his third driver's title in the series.

2001

MITSUBISHI: BIGGER AND BETTER?

While the 2000 World Rally Championship was still raging, Mitsubishi and Subaru launched their updated Lancer and Impreza models. The sixth-generation Lancer, the Cedia, went on sale on May 9, 2000. More angular, grownup styling distinguished the car from its predecessor, and it was also quite a bit bigger, riding a 3.9-inch longer wheelbase. Height was increased from 54.9 to 56.3 inches and width grew by 0.2 inches (the front track remained almost identical, though the rear wheels were moved outward to add further stability). Much of the engineering, including the engine and MacPherson strut front and multilink rear independent suspension, was carried over. However, it would still be several months before the Evolution version of this car (the VII) went on sale. Chief engineer Hiroshi Fuji and his team worked diligently to bring the new homologation special to market, as well as the very first automatic transmission-equipped Evo, the GT-A.

SUBARU: THE BATTLE FOR SHOWROOM SUPREMACY HEATS UP

On August 23, 2000, Subaru introduced its second-generation small sedan and wagon (internally coded GD), with a turbocharged WRX version launched alongside the regular, normally aspirated lineup.

From those used to the previous GC cars, the new Impreza's appearance was startling to say the least. Most of that had to do with the unusual front end, characterized by a pair of bug-eye headlights that incorporated turn signals in the upper portion. The sedans (there was no coupe version) featured bulging WRC-inspired fenders, both front and back, while wagons had flat-sided fenders and unique sheetmetal and styling pieces, save for the hood and the front and rear bumpers. Takeshi Ito, project leader for the new Impreza, had wanted to make the car considerably safer and stronger than its predecessor, and the unibody was deemed some 185 percent stiffer overall. Other key areas were improved interior ergonomics, with a revised center stack, shifter console, instrument cluster, and dash vents, along with

Subaru unveiled a brand-new Impreza in August of 2000, utilizing a new chassis, coded GD. A WRX version was offered, with sedans initially coming in a single trim level, coded WRX NB. The 'bug-eyed' nose proved somewhat controversial. Huw Evans

better-quality and softer texture materials and improved outward visibility. In addition, the new cars boasted a wider front and rear track for improved stability. Interestingly enough, the product mix on the new Impreza was heavily biased toward wagons, with no fewer than six models on offer, but just two sedans, both of which were dubbed WRX. Although the styling might have suggested otherwise, the absence of a WRX Type RA sedan (and wagon counterpart) indicated that Subaru was aiming for a more mainstream audience with this car.

The normally aspirated WRX sedan featured an EJ20 engine tuned for 155 bhp and 144 lb-ft of torque coupled to a five-speed manual or four-speed automatic, but we'll concern ourselves with the turbocharged WRX sedan and its wagon counterpart, the 20K. The engine used in these was considerably improved over those in first-generation GC Imprezas. ECU calibrations countered tightening emissions and fuel economy standards but also to provided drivers with more useable power and torque over a wider rpm range. Although compression remained unchanged at 9.0:1 and the internals mostly

The latest WRX featured a lighter and stronger suspension with an improved ride, yet boasted faster steering and stronger brakes. Buyers could order BBS wheels as a dealer option in 15-, 16-, or 17-inch sizes. Huw Evans

carried over, there were changes to the fuel system with a new design of fuel injector and a larger gas tank specific to turbo-engined cars. Considerable attention was paid to the exhaust, with revised piping for improved efficiency and a new catalytic converter design. A modified Mitsubishi TD04 turbocharger had a lightweight impeller for quicker spool up, plus a bigger wastegate and a larger capacity intercooler to maximize the new turbo's potential. Rated at 250 hp and 242 lb-ft of torque, this latest version of the EJ20 helped offset the additional weight of the new chassis it had to haul around.

For the new turbocharged WRX and 20K wagon, transmission choices were a five-speed manual or four-speed automatic. The five-speeder was specific to the blown engine with taller ratios than on the normally aspirated Impreza, including a 3.166 first cog and 0.738 fifth gear. The four-speed auto's ratios were taller still but identical to the lesser car's, though drivers still had the option of using the sport shift mode, where by the gear lever could be moved up and down manually, if so desired.

As in previous versions, stick-shift GD WRXs, along with the 20N and 20K wagons, came with a center viscous coupling for the AWD system. Plus, all turbocharged cars featured a special double-offset driveshaft between the front and rear wheels and Suretrac rear differentials. Normally aspirated automatic cars got an active torque-split system with power distributed to the front and rear wheels via an electrically operated hydraulic transfer clutch.

The suspension design was based heavily on the previous car's, being fully independent and sprung by MacPherson struts both front and rear, though Ito and his team made a number of improvements, including a new subframe to mount the front suspension (designed to further quell ride harshness) and aluminum lower control arms for the WRX sedans. The suspension points themselves were also strengthened. The turbocharged cars also featured quicker steering with a 15:1 ratio, while braking on both the EJ20-engined sedans and wagons came via vented front discs with dual-piston calipers and solid rear rotors with single-pot clampers and standard ABS. Combined with the wider track and 16-inch alloy wheels shod in P205/50R16 rubber, the turbocharged WRX NB, especially in stick-shift form, was an even more entertaining car to drive than its predecessor.

Equipment wise, the WRX sedans and the two-liter wagons largely mirrored each other. All came with standard front foglights, body-colored rocker panel extensions, and polished exhaust tips (the blown cars had twin outlets), and both the turbocharged versions wore 16-inch wheels and tires (the N/A cars came with 15s). Interestingly enough, the turbocharged WRX rims were carried over from the old GC, whereas the 20K's were a new design. Other standard features included a leather-stitched four-spoke Momo steering wheel (with shift buttons for the automatic cars), power windows, mirrors, and locks with keyless entry, automatic climate control, standard four-speaker stereo system with in-dash CD player, and specially bolstered sport front bucket seats with height adjustment for the driver. In Japan, buyers could order aftermarket BBS wheels in 15-, 16-, or 17-inch sizes, an upgraded six-speaker sound system, a special Safety Pack that added side airbags and three-point seat belts for all riders, a sunroof, plus tinted glass, though strangely, ordering that required the purchase of high-intensity discharge (HID) headlights as well. In time for the new car's release, STi dished up a plethora of accessories, particularly suspension pieces that included new springs and shocks, plus a strut brace kit, a fairly gaudy-looking rear spoiler, and a special gauge cluster and interior trim. As ever, the hard-core enthusiasts were waiting for the genuine STi models, which were announced later in October.

MORE EXPORTS

Just before STi took the wraps off its latest Impreza-based offerings, the new second-generation Impreza made its appearance in Europe. The place was the British Motor Show, which that year took place at the National Exhibition Centre in Birmingham, the city once home to the United Kingdom's car industry. Subaru United Kingdom's display included the brand new WRC 2001 rally car, but many buyers were drawn to the regular sedan and wagon. Compared to the GC

GLOBAL SUPREMACY

cars, which were then still trickling out of dealerships, the GD was a startling departure. A big change for the UK market was model nomenclature. Unlike Japan, the normally aspirated two-liter sedan and wagon were both called the GX, while the WRX moniker finally supplanted 2000 Turbo as the truly sporty offering.

As before, the UK-market WRX turbo differed somewhat from its Japanese counterpart. Although also equipped with the EJ20 engine and featuring a similar turbo, wastegate, and exhaust upgrades, it was tuned differently. It was designed to run on lower grade fuel and rated at 218 bhp and 215 lb-ft of torque. Also, it was coupled to a five-speed manual gearbox with different ratios to the home-market version, with a shorter 3.90:1 first gear and a taller 3.90:1 final drive (it was 4:11 on the JDM car). In addition, UK-spec WRXs also featured bigger brakes with vented rotors both front and back (11.6 inches and 14.4 inches, respectively), along with larger wheels and tires to clear, in this case, 17x7 five-spokes with P245/45/R17 Bridgestone rubber.

As the top-of-the-line Impreza in Britain, the car came fully loaded with standard air, CD stereo, power windows, locks, and mirrors, plus a theft immobilizer. The sport bucket seats were extra—not a standard fitment on the turbo car—and the instrument cluster was different, with a speedo calibrated in miles as per UK requirements and a different location for the tachometer. Because of the relatively strong yen at the time, the British WRX didn't seem a great buy by Japanese standards when it went on sale a month later in November 2000, especially in view of its somewhat lower performance. But with a top speed pushing 145 mph and reaching 0–60 in under six seconds, a MSRP of £21,995 wasn't bad compared with rivals on the UK market.

In Australia, the new Impreza was announced the day after the UK introduction. The Aussies got the GX variant, which wasn't that dissimilar from the British version. However, they also got something sportier called the RX, which was basically the WRX minus the hot-rod turbo powerplant. It was a shrewd marketing move, in light of the fact that running costs and insurance on the Rex put it out of the hands of most of those who really wanted to own it. The turbocharged

WRX debuted as the Australian flagship, priced at a $43,800—nearly 9 grand more than the RX. The four-door turbo car offered plenty of pep with 218 hp on tap, though both it and the slightly more expensive wagon counterpart were offered in stick-shift form only, unlike their Japanese counterparts.

STi'S NEW BREED

Back in Japan, a week after the Euro and Aussie cars launched, a fairly low-key unveiling of the STi range took place in Tokyo. As with previous versions, the latest STi featured a whole host of upgrades that distinguished it from the regular WRX NB, not the least in the engine compartment. Still a 1,994cc EJ20, the STi version was rated at 280 bhp at 6,400 rpm (again purely to satisfy Japanese regulations) with 274 lb-ft of torque at 4,000 rpm, giving a hint of the car's sprinting ability. The engine took much inspiration from the EJ22 featured on the old STi 22B. The block was a stronger, semiclosed deck design, with the cylinder heads incorporating sodium-filled intake and exhaust valves, metal head gaskets to improve sealing, plus shimless valve lifters for smoother operation and reduced parasitic loss. Like the

It wasn't long before a GD-chassis STi model was unveiled in Japan. This car boasted the most powerful EJ20 engine yet, with numerous features borrowed from the old STi 22B. It was also the first to receive a six-speed manual gearbox. The regular STi model is shown here (an RA was also offered). Subaru Global

regular WRX turbo mill, a slightly larger intercooler was fitted on top of the engine, requiring a larger mail-slot hood scoop. Water spray was once again employed, but with a larger tank for extended use. It had automatic and manual override modes, which the driver could control via a dash-mounted button. Engineers paid a great deal of attention to the turbocharger and exhaust. Unlike the Rex, the new STi models featured an IHI RHF55 turbine. The ECU was specifically tuned for this engine, and with an 8.0:1 compression ratio coupled with more boost, premium-grade fuel was mandatory.

The new STi's biggest party piece was the transmission, as Subaru installed a six-speed manual gearbox for the very first time in a street-going Impreza. This was a close-ratio unit encased in an incredibly strong and relatively light casting (far more sturdy than the five-speeder, in fact). It gave the car more flexibility and also provided a boost to fuel economy, something that had never been the Turbo Impreza's strong suit. First gear was a 3.636 ratio, with 2.375 for second, 1.761 on third, 1.346 for fourth, 1.062 for fifth, and 0.842 for sixth, with double syncros on first gear and third for smoother engagement. Combined with a 3.90:1 final drive (the same as that on the WRX export cars), the new STi boasted noticeably better range and fuel economy. But gas mileage was hardly the main reason most people bought an Impreza STi in the first place.

The driveline and suspension also received attention. A viscous coupling for the center differential controlled the front/rear wheel torque split, and the rear was given a Suretrac diff. The suspension received inverted front struts and rear shocks, specially calibrated spring rates, and changes to the rear links that increased the roll center in an effort to reduce the car's tendency to run wide under hard acceleration through corners. The steering was geared for 2.6 turns lock to lock (15:1). STis also received a special lightweight strut tower brace, supplied by Fuji Aerospace. The brakes were also state-of-the-art with standard ABS and monstrous four-piston Brembo calipers that clamped 12.6-inch diameter vented front discs, while single-piston calipers and vented discs were specified out back.

Special exterior touches included the de rigeur STi foglight covers, a special pink Subaru grille badge, and an STi callout on the rear decklid, but overall the car was the most subtle-looking since the very first version in 1993. It ran on wheels and tires that were similar to those on the WRX UK spec cars—7x17 five-spoke alloys—but finished in gold instead of silver, along with Bridgestone Potenza RE040 tires. Its standard Rex rear spoiler and fairly mild-looking front air dam and rocker extensions, made it tough to tell apart from the regular WRX NB (a slightly bigger hood scoop was pretty much the only clue). Inside was a similar story, with the same instrument cluster, steering wheel, and seats (though the latter featured blue inserts, as did the door panels). However, the instrument panel included a different tachometer that redlined at 8,000 rpm instead of seven on the NB, plus there was the addition of a brushed-metal bezel around the shifter boot and a dash-mounted shift light that the driver could adjust in 100 rpm increments to suit his or her particular driving style.

As with previous STi cars, there was also a stripped-down Type RA. In this case, it featured a driver-controlled center differential and a mechanical rear one; a quicker ratio (13:1) steering rack; smaller, non-ABS brakes; smaller wheels and tires (it rode on the old STi's 16-inch rims and rubber); and did without power windows, air conditioning, a premium sound system, and many interior embellishments, including the metal shifter boot trim. It did come with the same seats as the regular STi, even though they were somewhat plainer in appearance. However, RA buyers could step up to the Brembo brake package and the 17-inch wheels and tires, which also mandated ABS.

Outwardly, the Type RA was distinguished by its roof vent and external radio antenna, along with the fact it only came in Pure White; regular STis could be painted Silver Premium, Midnight Black Mica, or World Rally Blue Mica, in addition to white.

The third model in the 2001 STi lineup was the wagon, which sported 17-inch wheels of a unique design and featured the standard Impreza estate body without the bulging fenders of the sedans. Mechanically, it was very similar to the regular STi sedan, with much the same interior save for rear seat headrests and came in the same range of colors, except black.

Options on the factory list included high-intensity discharge (HID) headlights, privacy glass (tinted rear side windows, back light, and quarter windows for the regular sedan and wagon), a six-speaker sound system, and a then state-of-the-art satellite navigation system with a screen mounted in the middle of the center console stack.

Before the cars were actually launched, STi had been busy tooling up for a whole host of performance and styling upgrades for the three top Imprezas, and these were duly revealed at the Tokyo Auto Salon in January 2001. These included special high-performance timing belts, performance spark plugs, STi's own signature strut braces, a special pillow bushing suspension kit, lowering springs, performance cooling hoses (spec'd for higher temperatures), special cooling ducting, a STi-specific rear differential cover, subframe stiffeners, a special competition clutch and lightened aluminum flywheel, carbon fiber door mirrors, special badging, drilled aluminum pedals, and an upgraded instrument cluster with a 260 km/h speedometer (140 mph) and a tachometer that read all the way up to 11,000 rpm.

MITSUBISHI: THE EVO'S NEXT PHASE

Subaru got the jump on Mitsubishi with the release of its latest WRX and STi offerings, and a few cars made their way into the hands of road testers and journalists, where they were deemed more user-friendly than the outgoing Evo VI and the Tommi Makinen Edition. On January 26, 2001, the three-diamond concern introduced its counterattack, announcing the Cedia-based Evolution VII, which went on sale the following month.

What was actually quite amazing was, save for the hood, front doors, roof, trunk lid, and part of the floorpan, nothing else was shared between the Evo VII and its more pedestrian counterpart. With a considerably wider track, the front and rear fenders were noticeably bulged, with the rears extending right into the rear doors to meet Japanese tire/fender clearance requirements. Also, despite the basic

WRX vs. EVO

Mitsubishi's next iteration of the famed Evolution line, the VII, was launched on January 26, 2001. Based on the larger, sixth-generation Lancer Cedia, only the roof, front doors, hood, trunk lid, and part of the floor were shared with its more pedestrian counterpart. Mitsubishi Japan

Lancia Cedia chassis being considerably stiffer than the old fifth-generation car, for Evo VII duty, it was deemed necessary to add even more reinforcements, including stronger spot welds through the structure and between the body and frame rails, hardened suspension attachment points, the use of lighter materials (aluminum front fenders were employed), a standard strut tower brace, special gussets in stress-prone areas, plus a reinforced K-member on the GSR and RS models ordered with the big Brembo brakes and alloy wheel and tire combo.

However, a stiff chassis isn't anything without the right powerplant to get it moving. Central to the latest Evolution was, of course, a version of the veteran 4G63 engine that had been around for two decades. It was a proven workhorse that got numerous enhancements for duty in the VII, including a modified induction assembly, a new water intercooler spray system with three nozzles that could be manually overridden by the driver (a bit like that employed on the latest Subaru STi), a bigger capacity oil cooler to extend engine durability, a larger intercooler, and a new turbocharger with a smaller nozzle to improve performance—a Mitsubishi-built TD05HR-16G69-8T for the GSR model that sported Inconel

GLOBAL SUPREMACY

The veteran 2-liter 4G63 twin cam engine was uprated for use in the Evo VII, with a modified intake assembly, a larger intercooler with a new water spray cooling system, and a new turbocharger with lighter, stronger blades. **Huw** Evans

turbine blades. The hard-core RS model got a version of this turbo with lighter titanium blades for improved spooling and greater torque and throttle response (interestingly enough, GSR buyers could order the RS-spec turbo on their cars at a cost of ¥50,000—relatively inexpensive, considering). Power on this latest version of the two-liter, blown twin-cam was 280 bhp and 282 lb-ft.

The five-speed manual gearbox (the only transmission offered) was largely carried over from the VI and TME. Though it was strengthened to handle the extra torque with a stouter hydraulic clutch, actual pedal feel was lighter. The no-frills RS models got a different first gear (a 2.785 ratio cog instead of 2.928 for the GSR cars) but, if desired, RS buyers could order specific ratios on third, fourth, and fifth (1.444:1, 1.096, and 0.825—standard were 1.407, 1.031, and 0.720).

Like the IV, V, VI, and TME that preceded it, the Evolution VII GSR featured an AWD system with an updated version of the active center differential (ACD). Unlike previous Evos, which used a viscous coupling, this was a purely electronically controlled unit, which worked via a set of multiplate clutches. The ACD's function, as before, was to ensure maximum traction at all times by altering the torque split from front to back depending on which set of wheels needed the most power or the most grip, in view of the road surface or configuration the car was traveling on at that particular time (the normal torque split was 50:50 front/rear). The intelligent system was also designed to detect changes in road conditions and could even compensate for weather, e.g., dry tarmac, wet tarmac, gravel, snow, or icy pavement. Although a fully automated setup, the ACD could still be manually overridden by the driver, who could choose from three different settings for tarmac, gravel, or snow-covered road surfaces via a dash-mounted button. The Evolution VII also used an updated active yaw control (AYC) that worked in tandem with the ACD. Also electronically controlled, the AYC would alter torque distribution at the rear wheels from left to right to ensure the car took the most efficient cornering line possible when going through bends, ensuring optimum steering angle and response.

Suspension was largely carried over from the Evo VI, but engineers adjusted the shock valving and dialed in a greater degree of travel, which resulted in a ride that was somewhat less jarring than its predecessor.

Helping improve traction was a new, fully electronic Active Center Differential that could detect changes in road conditions and then alter front to rear wheel torque bias depending on which set of tires provided the most grip. Mitsubishi Japan

Coupled with the ACD/AYC system and a stiffer, stronger chassis, the car delivered almost mind-bending levels of handling and roadholding at statistically greater limits.

Brakes were one item that was essentially carried over from previous Evolutions. The GSR version of the VII sported a similar Brembo package to its older counterpart, with 12.6-inch front discs (vented) gripped by meaty four-piston calipers, while a pair of 11.6-inch rotors were carried out back and clamped by two-piston units. The intelligent ABS system fitted to this brake package featured sensors on each wheel that detected lateral and longitudinal g loading, speed, and also steering angle (a new feature) to further improve turning response when the car was under braking. Although the brake system delivered ample whoa power and then some, buyers who wanted every ounce of anchor ability available could order a dealer-installed brake cooling package that featured ducts that ran from the lower front fascia to just ahead of the front wheels.

The Evo VII GSR also came with 17-inch wheels to clear the brakes, but they were a new design and wider, being 17x8 multispoke Enkei alloys shod in meatier P235/45/ZR17 Yokohama Advan tires.

As the mainstream performance variant and essentially the flagship of the range at launch, the Evo VII GSR naturally came fully loaded. Power windows, locks, mirrors, and air conditioning were all standard, as were driver and front passenger airbags, an illuminated ignition lock cylinder (very Japanese, this), and rear window washer/wiper. Newly designed Recaro front bucket seats were fitted to the GSR, trimmed in a combination of dark gray, light gray, and blue, with blue stitching found on the steering wheel, shift boot, and parking brake, regardless of color. The Cedia interior was perhaps more sound ergonomically and the trim took a step up in quality, but it somehow lacked the feeling of cockpit-like intimacy found in older Evos. The instrument cluster was also more modern and paid homage to the TME with red readings and needles that were backlit (even in daylight). The tach, located to the right of the speedometer, also incorporated icons for the ACD override settings. The three spokes on the much more modern

WRX vs. EVO

A larger cabin was shared with the Cedia. Although the car was better-performing and more efficient, from behind the wheel the VII somewhat lacked the edginess of its predecessor. Mitsubishi Japan

Momo steering wheel were finished in brushed aluminum, as was the ring that circled the shift boot and the grab handles on the interior door panels.

Exterior colors on the GSR were comprised of Satellite Silver, a more somber Elsien Gray metallic, French Blue, Palma Red, Dandellion, something called Amethyst Black, and, of course, that good old standby, Scotia White.

As before, the stripped-down RS came exclusively in the latter color. The RS rode on steel 15-inch wheels and 205/65R15 tires that looked positively narrow thanks to the new car's bigger, wider, and more angular body. The RS was built strictly to order and remained very hard-core. It came with a version of the Evo IV's braking system that included smaller 11.6-inch front discs and no ABS. It also came standard without the electronic ACD or AYC system, had no air conditioning, and featured manual windows, locks, and mirrors and a pair of regular Lancer front bucket seats. It also had the old-style three-spoke steering wheel, sans airbag. Although the standard RS also came with minimal sound deadening, you could order a special lightened body for ¥10,000 that eliminated an additional 22 lbs. In addition, a special rear chassis brace was featured on all RS cars, which did not come standard on the GSR.

GLOBAL SUPREMACY

Incredibly bare bones by twenty-first-century standards, the Evo VII RS was intended to be used as the basis for a competition car. However, buyers could order much of the GSR kit, including the brakes, ACD, and AYC, along with that car's interior options, including the Recaro buckets, the new steering wheel, air, and power windows, locks, and mirrors. Heck, buyers could even order the GSR's optional sliding moonroof, projector headlights, and satellite navigation system (the last an item that was becoming increasingly popular on many vehicles in Japan). With the plethora of options available to RS buyers as in previous years, some truly unique and perhaps bizarre combinations could be put together simply by checking certain boxes on the order form.

Although it still clearly screamed its status as a rally-bred performance car—thanks to a prominent, front-mounted intercooler; bulging rear fenders; and sizeable rear wing—the Evo VII was more grownup looking and less of a cartoonish boy racer than the VI and Tommi Makinen Editions had been. And although it was heavier, the new car was more efficient and the performance numbers in most comparison tests were better than the older car. A brand new Evo VII GSR was taken out on the Nurburgring and was quicker than the older Makinen Edition over the same circuit. Most professional drivers and hard-core enthusiasts felt that, despite the new car's capabilities, the Evo VI and TME were still ultimately more rewarding to drive. However, for the average enthusiast, the more forgiving characteristics of the latest Evo only served to broaden the car's appeal, which was exactly what Mitsubishi wanted.

SUBARU: COMING TO AMERICA

The 2001 North American International Auto Show in Detroit finally marked the entry of the turbocharged Impreza WRX sedan and wagon into its biggest market. FHI had overcome the emissions hurdles that prevented previous versions from making it to North America. Key to meeting the Environmental Protection Agency Low Emissions Vehicle smog requirements was the use of three catalytic converters on a unique North American-spec exhaust system and special cylinder heads with tumble exhaust valves and electronic engine mapping tuned to run on the high-sulphur and relatively low-octane fuel prevalent in that part of the world.

Advertised at 227 hp at 6,000 rpm and 217 lb-ft of torque, the North American version of the EJ20 made less power than the JDM version, but more than the Antipodean and European export cars. The U.S. and Canadian cars also came with a five-speed manual gearbox that was near identical to that offered on the European cars and a four-speed auto that was the same as offered on home-market versions. The North American cars also featured European-style instrument clusters, with a centrally mounted speedometer and a high level of standard interior equipment, including climate control, power locks, windows, and mirrors, a six-speaker premium sound system with CD player, a Momo steering wheel, and automatic dimming rear view mirror. Visually, the car looked very similar to those in other markets, save for the functional side marker lights. North American cars rode on 7x16-inch five-spoke alloy wheels and Bridgestone Potenza P215/55/VR16

After years of being teased, North American enthusiasts were finally able to get their hands on the turbocharged WRX in 2001. The cars featured a 227 hp EJ20 engine and were sold as 2002 models. Derric Slocum

tires, similar to the home-market variants but different from the U.K. and European cars. Exterior colors were Platinum Silver, Midnight Black Mica, Sedona Red, Aspen White, World Rally Blue, and, for the less shy, a shocking color called Blaze Yellow was also available, though only for the sedan.

Launched in early 2001 (March to be precise), the North American cars were labeled as 2002 models and quickly found favor with a buying public that had been salivating over unobtainable turbocharged Imprezas for far too long. In fact the sales of the Rex sedan and wagon in the United States and Canada helped boost Subaru's sales to record levels in the North American market that year.

MITSUBISHI: IF YOU CAN BEAT 'EM, JOIN 'EM

Although the Evolution VII went on sale in Japan during early 2000, as far as Ralliart was concerned it would be a while before its WRC counterpart would see action. Thus for a considerable part of the 2001 season, MRE fielded updated Evo VI 1/2 Group A-spec cars for its top-flight effort. However, the once-dominant Evolution rally car was becoming outclassed by the World Rally Car machines of rivals Subaru, Ford, Toyota, and Peugeot.

Despite having a fairly disappointing Y2K season, MRE returned with the same driver lineup—Tommi Makinen and Freddy Loix—partnered up with the same guys as the previous year, Risto Mannisenmaki and Sven Smeets. As for the cars, they got newly tuned versions of the venerable 4G63 engine that delivered a meaty 400 lb-ft of torque, yet were still rated at 295 hp. In order to cope with the extra power, the front brakes were increased in diameter with nutty eight-piston calipers clamping them—the rears used four-slug units as on the 2000 season cars. As before, Loix's mount was campaigned as a Carisma GT, though in reality was a Lancer Evo in all but name (the real Carisma being an entirely different and much more pedestrian car).

Although the Mitsubishi team might have appeared outclassed, Tommi Makinen proved that the old warhorses should not be counted out just yet during the season opener in Monte Carlo. This year marked a return to traditional conditions, with plenty of slippery and snow-covered sections on the mountain stages, which proved challenging. By the end of Stage 6 on the first day, 21 of the original 56 cars that started were out, mostly due to accidents. Amid the carnage, Makinen and Mannisenmaki kept their cool, taking it steady through the opening leg. By the end of it, they were in second behind McRae and Grist in the Ford Focus. Choosing half-studded tires before starting leg two proved a wise choice for the Finns, as they kept up the pace and took the lead on the last day to secure Makinen's third straight victory on the Monte.

Loix and Smeets, in the other works entry, ran a good rally and picked up the pace on the last day to secure a sixth-place finish and two championship points. An excellent drive on the notoriously difficult Col de Turini stage helped move them up the order. In Group N, the Evos once again showed their dominance—five cars took the top five spots with the winning machine driven by Frenchman Olivier Gillet.

For Sweden, a third works car—another Carisma GT—was drafted in for local Thomas Nordstrom and co-driver Tina Thorner. The regulars didn't have a good time. Loix slid off the road twice during the first day, which hampered his progress on the way to a 13th-place finish. Makinen crashed out of contention just 20 km from the finish while doing his best to catch the leader Harri Rovanpera in the SEAT. Nordstrom managed to pick up the slack and gave Mitsubishi an excellent second-place finish.

Snow gave way to dust, rocks, and mud for Portugal. After disappointing efforts in the previous two years, MRE hoped the 2001 event would be better, even if its cars were fast approaching obsolescence. It appeared the conditions were going to be somewhat of an obstacle, with thick mud making the rally tough going as rain and fog hampered visibility. But Makinen put in the drive of his life and managed to fend off Carlos Sainz right to the end, winning his second rally of the year. Maybe the old Group A cars had some life left in them after all. Loix made excellent progress despite the tricky conditions; he was in fifth until his clutch let go on Special Stage 15.

Having won two races, Makinen now had a slight lead in the driver's championship, four points ahead of Sainz. Catalunya hadn't traditionally favored the Mitsubishis, and it was no different this time out. Struggling with traction issues throughout much of the event, Makinen simply couldn't catch the front-drive Citroens and Peugeots. However, on the last leg both Makinen and Freddy Loix showed an excellent turn of speed and ended the event as the top AWD finishers, in third and fourth, respectively.

Argentina started off with muddy, wet conditions, not unlike Portugal. Loix rolled his car during leg one, and Makinen, despite a valiant effort, found it tough to challenge the Fords of McRae and Sainz, along with the Subaru of Richard Burns. Still, a fourth-place finish garnered valuable championship points. Group N continued to be a Mitsubishi-dominated class, with Gabriel Pozzo wining his second event in a row.

The teams headed to Cyprus at the beginning of June, where Makinen unfortunately met retirement early on—his car slid off the road on Special Stage 4. Luckily, the presence of trees actually helped limit the damage, stopping the sliding Evo gently enough to allow Tommi and Risto to walk away. With Makinen out, it was left to Loix to uphold the Ralliart team's chance of a decent finish. He brought the Carisma GT home in fifth place to add points to the constructor's tally. Gustavo Trelles, meanwhile, fended off rival Mitsu driver Manfred Stohl to take top honors in Group N.

Greece arrived with Makinen leading Sainz by a single championship point. As ever, the hot, dusty conditions and rocky special stages took their toll on both cars and drivers, with only two teams finishing with their full complement of cars and pilots: Skoda and Mitsubishi. Makinen found the Acropolis tough going, struggling with steering issues and tires that weren't ideally suited. Still, a fourth-place finish earned three valuable championship points. Loix, dealing with delays after suffering from transmission problems and then a damaged wheel, drove valiantly to finish ninth.

Trading one punishing rally for another, the WRC teams headed for Kenya for the toughest event of them all, the Safari. While many of his rivals struggled with rocky roads, Makinen was simply flying. Despite an encounter with the natural flora and fauna, he kept his winning pace into the second and final legs, with the car proving a "dream to drive." Loix and Smeets were beset by mechanical problems, including an engine misfire. Once the car was fixed, Loix incurred penalties because of the repairs. Nevertheless, the Belgian duo came in fifth. Perhaps even more amazing was the progress of the Group N cars. Gabriel Pozzo came in sixth, just over a minute behind Loix, while Marcos Ligato drove an astounding first Safari to finish hot on the heels of Pozzo.

Heading to Finland, both Makinen and Mitsubishi were looking good in their respective championships, not bad going for a team

For the first part of the 2001 season, MRE continued to run versions of the Evo VI Group A-spec car. By this stage they were becoming outmoded, though in the Safari, Makinen was unstoppable and won the event. Mitsubishi Japan

fielding supposedly outclassed cars. However, by this stage MRE was well on its way to introducing a new machine, and the Lancer WRC had already been in testing, including a stint at the Millbrook Proving Grounds in Bedfordshire, United Kingdom, with Freddy Loix gaining valuable seat time. Still, the old cars were brought out for the Gravel Grand Prix. Makinen had a rough time of it, as he and Risto went off the course on the very first stage, retiring with a damaged front suspension. Loix and Finn Toni Gardemeister (who was given a third car to drive for the event) encountered plenty of obstacles of their own, suffering brake problems. On the last day, Gardemeister rolled his Carisma GT. Loix managed to bring the remaining car home in tenth place. Marcos Ligato was the top Group N finisher, beating out a whole host of local Finnish drivers, all of whom were driving Evos.

The Group A-spec Lancers were entered for one last time in New Zealand. Three cars were run, as Gardemeister was given another drive. It was a somewhat sad end to a car that had proved so dominant for so long. Makinen had the unenviable task of starting first, thanks to his championship lead, breaking in the road surface for the rest of the field. Not surprisingly, this meant that progress was slow; a spin on Special Stage 6 saw him end the first day in 14th place. Makinen's hopes of a top finish were dashed, but despite broken windshield wipers on day two, he managed to claw back enough time to finish eighth overall by the end of the rally, ahead of the two Hyundais of Alistair McRae and former MRE driver Kenneth Eriksson. Loix, after having problems of his own including a couple of spins on leg one, came in 11th, ahead of Francois Delecour. Gardemeister, who suffered a holed oil pan and transmission damage on the first day, finished in 15th place ahead of the Austrian Manfred Stohl, who again drove superbly to clinch Group N.

NEW RALLY CHALLENGER

The penultimate tarmac rally of the year saw MRE wheel out its new WRC Evo VII car. A more specialized rally machine, it featured an engine that was set further back along with a longer wheelbase and updated suspension with a brand new strut system at the rear. Combined with a 300-bhp engine that spun considerably faster, thanks to lighter internals, the new car looked every inch a winner. Both works cars were now official Evos (no more Carisma GT badging).

Although testing had proved successful, competition was a different matter entirely. In the San Remo, the results were mixed. Both Makinen and Loix suffered from mechanical woes, particularly the differentials not locking, which hampered traction and cost them valuable time. Just two stages from the end, Makinen crashed out when he hit a wall. Loix managed to finish, but he was well down on the leaderboard in 12th overall. After an already excellent season, Gabriel Pozzo clinched the Group N driver's title, becoming the first Argentine driver to do so.

Despite his disappointing performance in Italy, Makinen still had every chance of winning the championship as the WRC circus arrived in Corsica. However, while in eighth place, Tommi clipped a stone

The new Evo VII WRC machines finally made their debut in the San Remo. On their first outing both Makinen and Loix struggled with reliability issues, the former failing to finish.
Mitsubishi Japan

wall, which put the car on its roof and it slid for a few yards before coming to a halt. Makinen managed to climb out, but Mannisenmaki was injured and required paramedics to get him out of the car and to the hospital. As a result of this accident, the stage was cancelled. Two punctures (on different stages) cost Loix and Smeets a lot of time. Well out of contention, the Belgian decided to concentrate on getting used to the car and fine tuning his setup. He finished in 12th, behind Colin McRae. Gustavo Trelles, still driving an Evo VI Group N car, drove exceptionally well to win the class once again.

Although Makinen crashed early in the San Remo, the fact that McRae had finished outside the points meant the Finn still had a shot at the championship heading to Australia. With a new co-driver, Timo Hentunen, but suffering from pain sustained from the accident on the Tour de Corse, Makinen drove cannily to finish sixth and gain a championship point to remain in the running for the driver's crown. Loix, clearly enjoying the new car, was running ninth when a problem with the battery forced repairs and the Belgians incurred a penalty. They finally came home in 11th place, while local driver Ed Ordynski took Group N, coming in 17th overall, ahead of a gaggle of other Lancers, including the Pozzo machine.

With just one race left on the calendar—the RAC in Britain—2001 was shaping up to be one of the most closely fought seasons anybody could remember, with the driver's championship still undecided. However, the situation changed very quickly once the rally began. Makinen, who paired up with Kaj Lindstrom for this event, was out very early after an off-course excursion damaged a wheel and the suspension. Loix lasted until approximately mid-distance, when his transmission gave up the ghost. There was to be no fifth championship for the Finn, but despite a few late-season disappointments, he proved he was still one of the world's best rally drivers.

The final result might have been different if MRE had managed to stick with the older cars through the end of 2001, but the FIA required Mitsubishi to field a WRC-spec machine during the season. The team had hung on with Group A-spec offerings for as long as it could. Still, the Cedia-based car had shown its potential, particularly on gravel, and for 2002 the team would be much more prepared.

SUBARU: A CANNY SEASON

With the new GD Impreza sliding out onto the streets in sufficient numbers, it was obvious that a rebodied WRC car would make an appearance for the 2001 season. Considering that much of the engineering found in the new mount (particularly the suspension) had already been seen the prior season, clothed in the old Retna-based GC body, the new WRC car in many respects was already proven in competition even before the first round of rallying began.

Peter Stevens designed the exterior and cabin of the new machine. A coupe was no longer in the production car lineup, so the rally car reverted to a four-door configuration for the first time since 1996. The bulging fenders and projector headlights in the bug-eye housings made it look particularly aggressive, especially in tarmac trim with massive 18-inch OZ wheels and Pirelli tires. A wide track helped stability, while massive Alcon/Prodrive disc brakes helped it stop on a dime. The engine was once again a development of the proven 1,994cc boxer, with an IHI turbocharger tuned to deliver 300 bhp and 347 lb-ft of torque. The gearbox was a development of the existing Prodrive six-speed sequential manual, and the car employed three active, electro-hydraulically controlled differentials.

Richard Burns was once again the lead driver, but Juha Kankkunen's slot was taken over by the young Norwegian Petter Solberg, who, after having shown tremendous potential the previous year, was given a full-time works drive, as was Estonian Markko Martin. In addition, longtime stalwart Toshirio Arai was now part of the works team after spending the best part of a decade driving well in Group N cars.

The opening round in Monte Carlo posed more than a few difficulties for the Subaru team. Burns managed a fairly uneventful start, but Martin's car couldn't even get off the ramp because of engine problems. Solberg started off fine, but slippery conditions and a bit too much speed proved to be his undoing; he and co-driver Philip Mills

GLOBAL SUPREMACY

Richard Burns signed up for another season with Subaru for 2001, but the second driver slot was taken over by young Norwegian Petter Solberg (right), who showed tremendous promise in his debut year for the team. Subaru Global

slid off the road and into retirement on the first leg. Burns, in the only works car still running, started developing mechanical issues of his own toward the end of leg one and had to nurse his car back to base on Special Stage 5. There, he decided to retire to prevent any further engine damage. So, after just one day, all three works Subarus were out.

In Sweden, Burns got off to a decent start and was running well until Stage 3, when he slid off the road and into a snowbank. With nobody around to assist, he spent more than 10 minutes digging the car out to get back on the road. Having lost so much time, he was out of the running. He still put in a blazing performance on the last day, setting the fastest times on several stages. Markko Martin had in-car communication problems that left him unable to talk with co-driver Michael Park. He added insult to injury by hitting a rock, which took out a control arm. Although the damage was repaired, like Burns he had lost far too much time for any chance of a decent finish. Solberg, meanwhile, drove steadily on all three legs, and his sixth-place finish gave the team at least something to celebrate.

Rain, mud, and poor visibility made the 2001 TAP Rallye de Portugal a bit of a tough one. Four SWRT works cars were entered in this one for Burns, Solberg, Martin, and for Toshihiro Arai and Glenn MacNeall. Unfortunately, all retired except Burns, who, despite facing steering and gearbox issues early on, started charging hard toward the end of the first leg. He passed Freddy Loix and made a concerted effort to catch Marcus Gronholm, but in the end he had to settle for a fourth place. Still, it was more points toward the championship.

Catalunya was yet another disappointment for the Subaru team. Out of the three entries, Solberg was the first to retire when he went off course on Stage 3. Markko Martin, suffering from electrical problems, ended up calling it a day. After gearbox problems slowed him down and a tire blowout, Richard Burns did what he could, but on the twisty mountain roads the Impreza simply wasn't as competitive as the front-drive Peugeots and the new Citroen Xsara T4s, so a seventh-place finish was all that he could muster.

Fortunes began to change as the circus moved to Argentina. Burns, in excellent form, battled Colin McRae for much of the event, coming home a fine second behind the Scotsman, who himself had not been having much luck so far this season. Solberg drove steadily to come in fifth place, while Arai brought home the other car in eighth.

The slowest rally on the calendar—Cyprus—was next, where the rocky mountain roads have a nasty habit of taking their toll on both drivers and cars. Burns caught and then passed early leader Gronholm on the second leg, but a determined Colin McRae made Richard work for it. Ultimately, McRae passed the Subaru driver, but a strong second-place finish from Burns, despite Carlos Sainz closing the gap towards the end, added a healthy amount of points to the championship tally. Toshihiro Arai drove an excellent rally to bring a second SWRT works car home in a very strong fourth place. Solberg wasn't so lucky. An electrical short resulted in his car catching fire and dashed any hopes of a finish.

Greece, in terms of conditions, was pretty much a repeat of Cyprus, except faster. Four Subarus were entered once again, though, mysteriously, one of them caught fire again, only this time it was Arai driving. Burns made a silly mistake that cost him a finish, crashing out due to a lapse in concentration, while a broken wheel rim took out Markko Martin. That left Solberg as the only car still in the running; with a gutsy drive, he gave the Subaru team a third-place finish.

The Safari, traditionally a Burns favorite, proved to be Tommi Makinen's event this time out. On the very first special stage, after getting airborne, Richard and Robert's Impreza came crashing down so hard that one of the struts tore right through its top mounting, bringing the car to a halt. Arai also was out, and Solberg, despite losing a wheel, kept plugging away, even allowing co-driver Mills to lie across the hood to keep the now three-wheeled car upright. However, the car was too heavily damaged and eventually the Norwegian had no choice but to call it quits.

Back to Europe for the Neste Rally Finland, where things improved. All three Subarus were very much in contention. Right off the bat, Burns made steady progress, briefly taking the lead, but on leg two he was overtaken by Marcus Gronholm and Harri Rovanpera in the Peugeots. He fought back, passing a slowing Harri, but he couldn't quite catch Marcus and had to settle for second. A good drive by Markko Martin, despite damaging his exhaust on a jump and then spinning out, saw the Estonian gain his best result yet—a fifth-place finish—while Solberg brought the third car home in seventh behind Carlos Sainz.

There were changes at the top for New Zealand, with George Donaldson taking over as SWRT manager. A later date in the year also meant that the conditions were drier than usual. Marcus Gronholm was quickest on the opening leg, but before long Richard Burns assumed the lead. Despite Colin McRae's efforts, that's where the Englishman stayed to take his first victory of the year. Transmission problems plagued Petter Solberg's progress early on, but he overcame them and got into a real slugfest with Tommi Makinen. Solberg ultimately came out on top, finishing ahead of the Mitsubishi in seventh. Toshihiro Arai came in 14th and right ahead of him was Peter "Possum" Bourne, as N-Z was still part of the Asia-Pacific Championship.

In San Remo, which saw Mitsubishi introduce its new Cedia-based, WRC-spec car, two works Subaru entries once again didn't finish because of accidents, one on the very first stage (Burns) and then Martin, when he misjudged a corner and hit a wall. Solberg, despite damaging his suspension, stayed in contention and brought the remaining car home to take ninth overall.

Corsica, the last of the twisty tarmac events of the season, proved challenging as always, with the AWD machines struggling to keep pace with the Citroen of Jesus Puras and the Peugeots of Panizzi, Auriol, and Gronholm, until Gronholm retired. Burns had a light scrub with a wall on the first leg, but the damage wasn't bad enough to cause serious delay and he kept going, chasing down Auriol on the windy roads. Martin and Solberg also drove well, beating their team leader on several stages. By the end, Burns had clawed back enough time to take fourth overall, but Solberg and Martin finished right behind in fifth and sixth, which was a great result for the team.

Australia, the penultimate rally of the year, saw everything hanging in the balance. Colin McRae still had every chance of winning the driver's championship, as did Burns and Makinen, with just a single point separating the contenders. However, when Colin incurred a penalty and had to start at the head of the pack for leg two, he lost a lot of time. Gronholm in the Peugeot won the rally, and Burns, who was pushing hard to catch him, ultimately had to settle for second place. That still left Burns third in the driver's championship. Solberg plugged away to finish seventh. Arai and MacNeall, in the third car, didn't make it to the end.

The RAC started off as a real nail biter as the drivers left Cardiff on the opening leg. Makinen crashed out early on, leaving Burns and McRae as the only contenders to the crown. With a strong start, it looked like victory might go the Scotsman's way, but a crash on Special Stage 4,

GLOBAL SUPREMACY

As the season progressed, Burns' chances of becoming world champion grew. In the end it came down to the last event of the year, the RAC. With his main rivals out of the running, the Englishman came in third place to secure the points he needed to capture the driver's cup. Subaru Global

where he rolled and totaled the car, finished off his championship hopes. All Burns had to do now was stay in the running and finish fourth or better. Subaru's other two drivers, Martin and Solberg, both crashed out, the muddy Welsh forest stages getting the best of them.

Burns drove cannily to take third place and the driver's championship. Although he'd won just one event during the year, consistent high points finishes and careful driving had paid off. A Scoob driver was the champ, and despite a fourth-place finish in the constructor's championship, things were looking good at SWRT.

2002
SUBARU: MORE CHANGES

At about the same time as the WRC was getting ready for New Zealand, in September 2001, at the Tokyo Motor Show, Subaru introduced an updated Type B GD Impreza. Most of the differences were subtle, such as a slightly different grille opening with new mesh and a repositioned emblem. Others were more evident, such as the new projector-style headlights behind the glass lenses, aping those on the rally cars. HID bulbs were available, albeit only with tinted window glass. There were also a number of mechanical changes, including a stouter front chassis crossmember and reinforced suspension-mounting points, a more efficient automatic transmission calibrated for smoother shifting and better fuel economy, a revised 4.11:1 final drive for the automatic-equipped WRX NB, and new engine upgrades for the non-STi cars. Among the engine upgrades were new piston rings, revised cylinder heads with more cylindrical combustion chambers, a more efficient ignition system with improved spark plugs, and a lower-restriction intake manifold. Another feature made standard was electronic braking distribution, which along with ABS helped these new cars stop in a more controlled fashion than before, especially in panic or performance situations.

On the STi front, the HID headlights came standard on Japanese-spec cars, and the hard-core Type RA version was dropped (though only temporarily, as it turned out).

MORE HARD-CORE

It was only a couple of months before the STi Type RA was back and better than ever. On December 10 that year, Subaru took the wraps off the WRX STi Type RA Spec C. Power-to-weight ratio was the calling card of this monster. Thinner steel was used for the roof and trunk lid, sound deadening and insulation (particularly around the transmission) was reduced, the heavy front subframe was removed, and frills were absent (the car had no power windows and locks, nor airbags). Lighter front seats, different-design door beams, and front bumper mountings were included. The result was around 200 lbs in weight savings; combined with mechanical tweaks, this made for one serious performance car. The Spec C employed a variation of the familiar 1,994cc flat-four engine, but it used a version of the IHI RHF5H turbocharger found on the old GC chassis STi

GLOBAL SUPREMACY

22B. The engineers designed the engine to spin faster via a lighter valvetrain and new pistons that also featured reduced mass, along with a bigger-diameter intake tract and manifold and a recalibrated ECU with different mapping.

So, although power remained at 280 hp (metric), the engine's performance secret was in its torque curve. At 4,400 rpm, this boxer four made 283 lb-ft of torque. Yes, it was slightly less tractable on the street, but in the right hands, it was more rewarding. Although the six-speed manual gearbox was more than up to the job of harnessing the torque output, for Spec C duty it was fitted with a transmission cooler as a nod toward improved reliability. This version of the STi Type RA also came with a driver-controlled center and mechanical limited-slip rear differential, 4.11:1 final drive, and its own unique suspension calibrations, with specific-rate springs and a 10 mm lower ride height than the regular STi.

Other chassis touches were hardened mounting points for the suspension control arms, a Parnhard-type link, specific caster settings

By 2002, the GD Impreza WRX was becoming ever more popular with tuning enthusiasts. This U.S.-spec example boasts a raft of aftermarket performance upgrades and its World Rally Blue Mica paint and contrasting gold wheels pay homage to the car's rally heritage. Derric Slocum

for greater stability, and firmer control arm and spring bushings. It would be fairly credible to say that the car rode a bit like a buckboard, but the tradeoff was excellent handling and a level of grip that exceeded every previous STi. The fact it was a bit jarring over some road surfaces was a small price to pay, especially considering the car was built-to-order and aimed more at the hard-core enthusiast than the everyday motorist who wanted something a bit sporty. As befitting its bare-bones status, the car came equipped with standard 16-inch steel wheels, though a 17-inch alloy wheel and Bridgestone Potenza RE070 tire package was optional; ordering that got you the bigger Brembo brakes, too. A Type C equipped this way was not only a better performer through the turns, but also stopped better, too.

ANOTHER CLASH

By the time the Type C went on sale, various buff book magazines had already managed to perform comparison tests between the GD chassis STi and the Lancer Evolution VII. While the Evo won points for its superior at-the-limit performance in part because of its ACD and AYC system and a more involving overall driving experience, the Subaru was judged as the better car to live with every day. The STi's six-speed gearbox made for more relaxed cruising, whereas the buzz from the Mitsu's 4G63 engine and a relatively short fifth gear could make any longer journey somewhat tiresome. Despite the new Turbo Impreza's somewhat more refined and grownup character, at least bare-bones versions like the RA Type C offered the hard-core enthusiast driver a platform for balls-out performance, something that was becoming increasingly rare among new cars.

Before 2001 was over, Subaru introduced yet another turbocharged Impreza variant for the Japanese domestic market: the WRX Type NB-R. In many respects it was a standard Rex playing STi dress-up, sporting the requisite foglight covers and 17-inch wheel and tire combination, though in silver instead of the STi's gold finish. It did, however, feature a STi-spec suspension with inverted struts and different spring rates, though it retained the standard WRX-tune

GLOBAL SUPREMACY

EJ20 engine (with 250 bhp) and five-speed manual gearbox. It was offered in World Rally Blue Mica, but buyers could also choose Pure White, Midnight Black Mica, or Silver Premium.

AROUND THE WORLD

While Japanese buyers were the first ones to get their hands on the new GD STi models, the Europeans and Australians finally got their own versions, available for the first time through official channels. Australia was the first to actually get the car; it went on display at the Sydney Auto Show in November 2001 as production examples were already reaching Aussie shores. Dealer sales began the following month. The STi for this market was in many respects very similar to the JDM machine. It featured the upgraded suspension with inverted front struts, massive Brembo brakes (12.8-inch rotors with four-piston front calipers), Suretrac front and rear limited-slip differentials, the same spec of six-speed manual gearbox, 4:11:1 final-drive gearing, and a bigger capacity intercooler with water spray to boost power and throttle response. In Aussie tune, the STi's 1,994cc boxer engine was rated at 265 bhp and 253 lb-ft of torque, plus it came with the standard 17-inch gold-finished multispoke alloy wheels and Potenza RE040 tires.

In view of the Aussie preference for well-equipped cars, the STi also came with a standard six-speaker premium sound system, power windows, locks, and mirrors, air conditioning, and cruise control. De rigeur STi stitching was applied to the leather-rimmed, four-spoke Momo steering wheel and shifter boot, along with STi logos on the front seat backs. Outside, an offset pink grille badge and STi foglight covers were included. Priced at $55,130 (Australian), it cost over 10 grand more than a regular WRX—not that it seemed to matter, as the STi cars were quickly snapped up for the 2002 model year.

In Europe, it was a similar story, although with an earlier show introduction and later on-sale date. On the Subaru stand at the 2001 Frankfurt Motor Show was a Euro-spec STi; the production version of that car arrived on dealer lots a few months later; most

WRX vs. EVO

Bright red Recaro seats and RJS racing-style harnesses add to the competition-inspired look of this 2002 U.S.-spec, GD chassis WRX. Derric Slocum

of this production went to the United Kingdom. The official British cars (a few "gray" imports had already started trickling in) were mostly similar to the Japanese version, but they had a few changes to make them more suitable to the British climate. Among these were improved rust protection to cope with salted winter roads, an engine in a slightly different state of tune (very similar to the Australian version, in fact) rated at 261 bhp and 253 lb-ft of torque, a six-speed gearbox with slightly different gearing (taller ratios on five—0.971 versus 1.062—and six—0.756 to 0.842—in Japan) for improved fuel economy as an answer to astronomic fuel costs in Britain—especially important considering that the STi was rather thirsty at best. The British-spec STis also had a standard engine immobilizer, a satellite tracking system to deter car thieves, and high-intensity headlights, but not the tinted window glass (which wasn't legal). Suspension, brakes, wheels, and tires mirrored the Japanese- and Aussie-spec cars: Brembo anchors, 17x7-inch gold alloy rims, and Potenza P225/45R17 RE040s, plus the heavy-duty suspension with inverted Bilstein struts and shocks and 13:1 quick-ratio steering. The color choice mirrored

GLOBAL SUPREMACY

Japan and Australia, with just four hues available: World Rally Blue Mica, Midnight Black, Premium Silver, and, of course, Pure White. To sweeten the pot even more, there was also a UK-spec Prodrive-style version of the STi (see Appendix B: Special Edition Cars).

The Brits took to their first official STi as a fish does to water. *Autocar* magazine managed to get its hands on a Japanese-spec STi earlier in 2001 and came away impressed by the car's performance, especially in acceleration, compared with the standard WRX, the only turbocharged Impreza then on sale in the United Kingdom. When the official STi version arrived, the local press didn't waste any time before testing it. *Auto Express* clocked a Prodrive-style version at 5.2 seconds for the 0–60 mph dash with a top speed of 148 mph. Overall, the weekly publication remarked, "Few cars can match the STi's cross country pace." Few perhaps, except the Mitsubishi Lancer Evolution VII.

MITSUBISHI: TAKING IT TO EUROPE

Mitsubishi also chose the Frankfurt show to unveil its Euro-spec version of the latest Lancer Evolution, the VII. Like the VI before it, this was a true export car, offered in both right- and left-hand-drive form, with the greatest amount of interest coming from Germany and the United Kingdom. Model choices and specifications differed somewhat slightly from Japan, with the mainstream version being dubbed the RS II (equivalent to the JDM GSR), while the RS was the strict, built-to-order, bare-bones version, complete with steel 15-inch wheels and minimal sound deadening and creature comforts. British-spec cars featured a 4G63 engine rated at 276 bhp and 282 lb-ft of torque, a standard five-speed manual gearbox with the same ratios as the Japanese cars, but improved rust protection, a standard theft immobilizer (to combat high levels of car crime in Britain), plus other features designed to pass the UK's Single Vehicle Approval import regulations (standard rear foglights, folding side mirrors, and speedometers calibrated for mph, among others). Mitsubishi Ralliart United Kingdom group went to the trouble of serializing each officially imported VII so that HM customs, the department of transportation, and the driver and vehicle licensing agency all had records to prevent these cars from being confused with Japanese "gray" imports. British-spec Evo VIIs were offered in a choice of exterior colors: Scotia White (the only color available on the RS), Palma Red, French Blue, Dandelion, Satellite Silver, and Amethyst Black. Besides the RS and RS II, Ralliart United Kingdom also offered its own tuned version of the Evo VII specifically for British buyers – the monstrous FQ 300 (see Appendix B: Special Edition Cars).

TAMING THE BEAST

It probably wasn't surprising, given the growing number of performance cars sporting ever more creature comforts and refinement, that an automatic-equipped Lancer Evolution would make an appearance sooner or later. A brainchild of Mitsubishi's marketing department, the so-called Evo VII GT-A was aimed at broadening the car's appeal, and in many ways it succeeded. Based around the GSR, it featured extra sound deadening located in the unibody structure and a slightly detuned version of the two-liter 4G63 twin-cam four-cylinder engine rated at 272 bhp and 253 lb-ft of torque (versus 276 bhp and 282 lb-ft for the regular five-speed equipped GSR and RS) thanks in part to a different TD05 turbocharger with a smaller impeller and

Perhaps signifying the Evo's broadening appeal, in 2002 Mitsubishi launched the Evolution VII GT-A in the Japanese market. The "A" stood for automatic, making this car the first of its breed to be available with a self-shifting transmission. Mitsubishi Japan

revised nozzle, plus a different intake manifold and downpipe system tuned for reduced resonance in addition to specifically calibrated engine mapping.

Bolted to this softer four-banger was a version of Mitsubishi's INVECS (Intelligent and Innovative Vehicle Electronic Control System) II five-speed automatic with a manual-shift feature. Interestingly enough, the first-gear ratio on the GT-A was actually shorter than on the five-speed manual-equipped GSR. ACD and AYC were also standard. The suspension was retuned with slightly softer spring and damping rates, and the steering was given slower gearing for less of a kart-like response. Slightly narrower 225 section (as opposed to 235) Bridgestone tires were mounted on GSR-spec 17-inch wheels (with a unique polished finish). Outwardly, the GT-A was distinguished from the GSR by a plain hood without the twin hood scoops, a different front bumper with a centrally mounted license

The GTA was actually quite a different car, with unique Lapis blue seat inserts and dash trim. It also sported specially geared steering, befitting its role as a more Grand Touring-oriented vehicle. Mitsubishi Japan

plate bracket (instead of being offset to the left) and the deletion of the two small nostrils in the upper part of the bumper fascia. Special clear composite headlight and taillight assemblies were found on the GT-A, plus it could be optioned with a smaller rear deck wing in place of standard GSR piece.

Although it was a slightly gentler package in Evo terms (which meant it was still a serious barnstormer—try 0–60 mph in 5.5 seconds with insane levels of grip and tremendous stopping ability), the GT-A was an easier car to handle for the Everyman. It drew a bit of criticism, especially among Evo purists in the automotive press, but in most respects, it was still a killer all-around performance car and a ball to drive. Furthermore, the GT-A's INVECS II transmission was a welcome feature for those who'd seriously wanted an Evo, but for whom the standard five-speed manual made city driving a bit of a chore. Plus, the driver could still shift the gears manually when the road opened up again via the gear lever or steering wheel–mounted paddles.

Only 2,000 GT-As were released in Japan for the 2002 model year; all came equipped in a single trim level that largely mimicked the GSR (power everything, standard climate control, and a premium sound system), though GT-As did feature unique Lapis blue upholstery inserts and special trim around the dash vents and power window controls,

Keen spotters noticed a slightly different front fascia and smaller rear deck spoiler as distinguishing features on the GT-A model. Mitsubishi Japan

along with white-faced gauges and brushed-aluminum trim around the shifter boot. Leather-trimmed seating (the fronts being Recaros), a power sunroof, and satellite navigation were about the only options.

Although it might have appeared somewhat out-of-step with UK buyer tastes that generally ran toward hard-core performance in this particular segment, Mitsubishi's UK arm did decide to officially import the GT-A in small numbers. It found a following; *Auto Express* even went as far as to say that the cornering limits were still "above anything this side of touring car." Clearly the terms "sophisticated" and "civilized" were relative, especially concerning the Mitsubishi Lancer Evolution VII GT-A.

SUBARU: MAKINEN JOINS THE TEAM

Even though it had barely been two years since the introduction of the GD Impreza WRX and STi, by early 2002 there were signs that changes would be in store during the coming months. The bug-eyed styling hadn't been very well received, so plans were put in action for a face-lifted car to debut toward the end of the year.

Before that, STi announced the S202 model in Japan (based on the RA Spec C covered in more detail in Appendix B: Special Edition Cars), another limited-production special with some unique touches of its own. Also, there was still another season of world championship rallying to attend to, and SWRT wasn't about to sit still. The 2002-spec works rally cars appeared to be little changed on the outside, but they boasted a number of mechanical updates, including stronger six-speed gearboxes with revised ratios, lighter engine internals for a faster revving EJ20, changes to the IHI turbocharger, plus a more efficient four-into-one exhaust manifold (it had previously been a four-two-one arrangement) and throttle body. The front fascia splitter was also now made from rubber instead of carbon fiber, making it less prone to damage and easier to fix, while thinner rear glass helped shed some weight. For tarmac events, the cars ran on 18-inch OZ wheels and Pirelli rubber, with a braking system that employed six-piston front calipers with water cooling and a four-slug setup out back. For dirt and gravel, four-piston front brakes were specified, along with smaller rims and specific off-road tires.

Perhaps the biggest surprise was the signing of former Mitsubishi driver (and four-time world champion) Tommi Makinen, who took the place of Richard Burns (who went to Peugeot). British American Tobacco's 555 brand also returned as a major sponsor for the season. Petter Solberg renewed his contract, along with co-driver Phil Mills. Partnering Makinen was Kaj Lindstrom; Risto Mannisenmaki, because of the injuries incurred on the Tour de Corse the previous year, decided to sit out the season.

Things got off to an excellent start for Subaru in 2002. In the Monte Carlo, Makinen, despite still learning his new car, felt reasonably confident and finished the first leg in a solid second place, battling Frenchman Sebastian Loeb in the Citroen. After a bit of a shaky start, Solberg began gaining ground, and both Subarus proved highly competitive through all three days. On the final leg, Solberg actually set the pace, but it was Makinen who finished ahead overall. Battling Loeb until the end, the Finn would have been happy with a second place, but a penalty incurred by the Citroen driver over a controversial tire-changing incident made Makinen the winner, a week after the rally had been run. Solberg came in a respectable sixth, behind Gronholm and ahead of the Peugeots of Gilles Panizzi and his old teammate Richard Burns.

Sweden proved difficult for the Subarus. The conditions were a slushy mess, which made traction difficult and caused all kinds of problems. Makinen had an altercation with a snowbank early on during Stage 4, which plugged the radiator and caused his engine to overheat. He decided to retire on the first leg and concentrate his efforts on the Tour de Corse. Solberg lasted a little while longer, but on day two during Stage 6, his engine went south.

Serious rain showers during the Tour de Corse proved to be a boon to the Subaru works drivers. Makinen made excellent time, and Solberg, despite spinning out and damaging his rear suspension, claimed sixth by the end of the day. Makinen's luck ran out on day

GLOBAL SUPREMACY

Petter Solberg drove a solid season in 2002. During a particularly tough Rally Catalunya, he overcame seemingly impossible odds to finish well into the points in fifth place
Subaru Global

two, when in the slippery, wet conditions, his car went hydroplaning, damaging the front suspension and forcing him to retire. Solberg kept charging, setting good stage times and pushing to catch Carlos Sainz, whom he eventually overtook to claim fifth place.

In Catalunya, with similar conditions, the Peugeots and Citroens were again the cars to catch, but Solberg did a magnificent job despite being hampered by brake problems and then repairs that cost him a 10-second penalty. Further obstacles, including tire punctures, didn't deter him, and the Norwegian continued to push. He finished a respectable fifth once again. Makinen, after combating gearbox problems on the opening leg, finally got them resolved, only to slide off the road and into a ditch on the last special stage of the day. He recovered, but the car's cooling system had been damaged, and the engine croaked during the first stage on day two.

Back to rocks and gravel in Cyprus and a rally of attrition: Cars broke left, right, and center, and the fact that rain interfered with the

WRX vs. EVO

Former Mitsubishi star and four-time world champion Tommi Makinen signed up to drive for the Subaru team in 2002. He's seen here in action during the Cyprus Rally, a race of attrition where Tommi was one of the few top runners to finish. Subaru Global

event didn't help matters. Differential problems slowed Solberg in the very early stages, but he roared back and drove an excellent rally on the second day, eventually finishing fifth overall. Makinen drove well, too, and really picked up the pace on the last leg. He set the fastest stage times on four different occasions and battled Richard Burns for second until a half spin allowed the Brit to garner runner-up honors.

Argentina proved a heartbreaker, particularly for Makinen. It was Subaru against Peugeot and Tommi against Marcus Gronholm for much of it, with the Finn finishing top of the leader board by the end of leg two. However, on the last day, with victory within his grasp, Makinen hit a small bank on the road while running at considerable speed. This sent the car into a series of rolls, the worst accident of the Finn's career. Luckily, both he and co-driver Kaj Lindstrom managed to walk away with little more than minor bruising, though the car was utterly totaled. Solberg, suffering from stomach pains, drove an excellent rally considering, doing his best to fend off Carlos Sainz.

GLOBAL SUPREMACY

Although he ultimately was beaten to the finish by the Spaniard, Petter ended up finishing second overall; the Peugeots of Marcus Gronholm and Richard Burns were disqualified, handing victory to Sainz and Ford.

In Greece, the SWRT team fielded three works cars for Makinen, Solberg, and Toshihiro "Toshi" Arai. Tommi was an early casualty on the Acropolis, smashing into a huge rock on Special Stage 6, which damaged the car beyond repair. Petter, despite a spin early on the first day that delayed his start, recovered and kept pushing hard, setting the fastest time on three special stages and ended up scoring a fifth-place finish—remarkable because he'd started the rally in 27th. Toshi, in the other surviving works entry, came in a creditable 13th.

The Safari didn't prove kind to Subaru—Solberg developed engine problems on Stage 3 and was out with a blown engine by the end of the next one. Makinen, showing tremendous promise early on, was in the lead when he developed rear suspension problems on Stage 5. He made it back to the service interval, but on the following stage, the Subaru blew a tire. Although Tommi and Kaj managed to change it, the stop cost them 15 minutes. In the end, it didn't really matter, for on Stage 7 a front control arm gave way, and the Finn's rally was run.

As for the Neste Rally Finland, Makinen just couldn't match his usual place—his stage times were well down the scoreboard, and he plodded through to come in sixth place and score a single point in the driver's championship. That left Solberg to battle the Peugeots and Fords, which he did with enthusiasm, finishing third behind Gronholm and Richard Burns.

Four works entries were ambitiously entered for the new Rallye Deutschland (Germany). Besides the two regulars, Arai was given a drive, as was native German Achim Mortl, partnered with motorsports veteran Klaus Wicha. A bizarre incident on the very first stage saw Makinen yank on the parking brake so hard during a sharp corner that it broke off. This cost him a lot of time that he was unable to claw back. He ended up finishing a frustrating seventh overall, despite setting some quick stage times towards the end. Mortl lost a wheel on the opening stage but stayed in contention until a damaged suspension brought retirement on leg two. Arai also faced problems and was out on the second day; in his case, the transmission blew. This left Solberg and Makinen. The Norwegian drove as hard and fast as he could, and he was making good time when, on leg two during Special Stage 11, he hit a bump and went off into the bush, tearing off the right rear wheel. The car was pulled out, and Petter limped to the next service interval and retired shortly after.

In the San Remo, the Peugeots and Citroens once again proved the dominant force; the cars were ideally suited to the smooth, dry tarmac roads, with the likes of Gilles Panizzi, Gronholm, Burns, and Philippe Bugalski proving the men to catch. In the Subaru camp, both works cars were doing reasonably well, though Makinen's chances ended with a broken driveshaft on Stage 7. Solberg pressed on, gaining some ground by setting the fastest times on two stages during leg two and yet another on the final day. That was enough to deliver a third-place finish overall, behind the Peugeots of Panizzi and Gronholm.

New Zealand witnessed another sterling drive by Solberg, who outpaced teammate Makinen and won Special Stages 7 and 8 on the first day. Tommi came back, and the two teammates played cat and mouse almost until the end. Makinen ended up third overall, behind Marcus Gronholm, who provisionally secured his second driver's world championship, and Harri Rovanpera, in another Peugeot. Solberg, after running so well, retired within striking distance of the finish with a blown engine. In the Group N category, longtime Subaru driver and Kiwi Peter "Possum" Bourne took the top honors. This would be his last win in New Zealand, as he died tragically in a non-rally car accident the following spring.

Solberg got off to a fantastic start in Australia, setting the fastest time on the Super Special Stage opener in Langley Park, though Marcus Gronholm soon took the lead. Petter fought back, battling Marcus and Harri Rovanpera, setting the fastest time again on the last stage of leg two. The following day was more of the same, though the Peugeots ultimately proved quicker and the Norwegian had to settle for third (with this Gronholm officially claimed the driver's championship). Makinen had a disappointing end to his rally. He reached the end of the final stage in fourth place, but scrutineers later deemed that his car was underweight and he was disqualified—a frustrating turn of events.

Britain was a hotly contested rally, despite the championship having been locked up. It was unpredictable to say the least. Makinen spun his car early on but regained momentum and pushed on, steering through the Welsh mud to take a solid fourth overall. The biggest star of the event was Solberg. Hot on the heels of Marcus Gronholm until the Peugeot driver crashed out on leg two, the young Norwegian set a blinding pace on the second day and battled fiercely with Estonian Markko Martin in the Ford Focus. Solberg took the lead on three of the final day's stages and that was enough to secure his first WRC win—what a way to end the season! In addition, he finished runner-up in the driver's championship—an excellent result considering he had been competing against many more experienced drivers during the course of the year. Clearly, great things were around the corner for the young Norwegian and the Subaru team.

MITSUBISHI: TESTING TIMES

With the Cedia-based Evolution having proved a big hit on the streets, the question was how its WRC counterpart would fare during the 2002 season. Mitsubishi Ralliart Europe saw some major changes at the beginning of the season, notably an all-new driver lineup. Tommi Makinen left the team to head for archrival Subaru, and Freddy Loix went to Hyundai. The new number one seat was taken over by Frenchman Francois Delecour (a Ford stalwart for many years) and the second works entry by Alistair McRae (Colin's younger brother). The two wheelmen were partnered with Daniel Grataloup and David Senior, respectively.

MRE's strategy was to gain more experience with its first Evo VII World Rally Car spec machines (because the cars had only debuted toward the end of the 2001 season) before introducing an updated Version 2 car as soon as was deemed feasible.

In Monte Carlo, things didn't get off to the greatest start. Despite the fairly mild conditions, both Delecour and McRae found the opening leg frustrating, especially when Stage 2 on the Sisteron Pass was cancelled because of spectator overcrowding (MRE had chosen its tires based on getting a full run on this long, twisty section). However, with a very high attrition rate among the teams, the works Mitsubishi cars gained places as they kept going. Delecour came home in 9th place overall with McRae in 14th, despite hitting a wall earlier.

Three works cars were entered for Sweden, with Finn Jani Paasonen driving the third entry. Perhaps not surprisingly, Jani showed promise in the snow, making good progress and lying in fourth place until his car lost a wheel on day two. So much time was lost that the best the Finn could muster was a 14th-place finish. Delecour faced similar issues. Misjudging a corner on the first day, he went off the road and into a ditch. It took almost 20 minutes to get the Mitsubishi out, and by that stage any chances of a worthwhile finish were dashed. A bright spot was McRae. The young Scotsman drove an excellent rally, battling his older brother Colin and securing a fifth-place finish for the Mitsubishi team and the first points of the season. In the Group N category, the older Evolution VIs still proved dominant, and Daniel Carlsson won the class, with four of the top five finishers driving Mitsubishi Lancers and Carismas.

With no Portugal on the calendar, the next event was the Tour de Corse. Running on the twisty mountain roads earlier in the year than normal proved to be a challenge. On the opening leg, the roads were a bit wet and slippery, but Delecour was at home in Corsica. Although he couldn't catch the Peugeots of Panizzi, Gronholm, or Burns, he made steady progress despite a blown tire on Special Stage 13. He brought the lead works MRE car home in seventh place to score points in the constructor's championship. Meanwhile, McRae and Senior blew out a tire on the same stage. Also contending with vibration issues and brake problems on the first day, the duo battled on to finish tenth, ahead of Harri Rovanpera's Peugeot 206.

Group N was once again utterly dominated by Mitsubishis, the winning car an Evo VI piloted by Peruvian driver Ramon Ferreyros.

GLOBAL SUPREMACY

Proving how highly competitive the Evo VI was in production car–based rallying, all but one of the top 10 finishers were driving Mitsubishis—the lone exception being the second-in-class finisher Jean-Pierre Manzagol, driving a Peugeot 306.

Two weeks after Corsica, the teams found themselves in Catalunya for another fast, twisty tarmac event. Dry roads and fairly warm temperatures meant predictable driving for the most part, and with a revised chassis setup, Delecour was more confident with the car, charging harder than he had done in Corsica. Spectator concerns forced two of the three early stages on the second leg to be cancelled, but the Frenchman and his co-driver pressed on. Determined to clinch a manufacturer's point, Delecour almost lost it during one section on the final day, but he regained control and came home in ninth to get the desired point. McRae and Senior, despite a puncture on the first day and a spin on the last day, stayed in the running and came in 13th, behind the Peugeot of local driver Jesus Puras. If nothing else, the Evo VII WRC machines were proving to be reliable and consistent.

Back to gravel roads for Cyprus, which was run earlier in the season than past years. Unpredictable weather conditions and rain on the second leg made the going particularly tough for Delecour, who was stuck first with a broken gearbox, then a driveshaft, and, ultimately, nonfunctioning windshield wipers. With other cars dropping like flies, the Frenchman survived the tough Cypriot conditions to reach the end, but he came in out of the points in 13th. The other two works cars of McRae and gravel specialist Jani Passonen (who was drafted in with a third works machine) didn't fare so well. After suffering gearbox problems, McRae rolled his car on leg two in Stage 8 and was then finally out when his car lost all driven power on Stage 11. Passonen also retired on the second leg after plowing into a rock, which damaged the front suspension.

In Group N, the Evo VIIs were now starting to appear in significant numbers. Gustavo Trelles won the class in one of the new cars, followed by Italian Luca Baldini, driving another Evo VII.

Rally Argentina saw changes to the cars, namely revised gearboxes and driveshafts in light of the Cyprus failures. But at this rally, steering and suspension problems beset the drivers. McRae and Senior, after hitting a rock very early on, damaged their steering linkage and then had to contend with a slow puncture. On day two, a loss of turbo boost pressure hampered their progress. Still, the Scotsman kept plugging away and earned with an eighth-place finish and constructor's championship points. Delecour, after getting off to a good start, was forced to retire when his suspension collapsed on Special Stage 7. Mitsubishi again took top honors in the production car Group N class, with Ramon Ferreyros demonstrating excellent helmsman skills at the wheel of an Evo VII.

The Acropolis Rally lived up to its reputation as a real car breaker; by day three of competition, only around half of the original 84 machines that started were still running. The works Mitsubishi drivers fared better than most. Delecour got off to a slow start, but despite a puncture, a damaged shock absorber, and then steering issues, he survived the first day. So did McRae, but events took a turn for the bizarre when the laundry room in the team hotel caught fire on the second night, resulting in a sleepless hour and a half during the early morning. McRae's luck ran out on the morning of leg three when he damaged the steering enough to make repairs next to impossible. Delecour managed to bring the remaining works entry home in 11th place.

The WRC circuit left Greece behind for some fun in Africa and the even more punishing Safari. And what a rally it proved to be. Retirements and breakages were par for the course, and only 11 of the original 48 starting cars made it to the final day of competition. Among them was the MRE works machine of McRae and Senior. Despite suffering from brake and suspension problems on the first day, the young Scot drove well, posting some very respectable stage times on some of the toughest sections of the event. However, rear suspension issues, albeit fairly minor ones, meant that if McRae would gain any ground, it would be through attrition. By the last stage, he was still in the running and crossed the finish line in ninth place (his brother, Colin, won the event in his Ford Focus). Delecour had gone out early on the first leg when the engine overheated and then refused to start.

Of the 11 cars that finished, just two were Group N machines. One of those was the Evo VII of Rudi Stohl, who finished runner-up in class and was the last driver to reach Nairobi.

Mitsubishi Ralliart trundled out an updated Version 2 World Rally Car in time for Finland, and the team had high hopes. Jani Paasonen had been testing the car quite extensively, and on home turf a third works car was brought in for him. It proved a very wise move. Passonen knew the roads and conditions and made very good progress, setting some very fast stage times. On the first stage of leg three, he was hot on the heels of eventual second-place finisher Richard Burns, though on other sections, an abundance of loose gravel and big stones made progress a bit tougher. Still, Jani and co-driver Arto Kapanen finished eighth, which meant more points for the constructor's cup. Delecour's rally ended early when, after struggling with steering issues, a jump on Stage 9 caused the front suspension to collapse. McRae was making good time, despite a damaged shock on the first day, but then a fire caused by rear shock fluid leakage resulted in a serious time delay. The car was repaired and back in action for the final leg of competition, but more rear suspension problems brought about retirement on Stage 18.

Mitsubishi again scored top honors in Group N with local driver Jarkko Miettinen claiming the best result of his career, winning the class outright in his Evo VI. Italian Alex Fiorio's third-place finish in an Evo VII revived his chances of becoming the 2002 Group N champion.

Next on the calendar was a brand new WRC event in Germany, which didn't go too well for the works Mitsubishi team. Just two cars were entered. McRae was out of the running early on when his turbo blew on Stage 6. Delecour, not happy with his car's setup, found it slow going on the opening leg, but he picked up the pace considerably on day two. However, a lack of boost on the final day hampered progress, and the best the Frenchman could muster was ninth. Finn Kristian Sohlberg was the top finisher in Group N, not surprisingly behind the wheel of a Lancer Evolution VII.

The last tarmac rally of the year, the San Remo, saw the MRE team in good spirits, and Delecour (who tended to favor tarmac events) was looking to do well. However, more boost problems and a lack of power prevented the Frenchman from being competitive on several stages, but as the rally progressed, he started charging harder and faster. Delecour ultimately finished in tenth place, which at least garnered another constructor's point for Mitsubishi. McRae lost valuable time on the opening leg when the hood flew open after he had stopped to check for suspected engine problems. Given this state of affairs, team manager Derek Dauncey decided on the morning of the second leg that Alistair and David should be withdrawn as McRae's chances to

An all-new driver lineup of Francois Delecour and Alistair McRae (Colin's younger brother) was part of Mitsubishi's World Championship Rally effort in 2002. Boost problems plagued Delecour during the San Remo, but he did finish, albeit in 10th place.
Mitsubishi Japan

fight back were hampered by an injury suffered prior to the start of the rally.

In New Zealand, Passonen was once again brought in, this time to sub for McRae. He made excellent progress early, even setting the fastest overall time on Stage 5 and running quicker than the likes of Tommi Makinen and Marcus Gronholm on the opening leg. Sadly, Jani's charge came to a halt the following day when the Finn misjudged a left-hand corner and slid off the road, rolling down the embankment. Luckily, both driver and co-driver escaped uninjured, but thanks to a ruptured radiator, the car was done. Delecour, struggling with traction issues for much of the opening leg, ended up running at the front of the field on the second day, plowing the gravel and debris as he went. Still he managed to bring home the surviving car in ninth place and garner yet another points finish.

Accidents plagued both the works drivers in Australia. Paasonen, with limited experience in this event, wasn't really on the pace, and an accident on the second leg, where he rolled his car, cost valuable time. Repairs were conducted overnight, and he and Arto were back in

Young Finn Jani Paasonen was brought in for select rounds during the 2002 season, including Australia. With limited experience he struggled through and finished a well-deserved 9th. Mitsubishi Japan

action for the final day. Despite running toward the front of the pack, the Finn stayed the course to come home in ninth. Delecour and Grataloup had an interesting rally to say the least. While clipping a corner on the first day, Francois didn't see a tree stump, and the car banged into it, throwing the Evo across the road and smack into another tree that totaled the front end. Paramedics were called in, and although Francois suffered bruising, Daniel was in a far more serious condition with a broken ankle, bruised lung, and damaged pelvis. He would be out for the last race of the season, replaced by Dominique Savignoni.

In Group N, Austrian Manfred Stohl did exceedingly well, finishing an excellent tenth overall and taking top honors for the production car class.

The final round as usual saw the WRC circus head to dark, raining Wales for the RAC. Three cars were entered, one for Passonen, one for Delecour, and a third car for Justin Dale and co-driver Andrew Bargery. After a curate's egg season, the RAC wasn't kind to the works Mitsubishi team. Dale rolled his car on the very first stage and promptly retired when it was discovered the roll cage had been damaged. The two remaining cars lasted a while longer, but the slippery Welsh conditions got the better of them on leg two, when both Delecour and Passonen slid off the road and into the ditch—Francois on Stage 11 and then Jani in the same place as rally leader and world champion-to-be Marcus Gronholm. All the works MRE cars were out and, to add insult to injury, victory was claimed by archrival Subaru, with Petter Solberg and Phil Mills scoring their first-ever WRC win. In Group N at least, Swede Oscar Svedlund brought home the bacon for Mitsubishi, and in an old Evo VI at that!

SUBARU: FACELIFT

At the 2002 Paris Auto Salon in September, Subaru took the wraps off a face-lifted GD Impreza. The most obvious change was the front fascia. Gone were the previous bulging circular headlights and turn signals. In their place, trapezoidal lenses narrowed toward

GLOBAL SUPREMACY

Subaru launched a facelifted GD Impreza in the fall of 2002 at the Paris Auto Salon. The revised car would be a 2003 model in Japan and Europe, and a 2004 model in North America. The most noticeable difference was a restyled front fascia with new headlights, lower bumper, fenders, and hood. This is the "regular" WRX model. Subaru Global

the grille opening, giving the car a somewhat angry look. The front bumper was more rounded and the grille opening larger than before, with greater curvature around the edges. Also the front fenders and hood were modified to mate cleanly with the new front fascia. The rear was less noticeably altered, though keen spotters noted the revised taillight lenses with the clear backup portion now at the bottom instead of the top as before.

There were other changes, too. Slightly better quality materials were used inside the cabin. In a nod toward greater safety, there was a dual-zone front passenger airbag and standard side airbags in the sport rally front seats (they were previously optional on the WRX sedan). In addition, the front chairs now incorporated active head restraints. Other safety touches included an impact-absorbing brake pedal and new ISO-standard child tethers in the back seat. Mechanical changes were most evident on the WRX and STi models. The former got a retuned EJ20 with a power boost up to 225 bhp, thanks to new valvetrain components, revised air/fuel mapping, different exhaust tuning, and a hike in turbo boost. WRX models also featured revised suspension settings with differently calibrated spring and damping

Taillights were restyled on all GD Imprezas, though otherwise there was little change in the rear styling, unlike the front. Subaru Global

rates (the shocks featured multilayer valves that were able to adjust to different speeds and road surfaces, delivering improved handling and a more compliant ride). Gunmetal 16-inch multispoke alloys were also fitted as standard to the WRX cars.

On the STi version, power was bumped up to 265 bhp on the European-market cars, thanks to a redesigned intercooler water spray system. STis also benefited from a new front suspension with stiffer and stronger mounting points for the front control links, plus revised tie rod ends that, along with a new variable-assist power-steering pump, made wheel response even sharper than before. Outwardly, the STi was more boy racer than ever, with an aggressive lower front fascia, more prominent hood scoop, and a return to the shopping cart–style rear deck spoiler, which had been absent since 2000. The new cars were well received at the Paris show and soon found their way into

GLOBAL SUPREMACY

The STi shared its new front styling with other Imprezas and got a few mechanical tweaks as well. On European-market cars like this one, power was increased to 265 hp. Subaru Global

Although the cabin was similar inside, better-quality materials and soft-touch plastics appeared, and there were standard side airbags mounted in the front seats on WRX models. Subaru Global

showrooms (naturally Japan was first, getting the face-lifted cars in November 2002).

The freshened car's debut, aside from grabbing the attention of buyers, was meant to lay the groundwork for the next season of the World Rally Championship. As if to emphasize the point, Prodrive had one of its WRC 2003 contenders on the Subaru stand in Paris. In fact, WRC requirements largely dictated the need for an updated STi, not the other way around. Besides, as far as North America was concerned, there were bigger things on the horizon.

CHAPTER 5

STARS N' STRIPES

A little over three years into the new decade and the latest generation of Lancer Evolution and Subaru Impreza were gaining legions of fans around the world. In North America, the Evo and WRX/STi were like a forbidden fruit—given that neither car had ever been available there—which only increased the hunger for the Evo and STi.

Finally, after having been denied these amazing cars for close to a decade, North American enthusiasts were able to get in on the fun. The stateside Japanese car scene would never be the same.

2003

MITSUBISHI: A DREAM COME TRUE?

On January 2, 2003, Mitsubishi unveiled its latest version of the Lancer Evolution. This was notable in itself, of course, but the most important aspect of this date was that this introduction didn't take place in Japan, but across the Pacific, at the Los Angeles Auto Show. That's right: after years of being teased, the Americans were finally getting the Lancer Evolution in their showrooms. Given the high level of interest in Japanese performance cars and culture at the time, the rollout was a big one.

WRX vs. EVO

A few months after arch-rival Subaru debuted its WRX to a North American audience, Mitsubishi unveiled an updated Lancer Evolution at the Los Angeles International Auto Show. This was the first time the car was available officially on US soil. Equipped to comply with U.S. regulations, the American-spec Evo ended up being a rather unique species. Derric Slocum

However, the U.S.-spec Evo (no cars were offered for sale in Canada at this time because of regulations prohibiting the front-mounted intercooler) was quite different than the Japanese market version that would debut a few weeks later. For starters, in order to meet U.S. crash regulations, the American version featured stronger front and rear bumpers that added length and also weight. There was also a low-mounted composite fairing, designed to increase air flow underneath the car and reduce drag (an added bonus was improved cooling for hot U.S. summers). As with the VII, the hood and front fenders were made from stamped aluminum, which offset the weight increase a little. The front sheetmetal contours were curvier to blend with the new front fascia, and the previous dual hood vents were replaced by a single opening.

Contained within the front assembly was a larger grille opening, featuring a more prominent center divider housing the Mitsubishi

On the initial American-spec Evolution, the 4G63 engine was rated at 271 hp, less than on Japanese and European market cars. It had a less aggressive spark curve, needed to comply with California's ultra-strict emissions standards. Derric Slocum

logo, which would prove to a be feature unique to the 2003 and 2004 cars. Out back, the U.S. Evo also featured clear taillight lenses—à la the 2002 Evo VII GT-A. Mechanically, the new U.S. spec car was still powered by a version of the evergreen 1,996cc, 4G63 twin-cam four, but in order to comply with U.S. emission regulations (a major reason why it took so long for the car to arrive in this market), it was detuned slightly, with a less aggressive spark curve (compared with then-current Japanese machines) and thus rated at 271 bhp at 6,500 revs (SAE net) and 273 lb-ft of torque at 3,500. The twin-scroll turbocharger was set at a relatively high 19 lbs of boost, and to maximize power, the front-mounted intercooler featured a water spray system that could be overridden manually by the driver. The U.S.-market car featured a version of the JDM Evolution VII's W5M51 five-speed manual gearbox with the same ratios as found on the older Japanese car: 2.928 on first, 1.950 on second, 1.407 on third, 1.031 on fourth, and .720 on fifth. The driveline also differed from recent Japanese- and European-market Evo VIIs, in that the U.S. cars came without the helical limited-slip front differential, and while they featured a version of the active center differential, there was no active yaw control, much to the chagrin of hardcore U.S. enthusiasts. Still, being able to have any Evo was better than none at all.

Other features on the U.S. car included a uniquely sized, 11.7–imperial gallon (53 liter) fuel tank, standard strut tower brace, and a more rigid unibody structure with even stronger suspension mounting points than the VII (although changes to the spring and shock rates were very marginal). As for braking, the American-spec cars featured the Brembo package as fitted to the Evo VII GSR, along with ABS, which required 17-inch wheels to clear the rotors (in this case 8x17-inch Enkeis, on which were mounted P235/34/ZR17 Yokohama Advan tires).

Keen readers will note that U.S. cars did not use the VIII moniker. That's because Mitsubishi Motor Sales America (MMSA) labeled the car simply as Evolution at its introduction and initially only offered a single trim level. Amazingly, a small rear spoiler was standard and the massive trademark carbon fiber unit was optional. Although it cost $600, most buyers in the United States wanted it.

Inside, trim levels mirrored the Japanese GSR with full power accessories—windows, mirrors, locks—as well as air conditioning and a premium sound system (in this case a CD/AM/FM unit with a 140-watt six-speaker setup). Other unique touches included a 170-mph speedometer, special front seats with unique bolstering, and different cushions from the JDM GSR, plus somber black stitching on the steering wheel and shifter boot. Considering the car was a very hot commodity even before it went on sale, MMSA made sure every one was fitted with an engine immobilizer to deter thieves (much in the same fashion as the United Kingdom). Options on the U.S.-spec Evo were limited to the carbon fiber rear deck spoiler and a power sunroof. The cars went on sale in March 2003 and were quickly snapped up. Those fortunate enough to drive one reported mind-bending performance levels that lived up to the car's reputation, even in its less aggressive U.S. tune. *Car and Driver* tested one of the new U.S. Evos and recorded a 0–60 mph time of five seconds flat and a top speed pushing 160 mph, while *Motor Trend* dubbed its early tester "an outrageous little car."

It was easy to see why. Thanks to razor-sharp steering (by U.S. standards), tremendous grip, superb turn-in (even without AYC), and an engine that begged to be flogged mile after mile, the Evo offered a completely unique take on the concept of enthusiast driving for many Americans.

JAPAN GETS ITS OWN

On the last day of January, Mitsubishi offered up the Japanese domestic-market version of its latest hot rod: the Evolution VIII. As before, two versions were offered: a top-of-the-line GSR and a built-to-order, stripped-down RS version. The GSR looked very similar to the U.S. Evo, but there were significant differences. The front

Not long after the U.S. launch, an updated version was released in Japan as the Lancer Evolution VIII. Outwardly similar to the US car, it was mechanically quite different, with a more powerful engine, larger gas tank, updated AWD system, and new Super Active Yaw Control. Plus, on the GSR version, a new six-speed manual gearbox arrived.
National Motor Museum, Beaulieu, UK

bumper was nigh identical (it was easier to standardize it for the entire production run), but out back the JDM VIII retained the VII's shorter rear bumper assembly and cover.

Mechanically, the U.S.- and Japanese-spec cars parted ways. The Japanese GSR version featured a new six-speed manual gearbox (the first in an Evo and thus matching the rival Subaru STi). Ratios were spec'd at 2.909 for first, 1.944 for second, 1.434 for third, 1.1 on fourth, 0.863 on fifth, and 0.693 on top. The new transmission featured tall cogs on speeds one and two, but then shorter ratios on three through five to deliver more mid-range punch. A tall sixth gear helped boost overall fuel economy. Along with the new gearbox, the 4G63 engine was also updated on the JDM Evo VIII. Most of the alterations centered around the cooling system, which featured a larger, more efficient water pump and less restrictive cooling passages to reduce heat soak from the turbocharger. The engine internals were also modified, with a stronger bottom end—including forged steel connecting rods, a new crankshaft and stronger bolts, plus new forged alloy pistons designed to maximize power and improve durability. New lightweight valve springs and retainers were used (the Evo VIII engine was designed to run a specific synthetic blend of oil). Additional weight was saved in the exhaust system (thinner manifold), A/C bracket, and crankshaft pulley.

As per Japanese requirements, the engine was still rated at 276 hp, or 280 PS (metric horsepower), but the torque swelled to 289 lb-ft at 3,500 revs. Getting that power to all four wheels was an updated AWD system, the biggest change being a more sophisticated active center differential and a new super active yaw control (SAYC) that incorporated planetary instead of bevel gears. The result was that the system could transfer a much greater amount of torque between the rear wheels, thus further enhancing grip and cornering ability. GSR models now came with a massive 12.1–imperial gallon (55-liter) gas tank (even bigger than the U.S. cars) and minor changes to the suspension. The Brembo brakes were still standard on the GSR model, necessitating 17-inch wheels—Enkeis, much like those on the U.S.

STARS N' STRIPES

The Japanese domestic market Evolution was actually shorter than the US car, thanks to a narrower rear bumper that it shared with its predecessor, the Evo VII. Mitsubishi Japan

cars. Inside, the Evo VIII GSR was much like its older counterpart, save for black stitching, a 270-kph speedometer, and new blue inserts for the seats.

The RS model featured a number of differences, including a different TD05 turbocharger, and the intercooler spray system was optional (whereas it was standard on the GSR). RS models also came with the old Evo VII five-speed manual gearbox as standard (though the new six-speed could be specified if so desired). The RS had a smaller, 11–imperial gallon (50-liter) fuel tank and the old Evo IV-derived brakes as standard, plus 15-inch steel wheels and a very basic interior: no power options, passenger side airbag, or premium sound system. As a result, a bare-bones RS with the five-speed was almost 200 lbs lighter than its GSR counterpart and considerably cheaper; retail price was set at ¥2,740,000 (the GSR retailed for a shade under 3,300,000). As before only one color was available on RS cars—Solid White (the GSR was available in this color, plus Solid Red, Solid Yellow, Medium Purple, Cool Silver, and Black Mica).

Still, a plethora of options, both factory and dealer installed, enabled RS buyers to customize their cars simply by ticking off the right boxes. Adding the six-speed gearbox, the big Brembo brakes with ABS, Enkei 17-inch wheels (or even a set of special ultra-light RAYS

WRX vs. EVO

With improvements to the driveline, specifically the new Super AYC, which used planetary gears, grip and handling were even better than the Evo VII, resulting in car that was incredibly fast, yet controllable. Mitsubishi Japan

units—also optional on the GSR), 235-section Advan tires, plus the super active yaw control (only the ACD came as standard on the RS) could make for a truly interesting machine, with all of the performance attributes of the GSR but without the flash. In essence, such a machine was the perfect car for the dedicated road/rally enthusiast.

Besides this stuff, a plethora of Ralliart tuning parts were available to crank the performance on either Evo VIII model up a few notches, including exhaust, upgraded struts, shocks and springs, carbon fiber rally-style door mirrors, fascia strakes, and rally-style mud flaps.

The Japanese Evo VIII drew tremendous praise from the local motoring press, especially for its Super AYC and the torquier, more tractable engine in conjunction with the six-speed gearbox. Compared to the Evo VII, the new car was even faster through the corners and could waltz through a tight and twisty road course with the finesse of a ballerina at speeds where most cars would struggle to maintain grip—especially when the tarmac got slippery. As before, Japanese-market production was capped at 5,000 units across the board, and all of the cars quickly sold out.

STARS N' STRIPES

CONQUERING BRITAIN

In an era when the United Kingdom seemed to be increasingly governed by speed cameras and other forms of freedom-limiting surveillance, the introduction of the Lancer Evolution VIII was nothing short of a breath of fresh air. Not only was the new car cheaper than the VII, but it offered even better performance. In fact, the British Evo VIII models were among the fastest and baddest examples ever unleashed. The new cars were announced at the Autosport show in January 2003, with sales beginning in April. The RS II was joined by a pair of new Ralliart UK-prepped specials: the FQ 300 and, later in the year, the FQ 330, named after their horsepower ratings.

The British-spec Evo VIIIs all came equipped with the six-speed manual gearbox; thus fuel economy wasn't that bad (around 21 miles to the imperial gallon), in spite of the cars' insane performance capabilities. Because the UK cars weren't governed by the Japanese-required speed limiters—which restricted top speed to 180 kph (115 mph) —they could run all the way up to 157 mph (251 kph), though in Britain, congestion and the ever-watchful eye of the police provided few opportunities to do so, except perhaps on a disused runway.

SUBARU: GO BIG OR GO HOME

The hoopla surrounding Mitsubishi at the 2003 Los Angeles show with the unveiling of its Americanized Lancer Evolution did not go unnoticed by Subaru. Not content to let its archrival have all the fun in North America, precisely two weeks later at the North American International Auto Show in Detroit, Subaru revealed its challenger to the Evo, a fully fledged, North American-spec Subaru STi.

Like its Mitsubishi counterpart, this was a considerably different car to that offered in Japan or other export markets. The biggest change was the engine. Instead of the familiar 1,994cc EJ20, this latest version had a larger, 2.5-liter, horizontally opposed four. This engine featured hypereutectic pistons instead of forged-alloy slugs and, to one-up Mitsubishi, was tuned to deliver 300 hp (SAE) net at 6,000 rpm and 300 lb-ft of torque at 4,000 revs, though it required premium

WRX vs. EVO

Not to be upstaged by its arch rival in North America, Subaru took the wraps off its own federalized STi at the 2003 North American International Auto show. Like its Mitsubishi counterpart, this car was a unique breed, with a larger, torquier 2.5-liter engine rated at 300 hp. Subaru Global

91 octane fuel in the United States and Canada (that's right, unlike the Evo, the new STi was also sold north of the 49th parallel right from the get-go). A close-ratio six-speed manual gearbox was bolted to the back of the engine, and the car came with an adjustable center differential, a big Brembo brake package (with 12.6-inch diameter front discs), standard 17-inch BBS wheels with 225/45/ZR17 Pirelli tires, plus a standard Momo three-spoke steering wheel and dual front airbags.

Subaru announced that the car would go on sale in North America in the spring as an early 2004 model, but only 3,600 examples would be allocated for the year. Needless to say, considering the pent-up demand, each one was quickly accounted for. As the car found its way into the hands of road testers, it was every bit as good as expected—the wait, it seemed, had been worth it. Magazines reported 0–60 mph times of an astonishing 4.6 seconds, and the AWD monster blasted through the quarter-mile in just 13.2 seconds (quicker than many V-8 powered muscle cars, both new and old). The steering was judged to

STARS N' STRIPES

Thanks to extra chassis reinforcements and new front and rear subframes, which allowed the engineers to tune the suspension for more neutral cornering, the 2003-04 Impreza STi was the best-handling version yet. Subaru Global

be razor sharp. The only downsides were the brakes—which, although extremely powerful, were judged to lack feel, along with a firm ride, small back seat, and fuel economy that was rather atrocious for a four-cylinder car. Still, for U.S. and Canadian enthusiasts who'd waited so long to get their hands on it, the new STi was like a dream come true. Like Mitsubishi's Evolution, this North American-spec Scoob was a perfect example of the amount of influence public demand can have on a manufacturer's decision to sell a car in certain markets that it had not previously considered, in this case because of crash standards and strict emissions requirements. The fact that the STi was able to appear legally on North American shores was a testimonial to the triumph of human enthusiasm over government bureaucracy.

CHANGING SCENE

The introduction of the Evo and STi to North America was also significant in that it caused an epic shift in the so-called sport compact scene. Prior to the cars' arrival, most enthusiasts had only small, North American–market Hondas, Nissans, and Toyotas to modify, but these cars nevertheless inspired intense loyalty and provided the foundation for a new tuning community.

Yet for some reason, the companies that sold these cars were reluctant to bring their performance offerings to North America and provided stateside compact car enthusiasts with little in the way of performance aftermarket support. This was a complete contrast to Europe and Japan, where Honda's Type-R brand and Toyota Racing Development were major players.

The Evo and STi, despite being the products of smaller Japanese auto manufacturers, were able to forever change the face of the small car tuning scene in North America. Here were two machines that, in factory trim, raised the performance bar to an entirely different level. The WRX and STi, in particular, soon became stalwarts in the North American rally community, numerous examples being campaigned in the SCCA Pro Rally and Rally America. In particular, a young driver—well-known motocross racer and freestyle rider Travis Pastrana—soon made a name for himself behind the wheel of a STi with co-driver Christian Edstrom, first with the Vermont Sports Car Team and then with Subaru's Rally Team USA. He ultimately won the 2006 Rally USA championship and enjoyed battles with former WRC champion and Subaru driver Colin McRae, both in stateside rallying and the infamous X Games. There he beat the Scotsman in the Games' inaugural rally competition in Los Angeles that same year, after McRae rolled his car in spectacular fashion.

Besides rallying, both the WRX and Evo became popular mounts for road racing, particularly time attack, as their high-powered and extremely tweakable engines, combined with AWD, made them super quick at lapping. Companies such as Cobb Tuning and Robispec were soon pushing the envelope of performance with these incredible cars. Much like the Camaro versus Mustang wars that had raged for decades in North America, followers of Japanese performance cars now had their own fierce rivalry—only the contenders in this battle were packing small-displacement, high-winding turbo fours and all-wheel drive, instead of brute cubic inches and straight-line speed.

STARS N' STRIPES

IN BRITANNIA

Just prior to the North American announcement, Subaru was reporting brisk sales of the bug-eye GD chassis WRX and STi models in the United Kingdom. Late in October 2002, Prodrive announced a special performance pack for the British STi. This featured a tweaked engine management unit and a sports exhaust system with a high-flow catalytic converter. The tuning tweaks resulted in a substantial power hike—35 hp in fact—to a total of 300 bhp (DIN). Torque, meanwhile, swelled from 253 lb-ft to a mighty 299, making the car a real mover, capable of reaching 60 mph in 4.6 seconds and topping 150 mph (performance almost exactly on par with the forthcoming North American version, which relied on a bigger engine). The Prodrive pack cost just under £2000, which, considering the performance jump it provided, was money well spent, especially because cars fitted with it were still covered by Subaru UK's standard warranty of three years and 36,000 miles.

In February 2003, a month after the U.S. show debut, Subaru released the face-lifted WRX and STi onto the UK market. The former received an EJ20 engine with more power—up to 225 bhp at 5,000 rpm and 221 lb-ft of torque at four grand. In addition, with fuel prices in Britain reaching record levels, the new engine was tuned to run on both the regular grade of UK unleaded fuel (95 RON) as well as super unleaded (98 RON). Besides the obvious facelift, including the headlights, fenders, hood, and rear taillights, the WRX now shared its instrument cluster with the STi, including a nice set of brushed-metal trim rings around the gauges. Alongside the regular Rex model was an up-level SL version that added plush leather-covered, heated front bucket seats and a standard power sunroof at a price of around £22,000 (the standard WRX retailed for a shade under 20 grand).

The UK-spec STi variant came in just a single model, but packed into it was, as the Brits would say, "a lot of standard kit." The previously optional Prodrive body upgrades, including the rear spoiler, were made standard on the 2003 model, while a smaller Momo steering wheel was fitted and minor changes were made to the upholstery and interior trim. Power windows, locks, mirrors, air conditioning, and a premium sound system were also fitted, in keeping with the car's top-line image in the United Kingdom.

Along with the new looks adopted by the entire Impreza line, changes under the skin were evident, with stronger suspension-mounting points and a standard strut tower brace resulting in a tauter chassis and improved at-the-limit handling. The engine was also able to breathe better, thanks to a bigger-diameter intake and a more efficient intercooler setup for the IHI RF55 turbocharger; the changes improved throttle response and cut down the 0–60 mph dash to around 4.8 seconds in factory stock trim. As before, Prodrive offered up its performance packs for both the regular WRX and STi (boosting power to 265 and 300 bhp, respectively), which became available in February 2003. Although the price was increased slightly, at £1600 it was still a bargain in many respects and turned either car into a rocket ship.

PACIFIC RIM DEVELOPMENTS

In Australia, the new, face-lifted WRX, having been introduced alongside its lesser Impreza counterparts in December 2002, came in either sedan or wagon form with a choice of five-speed manual or four-speed automatic transmissions. Strangely, Australians couldn't get the new STi at this juncture. Instead the old bug-eye version continued for a few more months; though when the new, face-lifted STi did arrive, it was to much critical acclaim, which was followed by brisk sales.

Meanwhile, Japanese demand for the face-lifted GD WRX and STi cars had gotten off to a good start, and why not? There was a lot to like about the latest versions, including a raft of mechanical improvements. For the regular WRX, there were new, sodium-filled valves in the heads; lighter weight valve springs and retainers; a new, more efficient intercooler; and a revised, Mitsubishi-sourced TD04 turbo with a new, smaller and lighter impeller, designed to deliver boost more quickly and improve throttle response. At the other end, a redesigned exhaust system helped to better expel the nasty gases.

STARS N' STRIPES

Subaru also added the same instrument cluster as fitted to the European cars, with tasteful metal gauge trim rings, plus there was now a metal button for the parking brake. In addition, the wagon variant was simply now called **WRX Sports Wagon**, rather than the 20K, a logical choice given that a normally aspirated Impreza sedan was dubbed 20S.

The Japanese-market 2003 STi received a greater raft of changes than the WRX. Unlike the North American version, it retained a version of the EJ20 engine, with a stronger block, stouter bottom end (beefier crank and rods), plus new cast alloy pistons, though still on an 8.0:1 squeeze. The turbo and exhaust system were less restrictive and had more efficient piping, a bigger and more efficient intercooler, and a reshaped and enlarged intake manifold and tract. The result was an increase in torque up to 290 lb-ft, which came in higher than the European or North American cars (max grunt occurred at 4,400 revs). Horsepower, as per Japanese requirements, stayed at 280 hp, with max power still coming in at six grand on the tachometer.

Along with the engine, the STi's standard six-speed manual gearbox was also upgraded with a stronger casing and a new shift linkage fitted to try to smooth gear changes (they were a vast improvement over the early GC cars, but still quite notchy compared with many rivals).

Chassis alterations ran to new front and rear subframes with stronger mounting points and extra cross bracing at the front, which allowed the engineers to dial in more negative camber in order to further reduce understeer. The front wheel axis was pushed forward by 0.6 inches, and both front- and rear-drive axles were strengthened to cope with the increased torque of the engine and also higher cornering limits. A new ball-joint setup was added to the rear sway bar in an effort to provide more give and reduce the risk of the rear end skittering when exiting high-speed corners. The 12.6-inch Brembo brake package was carried over from the 2001 and 2002 cars, as were the wheels and tires.

The chassis and suspension changes, in particular, were noted by the automotive press—the latest STi judged to be more neutral with less understeer and capable of generating a tighter cornering line at higher speeds than its predecessor. Much like its U.S. counterpart, however, the big Brembo brakes, for all their stopping ability, were judged by Japan-based correspondent Peter Lyon to be somewhat "soggy and lacking precision."

Still, no car is perfect, and considering the price of admission, even in Japan, the new STi offered a tremendous amount of bang for the buck (or rather, yen).

Subaru also released another limited-production Type RA Spec C for 2003, announced in April of that year. This new Spec C variant actually came in two guises. The cheaper (¥2,740,000) version came with a front-mounted intercooler after the turbocharger (which was slightly different from that fitted on the regular STi, being a RHF5HB unit), standard 16-inch steel wheels and tires, quicker 13.1 steering, Suretrac front and rear differentials, plus a center unit that allowed the driver to adjust the torque split manually via a switch on the dash. The interior of this car was also very basic; for aside from the Momo steering wheel (with driver's airbag), it was virtually identical to a very pedestrian-looking, base Impreza interior. In fact, this car was so stripped-down and purpose-built that it weighed more than 260 lbs less than the regular STi.

The second Spec C (priced at ¥3,205,000) was a bit heavier and better equipped. It featured a central diff with automatic override as well as the manual driver-adjustable feature, 17-inch BBS multispoke alloy wheels (like those fitted to regular STis), the bigger Brembo brakes (as fitted to regular STis), front sport bucket seats, and a fairly discreet rear deck spoiler. Both Spec C variants could be ordered only in Pure White.

MITSUBISHI: A NEW APPROACH

By early 2003, it was becoming obvious that Mitsubishi's long period of success in WRC circles—including Makinen's four driver's titles in the late 1990s and early 2000s—was at an ebb. Mitsubishi was discovering that its reliance on Group A machinery long after its main rivals had adopted the World Rally Car format had ultimately proved a hindrance. With disappointing results from the 2002 season, including only one driver's point finish (courtesy of Alistair McRae), now was the time to take a serious look at the company's rally efforts and restructure where necessary. A full works effort for 2003 ended up being the casualty, with MRE deciding to run cars at only a few events—Sweden, New Zealand, and Germany.

A new management team was drafted in. Kimata was still in charge, but Sven Quandt was appointed Mitsubishi Ralliart team manager, while Mario Fornaris was brought over from Peugeot, a team that had been dominating the World Rally Championship in recent years.

The works team's main driver for the season was young Finn Kristian Sohlberg, who partnered up with Jakke Honkanen. McRae and Jani Paasonen were given a car for one event each (New Zealand and Germany, respectively).

Mitsubishi elected to run only a select few WRC events in 2003, with cars for Jani Paasonen and new driver Kristian Sohlberg. Here's Jani getting airborne in that year's Rally of Germany. Mitsubishi Japan

WRX vs. EVO

In Sweden, Sohlberg showed promise, demonstrating very canny and solid driving. His stage times enabled him to nudge into the top 10, but he ultimately settled for 12th overall, behind Mikko Hirvonen and ahead of former Mitsu works driver Armin Schwarz.

The next outing for the works Group A team was New Zealand, where McRae and Senior drove an excellent rally to take sixth place overall, finishing ahead of the great Tommi Makinen. Sohlberg didn't have as much luck, crashing out of the proceedings on the morning of the final leg.

Round five for the Group N class, in Germany, also marked the return of the top-flight WRC works entries, this time for Sohlberg and Paasonen. As a tarmac event, neither driver was really in his element. Sohlberg drove reasonably well, especially considering his limited tarmac experience and a steady amount of rain, which made the going quite slick. Despite his 14th-place finish, the experience gained by finishing the rally was valuable. Paasonen, who was also running his first event on tarmac, was doing reasonably well until he crashed out

Kristian Sohlberg battled slippery conditions in Germany to finish the event in 14th place overall, gaining much experience running tarmac events in the process.
Mitsubishi Japan

on the second leg during Stage 11. The accident was serious enough for Jani and co-driver Arto to be taken to the hospital, though luckily, neither of them had serious injuries and both were soon released.

SUBARU: A NEW CHAMPION

Although Subaru had chosen to display its new, updated WRC car at the 2002 Paris Auto Salon, it wasn't until just prior to the season's first event—the Monte Carlo—that the details became public. The new cars featured updated styling with the new headlights and front fascia, plus improved aerodynamics. The rally cars used a version of the venerable EJ20 four-banger, rated at 300 hp but a staggering 435 lb-ft of torque. The gearbox was an updated version of the Prodrive six-speed unit with sequential shifting, while the three differentials were electro-hydraulically activated (torque split was 50:50 under normal operating conditions). As before, the Subarus used OZ wheels and Pirelli tires.

The 71st running of the Monte wasn't a particularly memorable one for Subaru. Solberg retired on Special Stage 5 when his car was damaged from a meeting with the scenery. Makinen lasted a bit longer and pushed hard to catch Marcus Gronholm, but his race was over when a loose rock struck underneath the car and damaged the brake lines. Gronholm also retired after crashing out—leaving Sebastian Loeb to take top honors, followed by past Subaru drivers Colin McRae and Carlos Sainz, all of whom were driving Citroens.

The snowy conditions of Sweden proved better for the Subaru team. Despite dealing with familiar conditions, Solberg struggled to maintain competitive stage times (at least by his standards), though he later recalled that there weren't any problems with the car. Makinen was flying high and chased fellow Finn Gronholm, whom he was starting to reel in by the final leg. However, he ultimately came in second, and this, coupled with Solberg's sixth place, was much better than Monte.

The teams then headed to a brand new event on the WRC calendar, the Rally of Turkey. Both the Subarus suffered from attrition in the rocky conditions. Solberg was the first to go when he broke a steering

WRX vs. EVO

Tommi Makinen and Petter Solberg signed up to drive for the Subaru team during the 2003 season, though this would be Makinen's last. He's seen here in the Rally of Turkey, where he came in eighth place after fighting the event's very rough conditions.
Subaru Global

arm. Makinen plodded on but faced troubles of this own. Debris on several stages slowed his progress. Repairs to his car cost a sizeable amount of time, and the best he could finish was in eighth place.

Down in New Zealand, Makinen, suffering from illness, wasn't able to maintain his usual pace, but he stayed in the rally to come home in seventh overall. Solberg and Mills were simply flying, battling the Citroens of Burns and Loeb and trying to do their best to catch Gronholm, who appeared to be in a class of his own. Still, a third-place finish was enough to keep Petter in the running while the team gained valuable constructor's points.

In the works camp, Argentina proved to be a mixed bag. Attrition rates were high, especially on the first day, though both Solberg and Makinen made it into leg two. The Finn, who was not making much progress compared with his usual standard, decided to pull out and save his energy for another day. Solberg was left to fly the flag and brought the remaining works car home in fifth, garnering two points in the driver's points race—though by this stage, it seemed that Marcus Gronholm, after winning yet another rally, might take the crown for a second year in a row.

In Greece, plenty of cars once again succumbed to the rocky and hot conditions that marked nearly every stage. Solberg pushed hard, particularly on day three, where he set the fastest times on four of the six stages. This was enough for him to pass Richard Burns and claim a podium finish (Markko Martin won this one, driving his Ford Focus, with Sainz in the Citroen taking second). As for Tommi Makinen, he maintained a steady pace and ended the rally in fifth overall.

Cyprus was a good one for SWRT. Solberg drove a near perfect rally to take his first win of the season, beating the Peugeots and Citroens (Harri Rovanpera and Sebastian Loeb finished in second and third). Makinen was also making good progress until suspension damage caused his retirement.

On slippery tarmac in Germany, the misery was compounded for Solberg due to a fever. To his credit, the Norwegian stayed in the game until the end (by which point he was back to full health), finishing seventh overall in yet another Citroen- and Peugeot-dominated event. Makinen's troubles were of the mechanical kind; persistent electrical issues made his rally frustrating, and he ultimately retired when the alternator expired during Special Stage 6.

Markko Martin and his Focus set the pace in Finland; however, Solberg wasn't far behind, chasing the heels of second-place Gronholm on the first day, though he dropped down the leader board to fifth by the end of leg two. However, a fantastic performance on the last day saw Solberg battle fiercely for second place overall with Richard Burns. The Subaru driver ultimately won this battle, though the Englishman grabbed the lead in the driver's championship. Makinen drove steadily through all three days of the "Gravel Grand Prix" to take sixth overall.

The circus then moved back to the Pacific Rim for the Telstra Rally Australia, which as always, included stints on the infamous

Langley Park section. Here, Solberg, driving in top form, was locked in a game of cat and mouse with Sebastian Loeb, from which he emerged victorious. With Marcus Gronholm retiring, Petter now had a serious shot at the 2003 driver's championship. Makinen, although not quite matching the pace set by his teammate, drove steadily and brought the second works car home in sixth place, behind the Citroens of McRae and Sainz.

Three more tarmac rallies followed: San Remo, Corsica, and then Spain, events where the Citroens and Peugeots had triumphed in the last few years. Solberg didn't have much luck this time around; he ran out of fuel and thus was not allowed to restart, forcing retirement. For the San Remo, SWRT also decided to give Makinen and Lindstrom an updated car with new suspension settings. Although Tommi wasn't on the pace, he did at least finish to provide the team with valuable in-event testing data.

On the Tour de Corse, it all came together, though at the start it didn't appear things would go that well for Subaru. Solberg had crashed quite heavily in testing just prior to the event, although the car was repaired. On the opening leg, all eyes were on Sebastian Loeb, as he set fast time after fast time on the twisty mountain roads. However on day two, Solberg put in the drive of his life and won the last three stages, while Loeb lost a lot of time after spinning out in the rain. Solberg continued at a torrid pace on the final day of competition, and by the end, he had an amazing 36.6 second lead over his nearest challenger, Carlos Sainz, beating the Spaniard right to the last checkpoint. It was an amazing and well-deserved victory. Makinen brought the other works car home in seventh after another solid, steady drive, bagging a few more constructors' points for the team.

Catalunya didn't quite garner the same results, though both Subarus were the quickest cars on leg three, setting the fastest stage times and proving well suited to the smooth roads and wet conditions. Solberg finished fifth. With Gilles Panizzi claiming the win and Burns crashing out, plus Sainz finishing a disappointing seventh, Solberg was in a third place in the driver's cup, with Sainz and Loeb tied for first.

STARS N' STRIPES

Makinen had been off the pace for the first two days, but he was much happier on the final leg, both with the car and his progress. He finished eighth, behind Sainz.

The RAC, once again gloomy and damp and with many stages being run through the Welsh forests, turned out to be the championship decider—the finale to a hotly contested and unpredictable season. Solberg knew that he had to beat both Sebastian Loeb and Carlos Sainz to keep his championship hopes alive, but when the Spaniard was off on Special Stage Three, the battle narrowed to Petter and Sebastian.

Solberg, realizing that he had to drive all-out to stay ahead, proved exceedingly cool yet demonstrated amazing speed, both on the regular special stages and the super specials run around Cardiff. For the 13 of the 18 stages, he beat Loeb on the clock, but the Frenchman was persistent to the end, piling on the pressure during the last few stages and cutting into Solberg's once- substantial lead. It wasn't quite enough

The RAC rally was a spectacular one for Subaru as Petter Solberg clinched enough points to win the driver's championship. Winning the event was merely the icing on the cake. He's seen here celebrating the historic occasion as Makinen pours the victory champagne directly upon him! Subaru Global

to catch him, however, and Petter won his first WRC championship in the last event of the season (though thanks to the efforts of Loeb, McRae, and Sainz, Citroen won the manufacturer's cup). At the end of the final stage, Solberg jumped high in the air in celebration—what a victory! His teammate Makinen, who'd already announced his retirement from the WRC arena, came in a very strong third place for his final outing. With another Subaru driver clinching the crown, the stage was set for another raft of V-Limited special-edition Imprezas!

2004

MITSUBISHI: GOING RACING

Mitsubishi chose the 2003 Tokyo Motor Show to reveal yet another Evolution—a VIII subvariant, the sinister MR (for Mitsubishi Racing), signifying that the company's world championship program was very much back on and better than ever (the MR would go on sale in the home market the following February).

This latest car was offered in three guises: a full-jam GSR and two RS versions (one that was seriously bare bones and another with slightly more creature comforts but still less than the top-level GSR). Outwardly, MR models were distinguished from regular Evo VIIIs by darker tinted headlight units (with standard HID projector units), darker finished taillight housings, a dark gray insert for the carbon fiber rear spoiler, and a set of optional 17x8 BBS 10-spoke alloy wheels finished in gunmetal gray. Inside, the cabin was more somber and business-like than the standard Evolution VIII, thanks to black and gray inserts for the seats and door panels (instead of blue), a black Momo steering wheel, and carbon fiber dash and window switch trim, plus a special brushed-aluminum MR plaque around the shifter boot.

However, the new car featured considerably more than just cosmetic upgrades. The engine, still a version of the 4G63 and rated at 280 hp as per Japanese requirements, received a number of upgrades. There was a lighter balance shaft, new camshafts (fitted into a new cylinder head with revised cooling passages), plus a thicker and stronger block and a

STARS N' STRIPES

A new subvariant of the Lancer Evolution VIII was revealed at the 2003 Tokyo Motor show, the MR (for Mitsubishi Racing). This was an ultra high-performance variant with a fortified engine and less weight. With dark headlight housings and wheels and a new exterior color called Medium Purplish Grey, it was aggressive to say the least.
Mitsubishi Japan

more efficient, externally mounted oil cooler. In addition, the pistons also got new rings to cope with a revised turbocharger and exhaust plumbing. The turbos were upgraded to a Mitsu TD5HR 16G on the GSR and an even quicker-spooling TDHRA 16G for the RS cars. The wastegate was controlled by dual solenoids and, as a result, throttle response and power were improved through the mid- and upper-rev ranges, making the MR a peakier, more balls-out machine to drive.

The GSR and the up-level RS model came with a six-speed gearbox, using identical ratios as fitted to the regular Evo VIII, while the stripped-down MR RS retained the Evo VII's five-speed manual. Weight reduction was a major theme on the MR, with an aluminum roof, an aluminum instead of steel clutch carrier for the super active yaw control on the rear differential, and a lighter and more compact clutch that controlled power distribution between the rear wheels. The Super AYC, along with active center diff and the anti-lock braking system,

WRX vs. EVO

A peakier engine and quicker-reacting Super Active Yaw control made the Evo VIII MR the most deadly of the breed. It was the nearest thing to a street-going rally car you could buy at the time. Mitsubishi Japan

were also upgraded and more intelligent than before. In conjunction with suspension and chassis upgrades—stronger mounting points for the front and rear links and improved spot welding and body rigidity—the MR in any guise was a force to be reckoned with. The stripped-down, five-speed RS version—costing just ¥2,740,000—was the closest you could get to a full-on, street-legal rally car on the showroom floor.

As always, the RS models were built strictly to order and came in only one color: Solid White. The GSR version of the MR added a few more hues: Solid Red, Cool Silver, and an odd color called Medium Purplish Grey, a metallic color that looked gray from most angles though a little like parchment from others (especially in the sunlight). In fact, no matter what color a MR model was painted, it looked truly menacing and, unlike many cars, had the performance (and then some) to back up its all-business looks.

A WIDER SPREAD

Once the 2004 model year was in full swing, export markets started getting their hands on a spate of new Evolution VIII variants.

STARS N' STRIPES

In the United Kingdom, the Evo VIII 260 was introduced in an effort to steal sales away from the Subaru WRX. This car, which got its name from its horsepower rating (well, almost), featured a 4G63 engine tuned to deliver 263 bhp and 262 lb-ft of torque. Unlike other UK-spec cars, it featured the VII's five-speed manual gearbox and a slightly lower-spec interior, manual air conditioning, and lower-grade seats. It also came with a small rear spoiler, and at £23,999 it represented a relatively affordable way to get into an AWD homologation car.

The MR also arrived on British shores as a single, well-equipped model, called the MR 280, though without the Japanese-spec car's speed limiter and different equipment to meet British standards—such as improved rust proofing, slightly different exterior lighting, an imperial mph speedometer, and so on.

If that wasn't enough, there were the homegrown rally specials dished up by Mitsubishi UK, which could be created by souping up regular Evos or ordered as fully built, turnkey machines (See Appendix B: Special Edition Cars).

The early 2000s were interesting times for sure. Evo VIIIs started arriving in other countries, including Continental Europe and, of course, Australia and New Zealand. Among commonwealth countries, only Canada had yet to receive the car because of strict bumper laws. And while the Evo continued to whet the insatiable appetite of car aficionados everywhere, there was good news on the World Rally Championship front. Mitsubishi Motors, having undergone restructuring in the wake of major losses, credit problems, and product recalls, was starting to get back on its feet; naturally, motorsport was one arena that benefited.

SUBARU: SOLID PROGRESS

While a spate of limited-edition celebration WRXs and STis found owners in early 2004, the Subaru World Rally Team was busy getting ready for its defense of the WRC championship. For the first two events of the season, the team continued using the 2003-spec works cars, though with Tommi Makinen having retired from rallying, a new driver stepped into the legendary champion's place. A fellow Finn, Mikko Hirvonen was just 23 years old at the time and had already shown promise while driving for Ford in 2003. Now it was time to see if he'd make an even bigger impact at Subaru.

There were also other changes, notably the arrival of Luis Moya, the longtime co-driver of former Subaru WRC pilot Carlos Sainz. Moya's appointment as SWRT sports director brought the team a great deal of world rally experience and knowledge.

As always, the Monte Carlo kicked off the new rally season, but the Subarus got off to a bit of a shaky start. Solberg was doing very well by the third day, setting the fastest time on Special Stage 13. Though on the following special stage, frustration mounted when the car hit a patch of snow, sliding into a wall and damaging the front suspension. Solberg and Mills had to make roadside repairs and, as a result, lost huge amounts of time despite making it back into the rally; they crossed the line in seventh place overall. Hirvonen also suffered suspension damage, skidding out on Special Stage 9. Unable to make it back to the service area, he had to call it quits.

The old works cars were brought out for one final time in Sweden. The conditions were a bit challenging to say the least, with minimal snow, but Solberg drove steadily, finishing third overall despite suspension damage. Hirvonen slid off the road on Special Stage 9, but with some help he dug the car out and was able to continue, finishing in ninth place.

Mexico saw the introduction of the latest WRC 2004 Imprezas, and Solberg got off to a flying start, setting the pace for the opening leg. A five-minute penalty, incurred by spectator assistance, soured the proceedings and gave Solberg quite a mountain to climb. Still, the reigning champion did his best to make up for it, winning every single stage on the second leg and then 9 of the 15 special stages on the last day to come in fourth overall. Hirvonen scored his best result yet: an overall fifth place.

In New Zealand, Solberg played a game of cat and mouse with the Peugeots of Harri Rovanpera during the first leg and then Marcus

Gronholm, who mounted a serious challenge on the last day. Still, despite Gronholm winning the final stage of the event, Solberg and Phil Mills had set the fastest overall stage times by almost six seconds and that was enough for them to secure their first-ever win in New Zealand. Hirvonen and his co-driver Jarmo Lehtinen came home a solid seventh after a steady drive. In Group N, Australian Dean Herridge and his STi saw off the competition to collect a win in the production car category.

Rocky Cyprus lived up to its usual reputation. Solberg was very quick out of the gate, but several punctures and then an incident on Special Stage 4 that clogged his radiator full of dirt and gravel cost him a lot of time. He made up for it on the second day and ultimately brought the car home in sixth place. Hirvonen drove exceptionally well, despite the dusty and rocky road conditions, and maintained a steady pace to finish seventh.

In Greece, Solberg was on top form, winning five of the nine special stages on the first day. He continued his magnificent pace on the second leg despite losing his brakes on Special Stage 13, which forced him to drive just with the parking brake. On day three, he kept the momentum going, despite winning only one stage, but his overall times were enough to stay ahead of Sebastian Loeb (who claimed the most stage wins on day three) and win the event. Hirvonen damaged his braking system on the opening leg but kept going. Unfortunately, his rally came to an end on Special Stage 15 during leg two, when he couldn't avoid a boulder in the road, rolling his car and ending up on the roof. Luckily, neither he nor co-driver Lehtinen suffered serious injury, but the car was critically damaged.

Mud plagued the Rally Turkey, but Solberg ran strong once again, setting the third-fastest overall time on the first day of competition. Weather conditions improved on leg two, and the Norwegian pushed harder, winning the last two stages of the day and putting a bit of pressure on front runners Sebastian Loeb and Marcus Gronholm. He continued to push hard, winning the last three of the four remaining stages, but he simply ran out of time to beat Marcus for second place;

at least he got on the podium. Hirvonen continued to show a lot of promise despite his limited experience in this event, and he came home in an excellent sixth.

Argentina proved to be disappointing for Solberg and Mills who, after having enjoyed a very good season so far, ended up retiring on the opening leg after Special Stage 9, when the engine died. The remaining works car of Hirvonen and Lehtinen pressed on—the young Finn driving a sterling rally to finish fourth overall, ending the last stage of the day ahead of overall winner Carlos Sainz.

In Finland, both the works cars were casualties. Solberg was the first to retire, after running wide on a section of Special Stage 4, in which he was unable to avoid sliding off the road and into the ditch. To make matters worse, the car hit a rock before coming to rest, which damaged the front suspension. Hirvonen, while coming through a corner on the last stage on day one, clipped a barrier and shunted the car, causing damage to both the radiator and front suspension.

The first full tarmac rally of the season in Germany saw an additional top-spec car, driven by Stephane Sarrazin and backed by Subaru France, join the regular works cars. Despite being run at the height of summer, the event was soaked by major helpings of rain, making some sections very slippery and difficult. Solberg drove consistently and ended the first leg in a strong fourth, while Hirvonen was ninth. On day two, disaster struck on Special Stage 12, the day's longest and hardest, when Solberg slid off the road, smacking into a curbstone before rolling and coming to rest against another piece of heavy stone. Petter and Phil were airlifted to the hospital for checks, but luckily they suffered only minor injuries and made full recoveries for the next round in Japan. As a result of the accident, rally officials cancelled the stage. Meanwhile, Hirvonen pressed on, showing remarkable skill amid the conditions. He and Jarmo ultimately bagged eighth place. Sarrazin did a decent job, too, taking ninth place overall, finishing right behind the young Finn.

If ever there was a crucial rally during the 2004 season, Japan was it. With the top brass in attendance, SWRT knew it had to pull out all the

STARS N' STRIPES

stops. Solberg and Mills, back in action, were on good form once again, setting the pace and winning the first leg despite challenges, particularly from Sebastian Loeb. By the last day, Loeb and Gronholm were pushing hard, winning several stages between them, but Solberg was the most consistent and won the eighth rally of his career on Subaru's home turf and right in front of the company president, who'd stayed to watch the event reach its conclusion. Hirvonen was also on good form and maintained a steady pace despite suffering gearbox issues, collecting a couple of points for himself by finishing seventh overall.

The RAC was bumped up to September this year, which made the conditions somewhat better than usual, at least in terms of visibility. Solberg and co-driver Mills (on home turf, being from Wales) made a steady start, and from there things only got better. Solberg ended up winning three stages on the first leg, moving from fourth to third and finally second by the end of the day and taking a chunk out of Sebastien Loeb's lead. The situation was repeated on leg two, with

Reigning world champion Petter Solberg enjoyed an outstanding RAC, which was held earlier in the year than previous events, He finished first, making it three in a row in Britain. Subaru Global

Solberg storming through the Welsh forests and a tire change to give himself and Mills the advantage during some very slippery and muddy sections. On the final day, Solberg overtook Loeb and his Citroen to win the RAC yet again. Teammate Hirvonen also drove extremely well, despite an incident on the second leg that plugged his radiator full of mud; he came home in a strong seventh overall, sandwiched between the Peugeots of Harri Rovanpera and Manfred Stohl.

Success continued for SWRT, with Solberg again driving in top form during the new Rally Sardinia (which replaced the San Remo as the erstwhile Italian round). Although Hirvonen was out early with a gearbox problem on Special Stage 3, Solberg blasted off into the lead and, despite a cooling issue, was the top finisher by the end of the first day. On the second leg, he was just as dominant, winning all but one stage (Marcus Gronholm was quickest on Special Stage 11). By that point, Solberg was on his way to victory, which he clinched easily by winning four out of the six final stages and finishing more than two minutes ahead of overall runner-up Loeb.

From Sardinia, the teams moved to the island to the north, Corsica, for the "French" round. For this one, SWRT added a third works car (an old 2003) for Stephane Sarrazin and co-driver Patrick Pivato. Inclement weather conditions made some sections of the narrow, twisty mountain roads very slippery; both Solberg and Hirvonen struggled on the first leg, plagued partly by tires that didn't seem to work very well. They ended the day in a disappointing 7th and 12th, respectively. Day two was much the same with rain showers intermingled with drying spells, causing further difficulties. On the final leg, Solberg, much happier with the car, managed to win the first stage of the day, but ultimately the best finish he could muster overall was fifth, with teammate Hirvonen coming in a distant tenth. The biggest surprise was Sarrazin. He took to the course like a duck to water, and by the final stage, he had driven fast enough to take sixth overall, behind Solberg and Mills. On another note, the Tour de Corse saw Sebastien Loeb clinch the driver's title and Citroen take the manufacturer's cup, still with two rounds to go.

STARS N' STRIPES

Mikko Hirvonen replaced Makinen as a works Subaru driver in 2004. Seen here in Catalunya, which was the last tarmac event of the year, the young Finn managed to finish eighth. Subaru Global

The final tarmac rally of the year was Catalunya, which proved a bit of a challenge for Solberg and Hirvonen. Again, weather that changed virtually from one stage to the next made tire choice exceedingly difficult, but both drivers did their best and by day three had proved consistent enough to take fifth and eighth overall. Sarrazin, however, did even better in Spain than he had in Corsica, clearly at home amid the wet conditions. He set the fastest overall time on the first stage of leg three and claimed fourth overall by the end of the rally, finishing just over two seconds behind Carlos Sainz in fourth and ahead of Solberg.

Australia was the last rally on the calendar in 2004, and after a good season, Solberg exited the final round early when he hit a rock and damaged the steering linkage on his car. Hirvonen, despite dealing with brake problems, was quite happy with his car, and as the rally progressed, he got quicker, the car gaining more grip as the loose top level of gravel gave way to the harder stuff underneath. Mikko and co-driver Jarmo Lehtinen ultimately ended the event in a strong fourth place overall, the best of his career.

WRX vs. EVO

MITSUBISHI: SERIOUSLY DIFFERENT

The 2004 Mitsubishi Lancer Evolution World Rally Car was the most radical machine yet seen from the Japanese concern. Its resemblance to the production version was limited to say the least. Aerodynamics were a key part of the design, with a very low-mounted front fascia, fender openings that featured flat tops and strakes at the rear, plus a forward-mounted rear deck spoiler to keep the car planted on the road at speed. The 1,996cc 4G63 engine was moved back to improve weight distribution and linked to a five-speed sequential gearbox. The driveline still contained three differentials and a 50:50 torque split, but the diffs were now manually controlled instead of being active units as on the 2001 through 2003 cars. Brembo brakes were fitted as standard, and the car was unique in being the only one in the entire WRC field to run on Enkei wheels (everybody else used OZs), shod in Michelin tires.

After a re-alignment of its motorsports arm, Mitsubishi Ralliart fielded a more comprehensive WRC effort in for 2004. Its new contender was radical-looking to say the least. Mitsubishi Japan

STARS N' STRIPES

Two works cars were run for the season, with the driver lineup comprising former Peugeot man Gilles Panizzi in the number one car and young Italian Gianluigi Galli; Kristian Sohlberg (who returned from the 2003 season) and former Group N driver Daniel Sola shared the second car.

Naturally, the first event of the year was the classic Monte Carlo. Cars were entered for Panizzi and Galli. Despite the absence of a great amount of testing before the season opener, Panizzi and his co-driver, brother Herve, did a sterling job of proving the new car in battle. Things improved after the second leg, for despite incurring penalties for swapping the gearbox and new suspension settings, Panizzi became more comfortable with the car and ended up finishing sixth overall. Galli showed great promise early on, but his rally came to an abrupt end when the car slid off the road on Special Stage 5. It wasn't badly damaged, but it was so far off the course that it would take too much time to retrieve it.

For Sweden, Kristian Sohlberg replaced Galli in the second car, but things didn't go too well for the team. Panizzi was out early this time, retiring on Special Stage 4 when the car died and refused to start. Sohlberg and co-driver Kaj Lindstrom spun out on the first leg, losing a lot of time, though they managed to grab it back a bit and bumped up their position from 63rd to 34th on the leaderboard. Sadly, it was to no avail, because the following morning they were out too, with gearbox problems.

A period of intense testing then followed as the team got ready for the next round—Mexico. Galli was back in the second car with co-driver Guido D'Amore (Sohlberg was running Group N, as was Daniel Sola). Galli got off to a bit of a slow start, but he started gaining confidence. However, rocky road conditions during Special Stage 5 meant that the suspension took a pounding and ultimately serious enough damage to cause the Italian duo to retire once again. Panizzi, suffering from gearbox issues and then overheating, pressed on and picked up the pace on the last day, managing to come in eighth overall.

New Zealand was next, though it proved to be an unsuccessful rally for the Mitsubishi team, as neither of the two works cars finished. In fact, they were out at the very beginning, as both Panizzi and Sohlberg suffered electrical problems during the initial super special stage and the team decided to withdraw the cars.

For the works team, Cyprus wasn't a whole lot better than New Zealand. Both Panizzi and Sohlberg managed to complete the first leg, but it all went wrong on day two. Sohlberg's car died on the second stage after slowing considerably, and Panizzi, who'd been making decent time (he was in seventh) was also out before the start of Special Stage 10. At least the results of Evo drivers in Group N were better, with Andreas Tsouloftas taking the win and British driver Chris Armeftis finishing runner-up.

The Acropolis followed Cyprus, with very similar conditions. The Panizzi brothers had better luck, as their car was running much better. Gilles drove methodically to take seventh place by the end of the first leg, moving up to sixth by the following day. However, an engine problem slowed them down during the final stages, and they

Frenchman Gilles Panizi was Mitsubishi's number one driver for 2004, while a second car was driven either by Kristian Sohlberg, Gianluigi Galli, or Daniel Sola, depending on the event. This is Sohlberg in the Rally of New Zealand. Mitsubishi Japan

ended up coming in tenth. Daniel Sola, in his first outing as a works driver in a WRC-spec machine, did exceptionally well, though a rear-end collision on Special Stage 3 ended any chances of collecting championship points.

Like Mexico, the second WRC rally in Turkey represented untested waters for the Mitsubishi team, because it hadn't competed in 2003. A gravel course, it was similar to Greece and Cyprus, which meant it could very hard on cars, particularly the tires and suspension. Galli was back in the second works car, and this time out fared better than Panizzi, who was sidelined on Special Stage 4 with electrical problems and forced to retire. Galli and D'Amore, after dealing with turbo problems, moved up the field on the final day, ending the rally in tenth place overall, behind local Serkan Yazici in a Ford Focus. This event had shown that the young Italian was starting to show real potential, especially considering that the car was still very much brand new in many respects.

Two more gravel events followed Turkey, the first being Argentina, where Panizzi and his brother Herve got off to a great start, with stage times firmly within the top 10. This quick progress was then hampered, first by punctures and then by gearbox problems; a seventh-place finish was hardly shabby, all things considered. Kristian Sohlberg and Kaj Lindstrom, in the other works car for this one, also put in some very good early stages but on leg two, the car developed engine problems and was taken out the following morning.

The team also announced via Sven Quandt (now president of the Mitsubishi Motor Sport's German operation), that after Argentina, it would curtail its works rally activities and would not field cars in the Japanese through Australian rallies. Instead, the team would focus on testing and developing its new car to prepare for a full-blown assault on the World Rally Championship in 2005. As a result, its results would not count towards the 2004 championship.

In Group N, things were much better—Sola, back in a Group N car, drove extremely well and took the class win (his second of the season).

Rally Finland, with its long, fast gravel stretches, didn't prove highly suited to either the cars or the drivers. Panizzi struggled with driveline issues and, not wanting to break the car, played it safe for the early stages. The car's handling was not to his liking. Despite a charging issue later on, he managed to finish the event in 11th place. The Finnish duo of Sohlberg and Lindstrom were having a better time of it, running well until they hit a bump in the road on Special Stage 14, which put the car into a ditch.

Galli, who was given a privateer Group N drive in Finland, did better, winning the class and finishing more than four seconds ahead of the runner-up, local Kaj Kuistila—impressive considering that drivers from non-Nordic countries usually find the going tougher in Finland.

The penultimate world championship round for the works Mitsubishi team, Germany, didn't go too well. Daniel Sola and Xavier Amigo Colon got off to a blinding start, posting the third fastest time on the very first stage, less than 4.5 seconds adrift of the winner, Carlos Sainz. But in the slippery conditions, the Mitsubishi skidded off the road on Special Stage 2 and the young Spaniards had to call it a day. Gilles Panizzi and his brother Herve lasted a bit longer, treading more cautiously on the first leg, ending in a respectable sixth place overall. On the first stage of the second leg, disaster struck. Gilles hit a patch of wet grass, and the car slid off the road, down an embankment, and right into a tree. Luckily, the brothers only received minor bruising, but their rally was done.

Group N proved a bright spot with Xavier Pons, in his bright yellow Evolution VIII, snatching victory away from Niall McShea and Subaru.

The last event for Mitsubishi was another tarmac event, the Rally Catalunya. This time out, as far as the works team was concerned, things went a little better. Three cars were entered and all three managed to finish. The young guns impressed the most; Sola drove an excellent rally to take an impressive sixth overall, less than a minute behind reigning world champion Petter Solberg. Galli was also on form, coming in right behind his teammate in seventh. Panizzi, the most experienced driver on the team, proved the unluckiest. Having made a great start to sit in third place, he saw his progress hampered through the remainder of the event by a wrong tire choice and setup; he did finish, though, even if it was in 12th place. And with that, the season was effectively over for Mitsubishi, although success in the privateer Group N field continued right until the end in Australia.

2005

MITSUBISHI: EXPANDING PORTFOLIO

As 2005 dawned, things were fairly quiet on the home market, at least as far as the Lancer Evolution was concerned. Instead, noise was being made on the export front, particularly in the United States and Britain. For the former, there were now three versions on offer. The first was the full-jam American-spec Evolution, while a cheaper, more stripped-down RS version arrived for some three grand less (sticker price was $27,929). The RS did without the rear spoiler and featured featured black (instead of body-colored) mirrors and door handles; it also had no ABS brakes, power locks, or stereo, though unlike Japanese RS models, it came with standard alloy wheels and a greater choice of exterior colors (Rally Red, as well as traditional Scotia White). However, the biggest news was the arrival of a U.S.-spec Evolution MR model. This was, in many respects, a version of the Japanese-market Evolution VIII, featuring a more powerful 4G63 engine rated at 276 hp, thanks to changes to the electronics, turbocharger, and wastegate (torque was increased from 273 lb-ft to 286). This car also got the six-speed manual gearbox, active center differential, gunmetal-finished BBS alloy wheels with Yokohama Advan 235 section tires, uprated suspension with premium Bilstein shocks, aluminum roof, and dark-tinted headlight housings with HID projector bulbs, plus dark-tinted taillight lenses. Available for almost $35,000 as a single, well-equipped model, it was the most expensive of the trio, but the most capable. The two lesser U.S.-spec Evos also received the more powerful 4G63 twin-cam motor.

In testing, the MR was judged the quickest yet seen by the American press, with both *Car and Driver* and *Motor Trend* coming away impressed. Interestingly enough, *MT* tested the car side by side with a regular Evo and an RS version, and although the cheaper RS was quickest in the acceleration stakes, the MR's superior chassis setup made it quicker on the Streets of Willow road course (the standard Evo finished in the middle of the pack, with the RS bringing up the rear). Still, with the arrival of the MR, the Evo versus STi wars were really starting to heat up stateside.

While the Americans were starting to enjoy an expanding range of Evolution models, the Brits also had a sizeable number of choices. Carried over from 2004 was the entry-level Evolution 260, while Mitsubishi UK continued to offer a spate of limited, turnkey specials based around the six-speed MR (See Appendix B: Special Edition Cars).

FINAL VERSION

It was but a few days into 2005 when Mitsubishi made its latest announcement on the Lancer Evolution front: the unveiling of its

In 2005 it was time to introduce yet another development of the Lancer Evolution, the IX, which debuted at the Tokyo Auto Salon in January. It incorporated mild sheetmetal tweaks and a 4G63 engine with new lightweight pistons and revised ignition, making it the most powerful yet. Mitsubishi Japan

latest Cedia-based creation, the Evo IX, at the Tokyo Auto Salon. Outwardly, the Evo IX looked somewhat similar to the departed VIII, but keen spotters noticed a revised front end treatment, with a new, single-piece mesh grille, in which the tri-diamond logo floated instead of being attached to a pronounced center divider as before. The lower part of the fascia was also different, with a squared-up intercooler opening flanked by a pair of small "nostrils" that improved both aerodynamics and cooling efficiency. The rocker panel extensions and rear bumper cover were also slightly different and somewhat more linear than before, with a rear diffuser integrated into the latter. The big rear deck spoiler was also updated, and as a nod to cost savings, only the actual foil was now made from carbon fiber; the end plates instead were resin pieces. An aluminum roof was standard fitment on the IX as well, but the biggest news concerned the engine.

Although the engine was the familiar 4G63, now more than 20 years old, the venerable twin-cam four was given a considerable reworking. New pistons were specified, with thinner rings, and a new, stronger timing belt was installed in an effort to improve durability. More advanced engine electronics, with better-optimized air/fuel and spark control, helped improve power, fuel economy, and emissions. In Japanese-market trim, the revised engine was pegged at 280 bhp and a mighty 295 lb-ft of torque in GSR spec. Bolted to it was the Evo VIII's six-speed gearbox with unchanged ratios (on GSR models), though there were changes elsewhere in the driveline, including a revised super active yaw control system. Revised rear springs and Bilstein shocks were employed to improve handling and cornering.

Inside, the mainstream variant featured a greater use of sound deadening, new Recaro front seats with revised patterns, and special carbon fiber inserts on the dash, door panels, and around the shifter boot, along with a set of drilled aluminum pedals. Interestingly, a power sunroof could be specified on the GSR as a factory option, but ordering it substituted a steel roof panel for the aluminum piece.

Besides the GSR, two more variations of the IX were released: a hard-core RS version and the new GT. The latter was the mid-priced offering, providing much the same style as the GSR but with a few changes to keep the price down, including the absence of SAYC, a five-speed manual gearbox, slightly different interior trim (though still with the premium Recaro seats), and Yokohama tires with a lower speed rating than those fitted to the GSR. In many respects, this car had quite a bit in common with the U.S.-market regular Evolution, while having a few features uniquely its own.

The RS was still blessed with smaller, Evo IV–style brakes; 15-inch steel wheels as standard; and a five-speed manual gearbox. It had the most powerful version of the revised 4G63 engine, thanks to a revised turbocharger and exhaust with a new magnesium/aluminum/titanium impeller, a revised turbo housing to improve the flow of exhaust gases both into and out of it, plus slightly different engine mapping. (The RS-spec turbocharger was available as an extra-cost item on the GSR model.) While power was rated at the same 280 bhp as the other variants sold in Japan, torque stood at an impressive 300 lb-ft. Less sound deadening, along with the lighter five-speed gearbox and the absence of airbags, made the RS by far the quickest of the new breed—0–60 mph runs in the low four second range were easily possible. Then again, the primary purpose of this car was to be the base upon which to build a motorsport special, and it wasn't long before tuners in Japan started working their magic on the latest RS.

FLAMIN' QUICK

The same day the Evo IX went on sale in Japan on March 3, 2005, Mitsubishi took the wraps off the European version of the car at the Geneva Motor Show. Not long afterward, journalists in that part of the world were making their opinions known. The British new car weekly *Autocar*, after sampling the latest Evo, judged it to be "better than ever," before going on to say that the way the car "fuses supercar performance with advanced all-drive grip seems more the stuff of Gran Turismo than mechanical engineering." As far as most enthusiasts were concerned, they hit the nail on the head. Production-spec Evo IXs began arriving on British shores in June, with four models listed under the FQ banner depending on states of tune: the entry-level FQ 300 at a shade over £27,000, followed by the FQ-320, 340, and 360. At the top end, the £34,291 Evolution MR came complete with standard HID headlights and carbon fiber rear vortex generators mounted on the roof. Like all UK-spec Evos, it also came with a standard electronic engine immobilizer—by that time, the Evo was one of the most desirable cars among thieves and joy riders. The UK MR was capable of reaching 60 mph in well under four seconds (around 3.7), but the rest of the European range was now fitted with governors that limited top speed to 157 mph (without, the car was capable of theoretically reaching speeds of 175 mph-plus). With this kind of performance available right from the dealer, it kind of made you wonder if it was worth ponying up the funds for further upgrades, though in car-mad Britain, there were plenty of tuning operations that could do just that, for the right price.

On the other side of the Atlantic, the U.S. market was introduced to the latest Evolution at the 2005 New York International Auto Show in April (the author of this book was there to attend the launch and reception). Amid a cloud of dry ice fog, the latest U.S.-spec Evolution

The U.S.-spec Evolution IX was announced at the 2005 New York International Auto Show in April. The American-market cars got a more powerful engine, (now rated at 286 hp), but did without the Super Active Yaw Control. Derric Slocum

was rolled out onto the stage. For American buyers, as before, trim, equipment, and price varied considerably. Three different versions of the new car (which would ultimately go on sale as 2006 models) were announced: an entry-level-priced RS version, the regular Evolution IX, and the all-conquering MR.

The U.S. cars, like their Japanese counterparts, received upgrades to the 4G63 engine and turbo, with the result being a power hike to 286 hp and 289 lb-ft of torque (SAE). Interestingly enough, the Evo IX engine qualified for the EPA's Low Emissions Vehicle standards, quite an amazing feat considering the basic engine was more than two decades old. The regular and RS Evos came with the latest five-speed manual gearbox as fitted to the Japanese-market GT and RS, while the U.S. MR model carried on with the old VIII-version six-speed with unchanged ratios.

The U.S. cars came with helical limited-slip differentials, active center units, and mechanical rear diffs, but no super active yaw control. The MR received premium Bilstein struts and shocks and unique BBS multispoke wheels (the others rode on 17x8 Enkeis—even the RS). U.S. cars also featured a different rear bumper design to meet federal crash standards and were thus somewhat heavier than their Japanese counterparts. Still, the IX was the best-performing version yet, at least as far as the Americans were concerned. It wasn't long before several buff books pitted the new Mitsubishi against Subaru's 300-hp Impreza STi.

Edmunds.com decided to get in on the fun, with its editors comparing an example of each car, a regular U.S.-spec Evo IX with a decent mix of equipment and a fully laden STi. Through the winding roads of northern California's wine country, the two machines were pitched against each other on "roads that were damp, narrow, and riddled with sharp curves—perfect for testing a couple of rally cars like the Evo and STi." Afterward, both test victims were taken back down to southern California and flogged at the track. After the dust settled, the editors remarked, "Buy either one of these cars, and you're getting one of the best performance bargains out there." However, they also stated that the "manic Evo is still the more refined and capable machine. It's faster, turns in significantly better handling numbers, and supplies its driver with more feedback." It was dubbed "the one to get if you want the most fun for your hard-earned dollar," this despite the sample Evo stickering at over two grand more than the STi.

It was clear that a lot of U.S. buyers agreed, as the IX outsold the previous Evo by a considerable margin in its first year, becoming somewhat of a stalwart among the import tuning community. Examples began showing up in numerous racing series, including club racing, U.S. Time Attack, solo racing classes, and, of course, on the small (but growing) U.S. rally scene.

SUBARU: SUBTLE CHANGES

At a glance, the 2005 model year WRX and STi, introduced fairly early in June 2004, appeared to mainly mark time, but there were notable improvements. Interior trim was upgraded, an ergonomically improved center console was added, and a three-spoke steering wheel was made standard across the board. The Rex also got a new instrument

The WRX mainly marked time for 2005, though STi struts and improved steering sharpened the car's reflexes. The gearbox also got new syncros, answering a long-standing criticism of rough gear shifting. Derric Slocum

cluster with red instead of white icons. Technical changes included STi-style inverted struts for regular WRX models, a revised steering rack, aluminum rear control arms, and changes to the syncromesh on first gear in manual transmission models to reduce grinding. The braking system also received attention and was designed to deliver improved feedback to the driver—clearly somebody at Subaru had listened to the rantings of automotive testers over the previous months.

RAZOR REFLEX

The biggest changes of all were found on the STi, which got a shot in the arm via a more efficient intercooler and revised exhaust system. As a result, while power remained unchanged, torque on the Japanese spec version climbed to 303 lb-ft, giving the little EJ20 roughly the same amount of grunt as the bigger 2.5-liter four found on the North American cars. The driveline was also updated with a new, improved helical limited-slip differential. The driver-controlled center differential (DCCD), first seen in 2004, was now standard fitment on STi models, resulting in improved torque split, traction, and better rotation through corners. There were also major changes to the suspension, including lighter and stronger control arms at the back, along with new shocks, spring rates, and revised geometry, which actually increased rear track 0.39 inches (10mm). Up front, the strut mounts were changed, geometry was altered, and a new, quick ratio steering rack was fitted. With new sway bars both front and back, stronger front wheel hubs, and rims that were an inch wider (now 17x8s), along with fatter tires (235 instead of 225 /45/ZR17s), the latest Japanese-spec STi was more capable than ever.

Subaru also managed to launch another round of limited-edition specials, including an updated Spec C and the formidable STi S203 (see Appendix B: Special Edition Cars).

EMPIRE STRIKES

Although Japan was naturally the first to receive the updated 2005 models, the Brits and the Australians weren't far behind. In the

STARS N' STRIPES

Changes to the STi in 2005 included a more powerful EJ20 engine for the Japanese cars. Plus, the Driver Controlled Center Differential was now standard equipment instead of optional. The suspension was also revised, with new struts up front, stronger control arms at the back, and a wider rear track to improve stability. Subaru Global

United Kingdom, now regarded somewhat as Impreza turbo central, the latest WRX and STi began arriving in dealerships in November 2004. The British press largely waxed lyrical about both models, citing the STi as a more refined, complete, and grownup package. According to *Autocar*, the standard Rex was deemed to be, "a car that strikes that rare balance of compliance and composure, serving up performance whenever called for."

As before, British buyers had the option of adding a Prodrive performance pack to their cars for just under £2000. Considering that the STi model retailed for £26,995, about four grand less than a comparable Evo, it was the ultimate bang for the buck king. Plus, with the improved steering and other chassis and driveline upgrades that mirrored the Japanese-market car, the new model was by far the most involving to drive yet, with sharper turn in, improved grip, and less scrappy handling. The revised suspension settings also helped deliver a more compliant ride, though it still remained very much on the touring car side of firm.

With the 2005 model, Subaru clearly had one thing in mind with its latest STi: to seek and destroy the Evolution, both at home and abroad. This newest super Subie seemed to do just that, but the diamond-star brigade was not about to let this car walk all over it.

MITSUBISHI: BACK WITH A VENGENCE

After 2004's three-quarter season works rally campaign, Mitsubishi Motors was back with a full-fledged effort for 2005. Central to that was a new car. Although it looked somewhat similar to the 2004 version, the new WRC machine featured a new front fascia and redesigned fenders with larger flares, making it wider. Revised suspension settings (based on experience garnered from the previous season), along with new driveshafts and the adoption of Pirelli tires, promised to make the car more competitive. Changes to the engine management system, turbocharger, and wastegate, plus a revised six-speed semi-automatic gearbox with quicker shifting, were also incorporated to improve speed and throttle response.

Three drivers were signed up for the season: Gianluigi "Gigi" Galli, Gilles Panizzi (who would become the team's tarmac specialist), and a new number one, Finn Harri Rovanpera. Having amassed plenty of experience with Peugeot, Rovanpera was very quick on loose gravel and a welcome addition to the group.

STARS N' STRIPES

The team put together two cars for the Monte Carlo event, one for Gilles Panizzi and his brother Herve and the other for Rovanpera and co-driver Risto Pietilainen. It was Gilles who proved the star of the show as he drove consistently and skillfully during his home event. He set good stage times, ultimately enough to bag a podium finish and his best result to date with the team. It was Mitsubishi's most significant result in several years. Rovanpera, on his first tarmac outing since 2002, struggled a bit with the conditions but came through to take seventh and pick up a couple of constructor's points. Team technical director Mario Fornaris, clearly impressed with the results, declared that the 2005 Monte had been a "fantastic rally" for Mitsubishi and looked forward to the next round in cold, snowy Sweden.

For this one, Rovanpera and Pietilainen were joined by Galli and his co-driver Guido D'Amore in the second works car. The Italians impressed mightily and managed to finish the rally in a strong seventh place overall. Rovanpera and Pietilainen got off to a slow start but

Mitsubishi campaigned a full works effort for the 2005 WRC season with three cars, one for Gilles Panizzi, one for Gianluigi Galli, and another for Harri Rovanpera. The latter managed a decent fourth-place finish in Sweden. Mitsubishi Japan

started chipping away. Clearly more at home in Sweden than in Monte Carlo, they really picked up the pace on the last day. Claiming the fastest time on the very last stage, the Finns came in fourth overall, behind Toni Gardemeister in the Ford Focus.

Mexico proved to be a mixed bag. The cars had been given new active center differentials, but in Rovanpera's case it wasn't the driveline that proved problematic, rather the brakes and handling. On one downhill section, braking issues hampered his progress, but the Finn ended the day in seventh. Gilles Panizzi, in the second car, was plagued by punctures, but otherwise he drove spiritedly to finish the first leg in 11th place. Problems persisted for the remainder of the rally, with rocks damaging Rovanpera's oil pan and Panizzi having to contend with handling issues. Both drivers made it to the end, Rovanpera claiming fifth overall and the Panizzi brothers finishing in eighth place.

The next event, on the far side of the world, was New Zealand, with "Gigi" Galli replacing Panizzi in the second car for this one. After a brisk start, the young Italian was hit with mechanical trouble, first when the clutch let go at the end of the first stage and then when the alternator went on Special Stage 5, leaving the Italians limping along in safe mode. The car was repaired, and they pressed on but had to deal with tire issues. Ultimately, they overcame the obstacles to take eighth place. Teammates Rovanpera and Pietilainen were also plagued by tire troubles for much of the event, despite the car otherwise running fine, save for a minor overheating issue. Things finally came to a head right at the end of the final leg, when excessive tire wear caused both rears to give out after the last special stage (20). As a result, the team elected to withdraw Harri and Risto from the event, rather than risk serious damage or injury on the way back to base at Auckland.

Sardinia didn't prove kind to Mitsubishi. Galli's home event was a source of frustration, as his charge was halted by broken rear suspension on Special Stage 5, which caused a wheel to come off. Rovanpera got off to an impressive start, really piling the pressure on Marcus Gronholm during the opening stage and taking the second

STARS N' STRIPES

fastest time. He continued driving in excellent form and looked bound to take third overall, but cruel fate intervened on the second stage of the final leg, which saw the Finns hit a rock and retire with a damaged suspension.

Blistering heat (with temperatures as high as 110 degrees Fahrenheit) and rocky conditions saw plenty of cars and drivers slide into retirement during the opening leg of the 2005 Cyprus Rally. Both the works Mitsubishi drivers suffered problems of their own, Rovanpera hampered by a faulty rear diff that caused gear selection problems and Panizzi faced with engine and transmission issues, followed by a puncture on Special Stage 4. Rovanpera damaged his suspension on leg two, but he was able to restart the following morning and ultimately claimed 7th place. Panizzi finished 15th.

In Turkey, Galli got off to an amazing start, setting the second fastest times on the opening two stages before taking the lead on Special Stage 4, passing Sebastian Loeb. By the end of the first leg, Galli and D'Amore were lying in a very strong second, but a turbo problem the following morning saw them slide down the leaderboard to eighth, where they would stay for the remainder of the rally. Still, both driver and car had showed incredible promise, something that didn't go unnoticed by Mitsubishi Motorsports head Isao Torii. Rovanpera suffered disappointment, being forced to retire on the first day with damaged suspension while lying in a creditable sixth place.

Greece was tough as always, but Rovanpera at least had more luck this time out. He did a good job at mastering the rocky and dusty event, setting good times on several stages, though a gearbox issue and vibrations on the second leg cost a bit of time. Still, the Finn and his co-driver pushed hard to maintain a solid sixth position, trying desperately to catch Mikko Hirvonen in the Ford Focus. Galli and D'Amore, in only their second Acropolis rally (their first was in 2002), drove very respectably, and despite turbo problems, they were fast enough to bag seventh overall, right behind their teammates.

Down in Argentina, both Rovanpera and Galli were back in action, piloting the works cars. Rovanpera got off to a good start on the opening day, running consistently in the top six and battling Toni Gardemeister, but he struggled with a car not ideally set up for the conditions. Still, Rovanpera and his co-driver Pietilainen managed to take fifth overall, claiming more points for themselves and the team and proving that the Mitsubishis were very much competitive. Galli again showed his talent, even running third during the opening stage of the last leg, but gearbox problems, frustratingly, brought retirement.

At his home event in Finland, Rovanpera wasn't on the pace, with tall gearing hampering his ability to extract speed out of the car on the early stages. Nevertheless, he and Risto plowed on, and the car proved reliable. In the end, a finish was better than nothing, and by taking seventh overall, Harri was able to collect a few more constructor's points for the team. Galli and D'Amore, showing good speed on the opening stage, crashed before it ended, going off the road and losing a wheel.

It was back to tarmac roads for the Rally Deutschland, and this time, the Italians had something to celebrate. Galli was the quicker of the two works drivers and, despite finishing the first day in eighth, was right in the thick of the action, hot on the heels of Markko Martin. He steadily improved throughout the remainder of the event, finishing sixth fastest on leg two and then pushing hard to finish fifth overall by the end, besting Czech driver Roman Kresta. Rovanpera, on his first tarmac rally since the 2002 San Remo, elected to take it easy and brought the other works car home in tenth place.

The Wales Rally GB proved to be one of Harri and Risto's better events. Very quick in the Welsh forest stages, Rovanpera set the fastest time on the second stage of the day, Trawscoed. He looked set to take a podium finish, but gearbox problems on the second day held him and his co-driver back. A very good drive on the final day enabled Harri to take fourth overall, however, behind championship leader Sebastian Loeb. Teammates Galli and D'Amore, on their very first outing in the RAC, took 13th overall, setting some good stage times during the event. The rally was overshadowed by a horrendous accident on Special Stage 15 involving the Peugeot of Markko

Martin and co-driver Michael Park; Park ultimately succumbed to injuries suffered in the crash.

Japan, the team's first appearance at its home event, saw three works cars entered with the Panizzi brothers joining Rovanpera, Galli, and their respective co-drivers. Harri and Risto were by far the quickest here, battling and overhauling Chris Atkinson in the Subaru Impreza. A set of incidents on the last morning of competition, including a stalled engine and front end damage, cost valuable time, but Rovanpera made up for it and drove exceptionally well to take fifth overall, cheered on by crowds of Mitsubishi fans. Galli, running well until the last day, was in fourth when the left rear suspension gave way. He lost so much time that retirement proved inevitable, but again he was proving a real threat to the likes of Chris Atkinson and Sebastian Loeb before that happened. Gilles Panizzi, not comfortable with the setup on his car, drove a solid rally to claim 11th.

Corsica proved very disappointing for Mitsubishi in 2005, for despite entering three cars, none were on the pace. Rovanpera, with limited tarmac experience, finished in tenth place after having to deal with gear selector problems. Gilles and Herve Panizzi had a very frustrating Tour de Corse. A broken shock on the first day was bad enough, but handling issues persisted on leg two. Then the engine decided to call it quits on the last stage of the day. Galli, on his first outing in Corsica, couldn't match his usual pace, humorously stating that he was driving like his mother and aunt. Despite running on an unfamiliar course, he still managed to claim a couple of manufacturer points by finishing ninth overall, ahead of teammate Rovanpera.

In Spain, the young Italian was much quicker, running as high as fourth overall by the start of the second day. But just when things were looking rosy, inaccurate directions saw him and D'Amore slide off the road and into retirement. Rovanpera and Pietilainen, running a different setup on their car, were nowhere near as quick but at least managed to finish, once again in tenth place.

Australia was the last rally on the calendar in 2005, and for the Mitsubishi team, and Rovanpera in particular, it was an excellent

WRX vs. EVO

Two-thousand five would mark the last time that Mitsubishi actively fielded a full works rally effort, though the team made a lot of progress during its final season.
Mitsubishi Japan

conclusion to a mixed season. The Finn really drove his heart out and set the fastest time on the Perth Super Special, the last stage of the opening leg. From there, he battled Citroen driver Francois Duval to the bitter end and claimed an excellent second overall. Galli was predictably quick, though not quite on the same pace as his teammate. Still, a fifth place overall was hardly to be sniffed at. The fact that both cars finished well showed that things were really coming along well for the Mitsubishi team. For Andrew Cowan, the man who'd been involved with the company's rally efforts since the very early days, the event marked his last with Mitsubishi. Sadly, not long after the season ended, Mitsubishi announced that as part of the corporate revitalization plan, it would suspend any works World Championship Rally participation, though the company did say that it planned to return in 2008.

STARS N' STRIPES

SUBARU: HOLD THE LINE

With the start of a new year, it was of course time to gear up for yet another stab at the World Rally Championship. Petter Solberg renewed his contract for another full season as the main works driver; he was joined by young Frenchman and tarmac specialist Stephane Sarrazin, who had shown promise behind the wheel of a works Subaru in 2004. In addition, Chris Atkinson, the Australian who'd made quite a name for himself in Group N, was signed on as an additional works driver for the year.

As had become customary, the SWRT team ran with updated versions of the 2004 works cars for the opening events of the season, with the first race naturally being the classic Monte Carlo. With street super specials around the principality, twisty French mountain stages, and variable weather conditions, it proved as challenging as ever. Two cars were entered, one for Solberg and the other for Sarrazin. The Norwegian got off to a good start, but his charge came to a frustrating conclusion on the Col de Turini, when he hit a patch of snow and lost a wheel—this after he'd claimed a fastest stage time. Sarrazin, in the other works car, completed the event in 14th place but gained confidence with each passing day.

Sweden welcomed a three-car team from Subaru, with Australians Chris Atkinson and Glenn MacNeall joining the other works crews. Solberg and Mills had a much better time of it, getting off to a brilliant start and ultimately catching and passing Marcus Gronholm to finish first overall (Gronholm ultimately crashed out). Chris Atkinson, despite limited experience, was doing exceptionally well until he slid off the road on Special Stage 18, which saw him drop from 9th to 21st place. He managed to regain a bit of time and came home 19th. Sarrazin and co-driver Denis Giraudet were learning as they went along in Sweden, but managed to finish in 13th place.

Atkinson and Solberg were back in action for the team in Mexico. The young Aussie demonstrated good wheelmanship, both in the shakedown and on the first leg of the rally. A lost right front wheel after hitting a big rut on a right-hand corner was a frustrating end

WRX vs. EVO

A new recruit to the Subaru World Rally team in 2005 was the young Australian, Chris Atkinson. From the get-go he demonstrated tremendous potential. In Mexico he was doing well until a huge impact took out his right front suspension. Subaru Global

to his progress. Solberg, meanwhile, was strong right out of the gate. Battling with the Peugeots of Gronholm and Markko Martin, he set three fastest stage times and took the lead. There he would stay, giving himself and Subaru their second win in two events.

In New Zealand, Solberg and Mills were again the fastest out of the gate, but setting the fastest time on the opening stage would hamper them later, as they then had to start subsequent stages first and clear a path for those following behind. That gave the likes of Gronholm and Loeb the advantage, though Solberg fought back. After dropping to fourth, "Hollywood" Solberg recovered to take third overall by rally's end. Atkinson again showed tremendous potential, setting two fastest stage times on the opening leg and claiming seventh overall, his best result yet with the team.

Because he was leading the championship at that point, Solberg was first to start the Rally of Sardinia. Thus, he had to contend with clearing the loose gravel, giving the traction advantage to the drivers behind, allowing Sebastien Loeb to get the upper hand. However, a second-place finish was still an excellent result for the Subaru team. Atkinson picked up the pace early on, running as high as third, though severe damage to the steering linkage on day two slowed his progress. Still, the intrepid Aussie plodded on, taking 16th place overall. Sarrazin, on his first gravel rally, drove impressively and far quicker than many drivers with far greater experience. He was pleased to complete the event, having a good tussle with likes of Mark Higgins and Roman Kresta on the way to the finish.

From Sardinia, the circus moved to yet another Mediterranean island, Cyprus. After such a good run (at least in terms of reliability), mechanical gremlins struck hard. Atkinson struggled and his car was sidelined when his clutch went adios on Special Stage 2. Repairs were carried out back at base, and he was able to restart the rally. He and MacNeall managed to survive the heat and incredibly rough roads to finish, taking tenth place behind Janne Tuohino in the Skoda and ahead of Gilles Panizzi. Solberg, after a fairly good start, had to contend with increasing mechanical issues: overheating, a loss in turbo boost pressure, a slipping clutch, and finally retirement when the engine quit.

In Turkey, things didn't go well for Atkinson as an altercation with a rock on Special Stage 3 saw his rally come to an early and abrupt conclusion. Solberg and co-driver Mills fared much better this time out. Although they couldn't catch overall winner Loeb, they fought off Marcus Gronholm, claiming a stage win on the last day to finish a strong second overall.

Greece was not a good event for SWRT, as none of the works entries were competitive. Solberg slid off the road on the second stage of the rally, losing his decklid and rear spoiler in the process. His progress was further hampered later in the day when a driveshaft broke, knocking him down to 14th. He made a good recovery and pushed hard enough to finish the event in 9th place overall. Atkinson also didn't have much luck; his car died on the next-to-last stage of the first leg with engine trouble.

Argentina proved better for both drivers. Solberg and Mills once again found themselves locking horns with Marcus Gronholm and

Sebastian Loeb. Although the Frenchman and Finn were ultimately quicker, Petter still drove an outstanding rally, setting a record time on the Carlos Paz-Cabalango stage. Atkinson was also much happier, with a relatively trouble-free event seeing him reach the finish in ninth overall, sandwiched between the Citroens of Manfred Stohl and Xavier Pons.

Atkinson demonstrated his potential during the opening stages of Rally Finland, but on Special Stage 4 (Riihimaki), he clipped the left-hand corner of the car on a rock, which damaged his steering and suspension and put him out of the event. Solberg suffered a double whammy on Special Stage 8 when the rear spoiler was dislodged, causing his car to go airborne and land hard (sliding along a ditch for more than 200 feet in the process). Ultimately, he came home fourth, fending off a determined challenge from former teammate Mikko Hirvonen, now driving for Skoda.

Switching to tarmac for Germany, Solberg was happy with his car but was unable to catch the Citroens, which were ideally suited to the conditions. With a shift linkage problem, he dropped down from fourth to ninth place, but he recovered enough time to move up to seventh by the end. Sarrazin showed good speed during the early stages, but a spin on the first leg cost him time. He picked up the pace once again, proving very competitive and ran consistently within the top five and ultimately finished behind his teammate. Atkinson, with limited experience on tarmac events, finished a decent 11th, all things considered.

The Rally Wales GB once again proved a Solberg favorite. He played cat and mouse with Sebastien Loeb for much of it; this hotly contested event was ultimately decided in favor of the Norwegian. However, as mentioned in the Mitsubishi section, the whole event was overshadowed by the death of Markko Martin's co-driver, Michael Park, which made the win seem somewhat hollow. Atkinson and Sarrazin both had accidents during the second leg—the Aussie spinning on a corner and going off into the ditch, while Sarrazin plowed into a bank.

On Japanese turf, Solberg and Mills looked set to take the win, running strongly throughout both legs one and two and leading the pack by the start of the final day. However, fate intervened on the penultimate stage of the entire rally when a huge rock, flung up by one of the cars in front, lay in the path of Solberg's Subaru. The impact damaged the front suspension, and he was forced to retire within striking distance of the finish—a bitter blow to be sure. Atkinson, meanwhile, was enjoying the drive of his life. He was right in the thick of the action and at one point was even leading the rally. He and co-driver MacNeall ended up taking third overall and making the podium—their best result yet.

Corsica saw an excellent performance from Stephane Sarrazin in one of three works cars. The Frenchman, clearly at home on the tarmac roads, was well within the top five for much of the rally and the only one who came close to challenging Sebastian Loeb's supremacy—he finished in a strong fourth place. Solberg also did well. Facing a tough challenge against newly crowned champion Loeb and a strong-running Toni Gardemeister, plus a near-collision with a pig, he managed to secure a podium finish, adding another six points to his championship tally.

Just two more events were left on the 2005 WRC calendar, Catalunya and Australia, and Solberg was second in the drivers' championship. The last tarmac rally of the year wasn't a particularly memorable one for the Subaru team. Solberg hit a bank on only the second special stage, damaging his steering and putting him out of commission. Sarrazin didn't fare much better, going off the road on Special Stage 6 and causing major damage to the car. That meant only one works car, of Atkinson and MacNeall, was still left in the running. Gaining confidence as he went, Chris ended up finishing ninth—not bad considering he was still very much on a steep learning curve when it came to tarmac rallies.

The season finale was a disappointing one for Petter Solberg. While running in the lead, on the morning of the second leg a freak incident saw him collide with a stray kangaroo, which holed the radiator and left him with no choice but to retire. On home turf, Atkinson drove impressively, taking nine stage wins (more than any

WRX vs. EVO

The 2005 season was decidedly mixed for the Subaru Team, which finished fourth in the constructor's championship. Petter Solberg, seen here in Germany, won three events (including a fourth-straight Rally of Great Britain) during the course of the season and finished joint second in the driver's championship. Subaru Global

other driver during the event) and claiming a very strong fourth-place finish. Clearly, the young Australian and his co-driver were becoming a force to be reckoned with in the WRC.

Subaru finished fourth in the constructor's chase for 2005, behind Citroen, Ford, and Peugeot, with Solberg taking joint second in the driver's cup with Marcus Gronholm. The end of the season was tinged with further sadness when former Subaru driver and 2001 champion Richard Burns lost his battle with a brain tumor. A man of exceptional talent, Burns would be sorely missed by the rally community.

MITSUBISHI: SUPER HAULER

By mid-2005, Mitsubishi's development of a completely new generation Lancer was well underway. But as far as the Cedia-based cars were concerned, there was still one trump card in the deck: the Evolution IX wagon.

STARS N' STRIPES

An interesting variation on the Evolution IX theme was the Evo wagon, based on the Cedia of the same name. It was offered in both GT and GT-A guises and proved every bit as fast and fun as its sedan counterpart. Mitsubishi Japan

All Evolution IX wagons were produced strictly for the Japanese domestic market, and only 2,500 were built. That makes them exceedingly rare by anybody's standards. Mitsubishi Japan

WRX vs. EVO

The Evolution wagon featured the Cedia estate body, beefed up with front and rear fender flares, doors, and the aggressive front fascia cribbed from the Evo sedan, along with Enkei 17-inch wheels and massive Brembo brakes. Two versions of the hot hauler were offered, a GT and GT-A version. The GT was the hard-core model, employing the full-tilt, GSR-spec 4G63 engine, rated at 286 hp and 289 lb-ft of torque. It came with a standard six-speed manual gearbox and AWD with a helical front differential, ACD, super active yaw control, uprated suspension with specific spring and shock settings, and interior trim virtually identical to the GSR sedan. Combined with options like a rear strut tower bar, RS turbocharger, and other over-the-counter Ralliart goodies, an Evo GT wagon was one of the most interesting examples of the breed and just as potent as its sedan counterpart.

Along with the GT, a cheaper, more civilized GT-A wagon also debuted. This car took much of its inspiration from the 2002 sedan of the same name, employing an engine with a slightly milder state of tune thanks to different engine electronics and a unique TD05HR Mitsubishi turbocharger, plus revised exhaust plumbing. Rated at 282 hp and 253 lb-ft of torque, it was coupled with a version of the INVECS II five-speed automatic transaxle. The GT-A version also came without the GT's front helical limited-slip differential. Outwardly, GT-A models were distinguished from the GT by a different front fascia and a centrally mounted front license plate bracket (instead of being offset to the left); otherwise both wagons looked nigh identical. Both featured chrome around the headlights, a special rear bumper and roof-mounted spoiler, increased sound deadening (compared with their sedan counterparts), specially trimmed Recaro seats, a Momo steering wheel, and drilled aluminum foot pedals. Production was pegged at just 2,500 units strictly for the Japanese domestic market, so the wagons were not only extremely fast and well-equipped, but also rare. Those that managed to get their hands on one had the privilege of owning a truly unique automobile—one that marked the closing of one chapter of the Evolution's history and the opening of another.

STARS N' STRIPES

SUBARU: YET ANOTHER FACELIFT

In June 2005, Subaru launched a face-lifted Impreza (the GD chassis car's third revision in five years). The brainchild of chief designer Andreas Zapatinas, it was designed to give the Impreza a more consistent corporate look. The result was most noticeable at the front, with new headlight units, a new front fascia, front fenders, hood, and foglights. At the rear, more subtle alterations were found in projector-style taillight clusters with backup and turn-signal lenses mounted down below instead of above as before (wagons also got a new rear bumper cover). STi models also got a new, fairly subtle roof spoiler and now shared their mail-slot hood scoop with the standard WRX. Improved aerodynamics were also evident with redesigned door handles, while underneath the car smoother front and rear fairings were added, the latter ones doubling as a diffuser.

The WRX and STi sedans sported virtually identical body extensions, including the front fascia, rocker panels, and rear bumper cover, though, as before, standard front foglights were a giveaway on the Rex. Interiors were largely carried over, but attention to detail saw better use of materials, particularly the door panels and center console

Midway through 2005 (in June to be precise), Subaru launched a facelifted GD Impreza. The work of designer Andreas Zapatinas, it gave the car a less angry, more corporate look. Japanese-spec WRX models got gold painted 17-inch wheels as standard.
Subaru Global

stack. Interesting to note was the 260 km/h speedometer on both the WRX and STi, despite the cars being electronically limited to 180 in Japan. All WRX sedans came with gold 17x7-inch multispoke alloy wheels, while the wagons rode on argent painted versions. The STi got its own unique set of 17x8 wheels.

Mechanical changes on the STi centered around very subtly altered engine mapping on the EJ20 boxer four, resulting in an extra 7 lb-ft of torque for a total of 310. Tweaks to the driveline included a new Torsen center differential and a greater rear-drive bias under normal conditions—41 to 59 percent.

The DCCD system was also updated and there were new steering angle, yaw rate, and lateral G sensors to help optimize handling and grip. The result was an even quicker point-to-point car that retained a level of quirkiness one had come to expect from performance-oriented Subarus.

2006

SUBARU: MORE MUSCLE

Although the face-lifted cars started making waves on all export fronts during the latter half of 2005, the most dramatic changes centered on the European market. The new cars were displayed at Frankfurt that September, and the biggest surprise surrounded what lay under the hood. Both the WRX and STi models now featured a turbocharged EJ25 engine, instead of the more familiar (in this market) EJ20. In the WRX, the larger powerplant was rated at 227 bhp at 5,600 rpm and 236 lb-ft of torque at 3,600 revs. The latter was significant, as it gave the new car a sizeable increase in mid-range grunt, much to the delight of many enthusiasts. Truth be told, the real reason for introducing the 2.5-liter engine was that it was better able to meet upcoming European tier IV emissions regulations, designed to take effect beginning in 2006. European WRXs also got a standard rear deck spoiler, newly styled 17x7-inch alloy wheels and red brake calipers, plus a premium sound system and a leather-wrapped, three-spoke steering wheel.

For the European market WRX models got an enlarged 2.5-liter boxer engine rated at 227 hp and 236 lb-ft of torque. The larger motor was introduced mainly for easier compliance with upcoming emissions regulations. Subaru Global

As for the STi, the larger engine was rated at 276 bhp and 289 lbs-ft of torque, but it was more tractable than its predecessor. The car's six-speed manual gearbox got new ratios (3.64 for first, 2.23 for second, 1.52 for third, 1.14 on fourth, with fifth and sixth being 0.89 and 0.71, plus a 3.90:1 final drive); the result was an easier-to-drive car.

WRX vs. EVO

STis sold in Europe from mid 2005 onward also got a larger engine, though it only churned out 276 bhp and 289 lb-ft of torque. It was less peaky and more civilized, but still made the car ultra-fast. Subaru Global

Although performance was every bit as good as before, a little bit of civility had now been added to the mix. Magazine tests quoted 0–60 mph times in around five seconds flat and a top speed of 158 mph. Unfortunately, with ever-increasing numbers of the hated Gatso speed cameras appearing on British roads, the only places you could really exercise the latest STi's potential were track days or twisty mountain roads in Wales or Scotland. In these settings, STi owners were rewarded with a car that was truly fun to drive, allowing them to bring out their inner Petter Solberg.

Timed with the new car's launch in the United Kingdom, the release of various Prodrive performance upgrades enabled buyers to make their cars perform even better. The limited-edition STi Spec D also appeared (see Appendix B: Special Edition Cars).

NEW WORLD CHANGES

In North America, the face-lifted Imprezas were greeted with enthusiasm, especially the WRX and STi. Mechanically, the latter was very much the same, still featuring a 300-hp turbocharged and intercooled EJ25, six-speed gearbox, and all the goodies—though a revised mechanical limited-slip differential and driver-controlled center differential were added to the car, altering torque split to a more rearward bias, 41 to 59 percent. New composite engine mounts also were introduced on the STi, but these proved to be controversial and

STARS N' STRIPES

In North America it was similar situation to Europe. The WRX got the bigger 2.5-liter engine as standard fitment. Bigger brakes were also in the cards, as was a special TR or "Tuner Ready" model, roughly equivalent to Japan's Type RA. Derric Slocum

unpopular with many owners, resulting in a spate of recalls. As a result, Subaru reintroduced the steel mounts found on 2005 and earlier cars.

Probably the biggest news, like in other export markets, was the adoption of the 2.5 engine on the standard North American-spec WRX, although in a different state of tune—230 hp and 236 lb-ft of torque, peaking at a more useable 3,600 rpm instead of four grand as on the EJ20. This gave the car more grunt throughout the rev range and a character more in tune with U.S. and Canadian tastes and, hence, greater sales appeal, particularly with the optional four-speed automatic transaxle. Other changes included an improved braking system, which got bigger; four-piston front calipers; larger, 11.3-inch rear discs; and quicker steering for improved responsiveness. Aluminum lower control arms were installed at the front to reduce unsprung weight. Wider wheels (17x7 inches) were also specified, along with standard 215 section tires. The color palette and equipment were shuffled slightly, and enthusiasts were delighted at the launch of the WRX TR. The initials stood for Tuner Ready, and this car amounted to more or less a North American version of the Type RA. It had a more pedestrian interior, with cloth seats, a basic stereo, and air conditioning, and it came exclusively with the five-speed manual. It was more than $1,500 cheaper than the standard WRX sedan, which for many hard-core enthusiasts made a very shrewd buy, especially considering the performance on tap.

FINAL FURLONG

In calendar year 2006, Subaru added precious few changes to the hot GD chassis Imprezas, though the STis were now called STI models, with a capital I for International. Some fiddling resulted in a larger-capacity turbocharger with a revised impeller on Japanese cars for quicker spool up and improved throttle response through the rev range. In addition, the six-speed gearbox was given revised ratios to better match the spread of power. By this point, the JDM cars were the only ones still using the EJ20 as a standard powerplant; virtually every other market, including other Pacific Rim countries, was now receiving 2.5-liter STIs, including Australia, where the car was rated at 276 hp and found an eager audience.

THE MORE THINGS CHANGE...

Before long, it was time to gear up for yet another season in the World Rally Championship. The 2006 Subaru WRC car had been unveiled at the 2005 Tokyo Motor Show, with styling updates that mirrored its street counterparts. Revised regulations for the season required simplification or removal of the car's computerized systems; thus from the start, it looked like things would prove interesting. Petter Solberg continued as the number one driver, with Chris Atkinson as the full-time number two. Stephane Sarrazin returned primarily as a tarmac specialist, along with new co-driver Stephane Prevot.

The Monte Carlo kicked off the season with plenty of drama as always. Solberg struggled with tires that weren't suited to the conditions early on, but by the second half of the first leg, he was settling into his groove. On the last stage of the day, he recorded the second fastest time, finishing behind Marcus Gronholm, but on the transit back to base, his car developed an oil leak and was forced to retire. Both Sarrazin and Atkinson (on his first Monte) drove impressively, gaining confidence with each passing stage despite some very slippery sections. Stephane almost set the fastest stage time on Special Stage 17 and came home a strong fifth overall, while his teammate, demonstrating a level of maturity beyond his years, claimed sixth, securing valuable championship points in the first round of the year.

The teams moved to Sweden for the next round, though Solberg's run of bad luck continued. Having won this event in 2005, it was a bitter blow when almost from the start, he struggled with mechanical problems, including a broken differential and then gear selection problems. He ended the first leg in 26th place and without any chance of gaining a meaningful result. Atkinson also ran into some bad luck, colliding with a tree that took out his steering and cost him more than three minutes in penalties as he and MacNeall attempted roadside repairs. However, the car was fixed, and he finished in 11th place.

Things were much better in Mexico. Solberg blasted off to claim four stage wins and lead the rally on the opening day, but a steering issue on leg two saw Sebastien Loeb take the lead, leaving the Norwegian and co-driver Mills playing catch up. Needless to say, finishing second overall was a huge improvement over the first events of the season. Atkinson was doing well until he rolled the car on Special Stage 5. Although neither he nor MacNeall were injured, the car was badly damaged.

Two works cars were entered for Catalunya, one for Solberg and Mills, the other for Sarrazin and Prevot (Atkinson was also running this event for the first time, though he drove a Subaru Australia-backed entry). Although not able to match the Citroens or Fords on the twisty, tarmac roads, Solberg and Sarrazin managed to finish seventh and eighth, respectively, which at least garnered some championship points. Atkinson, struggling a bit with the course and getting involved in a few mishaps, came home in 11th place.

On the Tour de Corse, three cars were entered again, with Atkinson once again driving the Subaru Australia entry. The sharp corners and bumpy roads took their toll, however, as both Solberg and Atkinson had accidents on the first day, which in each case damaged the car's exhaust system, hampering progress. Things improved a little for them as the rally progressed, with Chris in particular picking up the pace. Day three witnessed better progress by Solberg, who managed to move up to 7th place by the end of the rally, having started off the day in 11th. Atkinson, getting to grips with the course, further improved his position and got into somewhat of a groove to finish the rally in 13th. Stephane Sarrazin, on his home course, put in the best performance of all until a puncture toward the end of the last leg cost him valuable time, which he was unable to claw back. Having been running in eighth place, he ended the rally in 11th.

Back to gravel and mud for Argentina, where SWRT was looking to improve its performance after a largely disappointing start to the season. Things got off to a much better start as Solberg set three fastest stage times on the first day, finishing the opening leg in a strong second place behind Loeb and his all-conquering Citroen. Atkinson, also more comfortable with the car and conditions, ran consistently within the top ten, moving from seventh up to sixth at one point, before incurring a penalty that saw him back down a spot. Petter continued to drive his best, and although he was unable to catch Loeb, a good second was an excellent result, this despite some gear selection problems on the second leg that cost him a bit of time.

The team fielded cars for Solberg/Mills and Atkinson/MacNeall in Sardinia, with its challenging combination of loose gravel surfaces and tight, twisting turns. Solberg spun his car early on, losing 18 seconds in the process; he ultimately retired after getting three punctures. Atkinson was off like a shot and, on the opening stage, he posted the second fastest time behind Marcus Gronholm. Although he fell back to fifth, an excellent result and the fastest stage time on Special Stage 14 showed the young Australian's potential. However, an accident on the very last stage damaged his suspension and steering. He was awarded a tenth-place finish, rather frustrating considering his steady progress up to that point.

STARS N' STRIPES

Greece, with much rockier conditions, did provide the drivers with wider and faster sections than Sardinia, though the cars were set up in similar fashion. In addition, the 2006 Acropolis Rally was also based exclusively in and around Athens, unlike years past. Solberg was hot on the heels of Marcus Gronholm and his Ford Focus, and everything was going well until, on the transit between Special Stages 12 and 13, the Norwegian had to swerve to avoid an oncoming car, which was traveling on the wrong side of the road. He had no choice but to put the Impreza 2006 WRC into a wall, which caused a serious amount of damage. The car was repaired, and Solberg and Mills were back in action for the final day, winning three of the four stages, but it wasn't enough to allow a top five finish; the duo ended the event in seventh. Atkinson and MacNeall got a decent start, too, but the rocks, dust, and heat proved unforgiving, and Atkinson's machine broke a steering arm on Special Stage 12. It cost him time, but he also was able to restart and complete the event to take 11th place overall.

Having joined SWRT for select rounds beginning in 2004, Stephane Sarrazin returned for a third season in '06. A tarmac specialist, he could be exceedingly quick. His season was fraught with mishaps, however, including Germany, where he went off the road and toasted the transmission. Subaru Global

SWRT designated Stephane Sarrazin to drive in Germany, so Atkinson would be piloting a Subaru Australia entry this time out. Solberg got off to a bit of a rocky start, crashing on the preview, but a new car was ready in time to start the actual rally. The Norwegian was in fifth place when an engine problem forced him to retire on the second morning. Sarrazin and Atkinson both struggled with road conditions that seemed to change from one minute to the next. Sarrazin went off the road on the last day and, in his efforts to escape, he threw the car in reverse and broke the gearbox. Atkinson, the last of the trio still in the running, braved the odds to take eighth, ahead of plucky Finn Mikko Hirvonen.

The "Gravel Grand Prix" in Finland proved to be exciting and fast as usual. Chris Atkinson, on only his second outing, drove well in the opening stages, though overheating problems set him back; further mechanical woes saw him slide all the way from 6th to 21st. Solberg also ran into some more bad luck. On Special Stage 11, Ouninpohja (considered one of the toughest in the WRC), while on his way to set a record stage time, his Subaru landed wide after a crest and plowed into a bank at more than 70 mph, causing it to roll. Both Petter Solberg and Phil Mills were uninjured, but the car was a wreck. Atkinson and MacNeall were able to continue and, despite fighting for traction for much of the last day, were able to move up several places and take 11th.

As the teams got ready for Rally Japan, the stakes were high, particularly for Subaru. Three cars were entered, one for Solberg and Mills, one for Atkinson and MacNeall, and a third car for Toshi Arai and Tony Sircombe. Japan proved to be a so-so event in terms of results. Atkinson proved the quickest overall, setting good stage times consistently within the top five, while Arai and Sircombe demonstrated their experience, again driving consistently well—Arai came home in sixth place. Solberg was beset by more mechanical problems, particularly the brakes. He did finish in seventh, but it proved a frustrating event overall.

Cyprus was moved back on the calendar this year (Cyprus was also run in 2005, but earlier in the season). The weather was cooler, though running the event later in the year also brought with it a greater risk of rain showers, which had the potential to make things very interesting indeed. Sure enough, traction did prove an issue for many drivers, including Solberg. The 2003 champion and his co-driver Mills got off to a good start, even setting the fastest time on Special Stage 4, but while catching Manfred Stohl, Solberg developed gearbox problems, and he dropped down from 5th all the way to 11th. He pushed back on day two and was up to seventh when, on the last stage of the event, he hit a rock and bent a rim, losing a spot to come home eighth. Atkinson was doing very well, maintaining a solid fifth place overall, when his engine cut out and he crashed into a ditch on the second leg. He was able to restart under Super Rally regs (whereby drivers could re-enter the event but were given time penalties for each rally stage missed) and finished ninth.

With Cyprus yet another disappointment, the SWRT bit its teeth, ready for the next round in Turkey. Due to rains, many of the stages were bogged down with mud and badly rutted, and several were cancelled. As the event wore on, Solberg began to pick up the pace, the car performing well and the Norwegian gaining confidence out on the course. He set the fastest time on the last three stages of the opening leg, though his charge came to an abrupt end when his car collided with a rock on Special Stage 15. Atkinson did very well and was set for a podium finish when a spin cost him valuable time, ultimately dropping him to sixth, though at least he still finished well into the points.

In his home event in Australia, Atkinson went all-out. He charged into the lead on Special Stage 4 and set the fastest time on the next two stages. He misjudged a corner, though, running wide and wedging the car into a bank. The car subsequently caught fire, ending his day and with it any chances of a top-three finish. Solberg fared much better. After briefly leading the rally, he was bumped down to second place, but he consolidated his position with a fine drive and an excellent finish, equaling his best result so far this year.

Traction again proved a problem in New Zealand, which was dogged by on-and-off rain showers. Solberg and Mills, while not

WRX vs. EVO

A very wet and muddy Rally of New Zealand made the going tough at times, but Petter Solberg and co-driver Phil Mills managed to come home in sixth place, accumulating valuable championship points. Subaru Global

able to match the pace of Loeb or Gronholm, drove sure and steady, picking up a sixth-place finish for the team. Atkinson, after ending the first day in ninth, was pushing hard on leg two and set two fastest stage times before slamming into a rock and into retirement.

The last rally of the season, getting back to a more traditional format, was the Rally Wales GB, the site of Solberg's first ever WRC win and his 2003 championship victory. For the Subaru team, this event proved to be one of the better results of the season, with Solberg and Mills running strongly through the three days and finishing third overall, behind Marcus Gronholm and Manfred Stohl. Atkinson and MacNeall also came through, finishing in sixth place.

On reflection, 2006 had been a disappointing year for SWRT, with a spate of accidents and technical problems hampering progress. The Citroens, Fords, and Peugeots were clearly faster and needed to be countered. A thoroughly revised Subaru WRC spec Impreza was well into the development stages by the end of the 2006 season.

2007
SUBARU: BLAZE OF GLORY

By early 2007, the days of the GD chassis Impreza were numbered. In an effort to reduce cost, the control arms on the WRX reverted from aluminum back to steel. On the STI front, a number of changes were instigated, particularly on cars destined for North America as new LEV2 emissions regulations came into effect. Chief among them were new pistons and cylinder heads with revised intake and exhaust valves, to promote cleaner combustion and improved cooling. Engine mapping was also changed, and a new turbocharger and bigger wastegate were added, along with a revised mechanical boost controller. Cost savings were evident on the suspension front, with control arms now shared with regular JDM cars, not the Spec C homologation variant. There was also reduced front caster angle and a smaller rear sway bar. The

Changes to the Impreza STI for 2007 included elimination of the smoker's package and a new Torsen rear differential. By this stage the GD chassis car was entering the twilight of its production run. Subaru Global

six-speed gearbox got taller cogs on second through top gears in an effort to boost fuel economy, which among four-cylinder performance cars had been marginal at best. Other changes included the return of steel engine mounts (due to warranty issues in 2005 and 2006), the elimination of the smoker's package for the interior, and a new Torsen differential in place of the helical limited-slip rear.

As production drew to a close, a number of special edition variants, based both on the WRX and STI, were rolled out and quickly snapped up. As with the plethora of others that had gone before them, these cars are covered in detail in Appendix B: Special Edition Cars.

By 2007, the Evolution versus WRX/STI battle had been raging for almost a full 15 years. With thoroughly new cars due from each manufacturer in 2008, this was one rivalry that showed little signs of slowing down. If anything it was about to get even more intense ...

ONE FINAL HURRAH

Although the GD chassis Impreza was clearly on its way out by 2007, as far as SWRT was concerned, there was still life in the old girl yet. An improved WRC version was slated for introduction in Mexico, so for the first three events of the season the team used the old 2006 car.

As before, there were three machines fielded as official works entries: one for Solberg and Mills, another for Atkinson and MacNeall, and a third car at select events for young Spaniard Xavier Pons and co-driver Xavier Amigo. One thing that did differ, however, was the choice of tire supplier; Subaru had signed a contract to partner with BF Goodrich for 2007 instead of Pirelli. The unfamiliar rubber provided its own set of challenges, particularly in the opening rounds.

As ever, the season began in Monte Carlo, which was blessed with rather mild weather this year. Team directives were to bring both cars home, preferably within the points. During the first leg, there was little to suggest this would not happen. Although it was dark as the cars roared off, it was relatively dry. Solberg drove steadily, setting the fourth-fastest time on the first stage and, by the end of leg one, was in

STARS N' STRIPES

Petter Solberg charged into the lead early during the 2007 Swedish Rally, but a later excursion into a ditch ended his chances of a decent finish. Subaru Global

fifth overall with Atkinson right behind. Atkinson got off to a blinding start on leg two, clawing his way up to fourth, where he stayed until the end. Solberg fell into a bit of a sluggish pace, but he did his best to make up for lost time and finished in sixth place—a personal best.

Things didn't go quite so well in Sweden. Solberg and Mills did very well in the opening leg, securing the lead by the end of the day. However, the following morning, on Special Stage 10, Petter misjudged a turn and ended in the ditch. It took almost 15 minutes to get the car out again, after which he'd lost so much time he ended up pulling out of the rally. Atkinson, still not that familiar with driving on snow, put in an impressive turn, winning Special Stage 16. However, rising temperatures and melting snow made the conditions ever more treacherous; two stages later, Chris lost grip, putting the car into a ditch and plugging the radiator with snow. The car was still drivable, but rather than push the pace Atkinson and MacNeall elected to finish intact, coming in eighth overall.

WRX vs. EVO

A new rally this year was Norway, Petter's home country, just four days after Sweden. Not surprisingly, there was an urge to do well. He drove steadily to claim fourth by the end of the first day. He picked up more speed on leg two, managing to muscle past Sebastien Loeb to take third. On the last day of competition, it was cold but clear, though with no more large studded tires available, Petter lost a bit of time. He managed to bring the car home in fourth. Atkinson didn't fare quite so well. A spin on the second leg knocked him out of the top 10. He drove the remainder of the rally with the goal of gaining familiarity with the conditions and finishing, which he did, in 19th place.

Mexico brought higher temperatures and a new car to boot. Narrow, tight sections and plenty of dust make Mexico challenging at the best of times, but in the opening leg that didn't seem to faze Solberg or Atkinson. Both drivers put in excellent performances, though Solberg was beset by engine trouble on Special Stage 5 while leading, forcing him into retirement. Atkinson won a stage on the first day and continued to press hard, eventually finishing fifth overall.

Back to Europe for Portugal, where Solberg and Mills had better luck. A spin on Special Stage 6 cost them valuable time. Nevertheless, they plugged away for the remainder of the rally, finishing in fourth and collecting five valuable championship points. Atkinson struggled, not happy with the setup on his car. After picking up speed his luck ran out, when on Special Stage 10, he crashed out of contention.

Argentina was plagued by unpredictable weather in 2007, and a number of stages were cancelled, with others modified. The rally marked the 100th event for Solberg and Mills with SWRT. Leg one consisted of just two stages, but Atkinson and Solberg drove well. The Australian set the fourth-fastest time in the Estadio Cordoba Super Special, remarkable considering he was working with a new co-driver, Stephane Prevot. The following day, weather conditions improved, but mechanical trouble brought retirement for Solberg and Mills. That left Atkinson and Prevot to press on, which they did, finishing seventh overall and collecting more crucial championship points.

STARS N' STRIPES

Argentina 2007 marked the 100th rally for Petter Solberg and Phil Mills, but after a strong start they retired with mechanical problems, leaving Chris Atkinson and Stephane Prevot (seen here on the Estadio Cordoba Super Special) to come home seventh.
Subaru Global

In Sardinia, Atkinson and Prevot hit some rocks on the opening leg, which damaged the suspension and caused them to miss the last two stages of the day. However, once the car was repaired, they pressed on, finishing the rally in 11th place. Solberg started off in high spirits but struggled with his car setup on the second day, and he elected to just try and maintain the best position he could. Ultimately, he was able to bring the car home in fifth place, behind his brother, Henning, in a Ford Focus.

In challenging Greece, Solberg's primary objective was to get through to the end, which he did; a canny drive netted him and Mills a well-deserved podium finish. Atkinson's start was decent enough, but on leg two the rocks gave his suspension a pounding and he lost time due to tire punctures. Still, he made decent enough progress to come in sixth place.

In Finland, Atkinson was on fine form, setting a succession of fast stage times to end the first leg in fourth place. He maintained his pace throughout the remainder of the rally, keeping his strong fourth behind

Sebastien Loeb. Solberg wasn't so lucky. Driveline issues hampered his progress from the very start and he retired on Special Stage 16 with suspension issues. Spaniard Xavier Pons, in the third works car, drove an excellent rally to come home in sixth place.

Germany hadn't proved favorable to the Subaru team in years past, and at the start, it looked like the 2007 event would prove no different. Solberg hit a rock on Special Stage 5, and although the car was repaired, it cost time. Ultimately, he finished in sixth place, collecting three constructor's points in the process. Atkinson was running very well, gaining ground on stage two and setting stage times within the top five. Perhaps he pushed a bit too hard, though, as an accident on the last day dashed his hopes of a decent finish. Pons, in his first tarmac event with the team, showed tremendous promise, running as high as seventh, but his engine went south on the last leg, bringing retirement.

New Zealand proved very frustrating for Solberg in the opening stages. He struggled with a car that didn't handle to his liking. An overnight servicing helped, and on the final leg Petter felt much more confident; he plugged away to finish seventh overall. Atkinson put in an excellent drive, and in a similar style to Finland, he brought his car home in a very solid fourth. Xavier Pons left the road on Special Stage 3, misjudging a corner and getting his car wedged in soft mud. He restarted under Super Rally regs the next day, but a further incident saw him roll the car, ending any chances of finishing.

Back to Europe and tarmac in Catalunya. Three cars were entered: one for Solberg/Mills, one for Atkinson/Prevot, and a third for Pons and co-driver Xavier Amigo, who were on home turf. At the start, conditions were slippery, but all three cars made it through the opening leg. Solberg finished sixth overall. Atkinson, despite suffering a near rollover, stayed on course to come in eighth. Teammate Pons, despite pushing hard to catch him, came in ninth.

In Corsica, the Subarus were unable to catch the Citroens and Fords, but the team did well overall. Solberg battled Focus driver Jari-Matti Latvala for much of the event, though he ultimately failed to catch the Finn and finished in fifth place. Atkinson, despite not feeling too comfortable with the suspension settings on his car, gained confidence on legs two and three to finish a respectable sixth. Xavier Pons had a couple of punctures on the last day that cost him valuable time, but an eighth-place finish was more than respectable.

Japan, a crucial event as far as the team was concerned, didn't get off to the greatest start. Solberg retired with gearbox problems, though he was able to restart under the Super Rally regulations the following morning. Still, any chances of a good points finish were dashed. Atkinson ran wide on Super Stage 6 and slid into a tree. Although he and Stephane weren't injured, the car was a mess. Pons was the only driver to make it through the first day. However, on leg two during Special Stage 12, he damaged the front suspension, and the car went off the road and into soft mud, ending his chances of a decent finish.

Ireland, a new addition to the WRC calendar, was a tarmac event, though bumpy roads and inclement weather (it was run in November) made things rather tricky. Pons was out on the opening leg after sliding off the road on Special Stage 4, damaging the engine and forcing retirement. Atkinson did well in the opening Super Special, but amid the rain and badly rutted roads he also slid off the road on Stage 4. He nursed the car back to the service area and it was repaired, but the following morning, the car was withdrawn with engine problems. Solberg and Mills were the only ones to survive the event. They got off to a decent start, ending the first leg in fifth place, where they stayed, despite a puncture on the final morning. Petter set the fastest time on the very last stage.

Last, but not least was the Rally Wales GB. Traditionally a Solberg favorite, the Norwegian was looking to do well, but the conditions were treacherous and Petter was lucky not to sustain any damage during a high-speed spin on the first leg. He and Mills battled the fog, rain, and mud to finish a solid fourth. Atkinson and Pons had better luck this time out, and although both of them nearly went off and suffered visibility problems from fogged up windshields, they managed to finish in sixth and ninth, respectively.

SWRT finished third in the constructor's championship for 2007, behind Ford and Citroen, while Solberg was fifth in the driver's cup. And although it had been a mixed season, the team looked forward to 2008, when it would be back in action with an almost completely new car.

Sadly, 2007 was also a season tinged with sadness for WRC and Subaru fans, as former world champion and SWRT pilot Colin McRae lost his life in a helicopter accident in his native Scotland, along with his son and two family friends. It was a bitter blow; as perhaps the greatest rally driver of his generation, McRae would be sorely missed.

CHAPTER 6

GROWING UP

Both Mitsubishi and Subaru elected to update their rally-bred performance offerings for 2008. As always, although the two cars were created with the same mission in mind, each dished up a different flavor when it came to behind-the-wheel thrills. The cars were by far the most refined examples of the breed, but some enthusiasts bemoaned the passing of the old guard, in the form of Mitsubishi's veteran 4G63 engine and Subaru's truly quirky identity.

2008
MITSUBISHI: CONCEPTUALIZING THE FUTURE

At the 2005 Tokyo Motor Show, Mitsubishi wowed the crowds by unveiling the Concept X. Very much following the process of concept to market, this vehicle was a trial balloon for the eighth-generation Mitsubishi Lancer as well as the next Evolution model, the X. Its massive fender flares, a very low front air dam, rear under-bumper diffuser, and prominent rear deck spoiler gave the car a somewhat Hot Wheels appearance, but that aside, the look of this latest concept clearly indicated that the next Lancer would be more grown up in both looks and character. Later on that year at Frankfurt, the company teased onlookers with its Concept Sportback, which sported similar design cues to the X.

WRX vs. EVO

In September 2005, Mitsubishi unveiled the Concept X at the annual Tokyo Motor Show. It was a trial balloon for the upcoming tenth iteration of the Lancer Evolution and it featured a novel dual-clutch transmission. Mitsubishi Japan

Approximately 18 months later, at the 2007 North American International Auto Show in Detroit, Mitsubishi took the wraps off the new production Lancer. In U.S. trim, the car would come with a new 2.0-liter four-cylinder twin-cam engine, the 4B11, as well as the option of a five-speed manual gearbox or a new constantly variable transmission (CVT).

The new car was bigger, taller, plusher, and more refined than any Lancer before it; in fact, it was perhaps more akin to a Galant, which brings up an interesting point.

On August 23 that year, the new base model went on sale in Japan, dubbed, of all things, Galant Fortis. Clearly, Mitsubishi was taking its economy-minded sedan upmarket and toward the mid-size executive sector (the car was still called Lancer in other markets—though in several countries, including Singapore, Indonesia, and parts of South America, it was sold alongside the Cedia based-car for several seasons, as the former continued to prove popular with buyers).

GROWING UP

Approximately two years after the Concept X, the JDM production version of the Lancer Evolution X was revealed. It was based on the curiously named Galant Fortis, even though the new car was called Lancer in markets outside of Japan. Mitsubishi Japan

X MARKS THE SPOT

With the new Lancer, enthusiasts were no doubt wondering if the latest Evolution would perhaps be a bit soft—more grand tourer than rally-bred performance machine. They needn't have worried.

When the eighth-generation Lancer was launched at NAIAS 2007, Mitsubishi again teased enthusiasts, revealing a further developed, less-stylized version of the Concept X, dubbed Prototype X, which was clearly the next Evo. It would be a few more months before the public actually got a chance to sample the production version, in October. Japanese sales of the Evolution X began on October 1, and although there was clearly a lineage to the past, there was also a break with tradition. It was the biggest and heaviest Evo yet, fully loaded examples weighing over 3,500 lbs, though an aluminum roof skin, front fenders, and rear spoiler were designed to keep mass down

Besides employing a new body structure, the latest Evolution also had a new engine in the shape of Mitsubishi's corporate 4B11 2.0-liter twin cam four. Although rated at 280 ps in Japan, it actually made 300 metric horsepower and a meaty 311 lb-ft of torque, thanks to aggressive ECU mapping and a very efficient TD06 turbocharger.
Mitsubishi Japan

as best as possible. Among Evos it was the stiffest (structural rigidity was improved by some 40 percent) and also the most stable, thanks to a longer wheelbase (104.3 inches) and wider track, both front and rear.

Perhaps the biggest difference was a new engine. The veteran 4G63 had done its job well, but ever-tightening emissions requirements meant its days had been numbered. In its place was a version of the new corporate 4B11, 2.0-liter twin-cam four, boasting a die-cast aluminum block, timing, and valve covers. Mitsubishi's MIVEC continuously variable valve timing system was employed on both the intake and exhaust camshafts, in the interest of maximizing power delivery at various engine speeds while reducing emissions (Mitsubishi press materials said that the new engine earned a three-star rating under Japanese requirements for smog emissions, which were some 50 percent lower than 2005 standards). Another interesting aspect of this engine in Evo X was the exhaust plumbing. The TD06 turbocharger

GROWING UP

boasted a specially shaped housing, titanium-alloy turbine wheel, and aluminum alloy compressor wheel. The latter was shaped to maximize boost and minimize spool up time for snappy throttle response. The exhaust manifold was now mounted behind instead of in front of the engine, freeing up more space and allowing the motor to be mounted lower in the car, improving the center of gravity. The design also promoted more efficient flow of spent exhaust gases, helping the emissions cause. In Japanese-spec trim, despite the low-key official rating of 280 PS, the new engine actually put out 296 hp, or 300 PS (metric horsepower).

Even bigger news was the adoption of a six-speed twin clutch gearbox with sequential shifting, eliminating the need for a traditional-style clutch. Odd and even speeds were split between each clutch, and

An interesting feature available on the JDM GSR model was the new Sequential Shift Transmission that used dual clutches to execute ultra-quick gear changes. The driver could change speeds through the lever or via paddles mounted on the steering wheel.
Mitsubishi Japan

The dual-clutch gearbox divided odd and even speeds between two different clutches. The transmission could operate in automatic mode, whereby it controlled shifting itself. A console-mounted switch allowed the driver to fine-tune the transmission's behavior. Three settings enabled the gearbox to optimize shifting to suit differing road conditions.
Mitsubishi Japan

the transmission could either work in fully automated mode—whereby it controlled shifting—or manual mode, which allowed the driver to change gears via paddles mounted on either side of the steering wheel. Further complicating matters was the addition of Normal, Sport, and Super Sport modes, each activated by a console-mounted toggle switch behind the shifter boot. These were designed to optimize gear-changing depending on road conditions—in town, highway, or winding open road. The new transmission was a radical departure from those on previous Evos, though hard-core purists could still opt for a traditional five-speed manual that had been strengthened to handle the extra torque of the new engine, some 311 lb-ft.

GROWING UP

The suspension was based on that used in the Cedia: fully independent with MacPherson struts employed up front and a multilink rear, but with the struts and location points pushed further out improved stability. The hard points were also stronger than before to reduce lateral deflection over rough surfaces. A factory-fitted high-performance package comprised Bilstein monotube shocks and Eibach performance springs, derived from those used on the old Evo IX MR, which further aided the handling cause.

The Evo X was offered in full-jam GSR and stripped-down RS models, as per its predecessors. Evolution X GSR models came with a standard Super All Wheel Control system that offered different modes for tarmac, gravel, or snow. This system was basically an umbrella that was designed to make sure the Evo's other driveline systems operated in harmony with each other in order to deliver the maximum amount of grip and traction at all times. These other systems included an updated active center differential, with an electronically operated clutch that controlled torque split from the front to rear wheels, and a development of the active yaw control system, to control side-to-side torque transmission between the rear tires; these now utilized a yaw rate sensor to more precisely measure cornering dynamics. A new addition to the driveline—active stability control—modulated engine

As with previous versions in Japan, two models of the Evolution X were initially offered – the GSR (seen here) and a stripped-down RS. Mitsubishi Japan

WRX vs. EVO

Mitsubishi's new Super All-Wheel Control System grouped together the car's driveline features, including the Active Center Differential and Active Yaw Control system. It was designed to optimize grip at all times. Mitsubishi Japan

GROWING UP

power and braking to each wheel to reduce the risk of skidding and improve grip, particularly on slippery surfaces.

Anti-lock brakes were fitted as standard. As on the IX, GSR models came with standard Brembo brakes, in this case massive vented discs with four-piston calipers up front and two-piston units out back. Wheels were 18-inch Enkei high-strength multispoke alloys, wrapped around P245/40ZR18 tires.

Inside, GSRs were as opulent as ever, with standard Recaro multi-adjustable front bucket seats, power windows, locks, mirrors, sunroof (if ordered), air conditioning, and an available factory-fitted premium sound system with MP3 capability (courtesy of Rockford-Fosgate) that incorporated a total of nine speakers and a 650-watt amplifier. Also optional: a computer/navigation system with a built-in 30gb hard drive and seven-inch liquid crystal display screen in the center stack. On the safety front, the new Evo GSR came with adaptive front headlights featuring HID bulbs (the auxiliary lights turned with the steering, a modern variation of the swivel lighting systems found on cars like the 1948 Tucker Torpedo and 1967 Citroen DS), rain-sensitive wipers, dual-stage front driver and passenger airbags, side knee airbags, and, to deter thieves, a standard engine immobilizer and theft alarm.

Japanese market GSR Evolution Xs sported massive 18-inch Enkei wheels and P245/40ZR18 tires. Brembo brakes were also standard. Mitsubishi Japan

WRX vs. EVO

Like the exterior, the new Evo's cabin was more mature, with improved ergonomics over the Cedia-based cars. As before GSR models got standard Recaro front bucket seats and came fully-loaded. Shown here is a car equipped with the five-speed manual gearbox. Mitsubishi Japan

In Japan, the RS Evolution X, like previous incarnations, was the hardcore performance variant. It came in just one color, Scotia White. 17-inch wheels and tires were standard, though many buyers upgraded after buying their cars. Mitsubishi Japan

GROWING UP

RS models featured a more basic interior compared with the GSR model, including regular Galant Fortis front seats and no premium sound system. A five-speed manual was the only gearbox available. Mitsubishi Japan

The RS model, as before, came strictly in one color, Scotia White, with black instead of body color mirrors, and it did without the rear spoiler. The RS model ran on the Evo IX's 17-inch wheels instead of the big 18-inch Enkeis and deleted the Brembo brakes, antitheft alarm, passenger-side front airbag, Recaro seats, and premium sound system. It also came exclusively with the five-speed manual gearbox. Weighing some 200 lbs less, it was still the hard-core enthusiast's choice.

At launch, Mitsubishi set pricing at ¥3,750,000 for the GSR model with the SST sequential gearbox, ¥3,450,000 for the GSR with a standard five-speed manual, and a rather affordable ¥2,997,750 for the stripped-down RS version.

Although the new car was clearly the most sophisticated and capable Evo ever, there were some, especially among the enthusiast community, who felt that a little of the Evo's raw-edged, pure driving persona had been lost. In testing, however, no doubt helped by the dual-clutch gearbox and Super All-Wheel Control system, the Evo X GSR was noticeably quicker around the track than either the IX

WRX vs. EVO

North American deliveries of the Lancer Evolution X, initially offered in GSR trim, began in January 2008. US buff book Road & Track *called it a car with a "wild side to thrill anyone."* Mitsubishi Motor Sales Canada

or VIII and was still just about the fastest thing you could buy for the money. Yet, although the cold hard numbers said otherwise, the car somehow just didn't feel as fast as its predecessors.

BANG FOR THE BUCK

A few months after the Japanese launch, Americans got their hands on the first examples of the new Evo X, in January 2008. U.S. cars differed somewhat from their Japanese counterparts, featuring a slightly detuned engine (rated at 281 hp—295 PS) and a slightly different equipment mix, initially with the GSR model and soon joined by the MR and MR Premium, as that version of the VIII and IX already had strong brand equity in the United States. The GSR was actually the stripper version in America, coming only with the five-speed manual, though it did have the 18-inch wheels, Brembo brakes, fully equipped cabin, rear spoiler, and super active yaw control, including stability control, found on the Japanese version.

GROWING UP

In the US and Canada, the new Evolution featured a slightly different state of tune, with the 4B11 engine rated at 281 horsepower (SAE Net). A new MR model added the Dual Clutch six-speed gearbox that debuted to rave reviews. Mitsubishi Motor Sales Canada

Like their Japanese market counterparts, North American Evos got 18-inch wheels and the big Brembo brakes as standard. This was also the first Evo variant to be officially sold in Canada. Mitsubishi Motor Sales Canada

WRX vs. EVO

North American cars finally got Super Active Yaw Control. As a result, the X was the quickest car, point-to-point, of all Evos sold in that part of the world, even though the car's larger dimensions and extra weight might have suggested otherwise.
Mitsubishi Motor Sales Canada

The U.S. MR got the factory high-performance suspension package, with the Bilstein shocks and Eibach springs as standard, along with the six-speed SST gearbox, Xenon HID headlights, leather seating surfaces, and Bluetooth communications, by that stage all the rage in North America. The MR Premium added the Rockford Fosgate nine-speaker sound system. At $33,000 for the GSR and $37,000 for the MR, the latest Evo was by all accounts a very attractive buy in the United States, especially considering that for the money, few performance cars could touch it.

That was further established in a comparison test by *Road & Track* magazine, which pitted the new car against its rival, the also-redesigned 2008 Subaru Impreza WRX STI, in the March 2008 issue. In testing, the magazine's MR recorded a lap time of just 1 minute 31 seconds on the Streets of Willow course, north of Los Angeles, with Indy car driver Roger Yasukawa at the wheel. Yasukawa stated that the Bilstein/Eibach suspension package "gives the car good turn-in

GROWING UP

stability, and the TC-SST gearbox is really impressive. It's the only one I know of that runs better in full automatic mode." International editor Sam Mitani stated that, although the new car was "heavier and lacks the sharp-edged nature of the previous car, it's just as fast around the track, if not faster. The [Evolution] is no longer just for weekend boy racers; it has evolved into the complete sports sedan, one with a wild side to thrill anyone."

Those thrills could now be mixed with chills, as for the first time Canadian buyers could also get their hands on an Evolution through official channels. Previous versions didn't comply with Canada's five-mph bumper laws because of the location of the front-mounted intercooler—a bane to Canadian enthusiasts who'd been wanting to get their hands on Mitsubishi's rally superstar forever. Canadian sales began in February, approximately a month after U.S. deliveries started.

CENTER STAGE

In Europe, perhaps not surprisingly, the United Kingdom was the first country to receive the new Evo X, with deliveries beginning in March 2008. As before, UK-spec cars introduced some unique features of their own and came in three basic configurations: GS (which was roughly equivalent to the Japanese GSR), GSR, and GSR-SST. The former included all of the GSR hardware, including the super active yaw control, 18-inch wheels, Brembo brakes, and Recaro seats, but it only came with the five-speed manual gearbox and six-speaker sound system. The GSR version was largely the same, but it added the premium Rockford Fosgate sound system as well as the satellite navigation system and MP3 capability.

The GSR SST, as its name suggested, featured the six-speed twin-clutch sequential gearbox and was priced as the premium version, a logical move considering that in Britain the preference for many pur sang sport sedans was to have proper manual gearboxes, even in the early twenty-first century.

Car magazine managed to get its hands on early Evo X tester and waxed lyrical, particularly about the car's grip and handling, stating,

WRX vs. EVO

Capable of accelerating to 60 mph in under five seconds, this was the view most competitors got of the Evolution X. Mitsubishi Motor Sales Canada

"You'll need a 911 Turbo to keep pace over wet, badly surfaced British roads. You can feel which wheel has the most grip and can take the most torque—it's weird, slightly artificial, but devastatingly effective and, for some, central to the Evo's appeal." The magazine also came up with its own acronym, playing on the car's SAWC and SYC, which it dubbed TBC for "Totally Bonkers Cornering."

UK cars also received the FQ moniker, relating to the state of engine tuning, thus the entry-level model was officially called the Lancer Evolution X GS FQ 300. The entry-level UK car could accelerate from 0–60 mph in around 4.5 seconds and retailed for £28,995, which by UK standards was a relative bargain. An even hotter and faster version, the GS FQ330, with an engine rated at 324 bhp and 322 lb-ft of torque, started at £31,498. The UK GSR was, like the GS, available with engines in FQ300 or 330 form, while the GST, which incorporated the sequential gearbox, was offered as the FQ300 only.

Top-of-the-line in Britain was the monstrous GSR FQ 360 that featured a 4B11 engine tuned to deliver a staggering 354 bhp and 362 lb-ft of torque via a tweaked ECU, cold air intake kit, revised

GROWING UP

fuel system, and free-flowing exhaust. Equipped exclusively with the five-speed manual gearbox (because the SST unit was considered not up to handling the extra torque), the FQ 360 cost a not insubstantial £38,999. However, for that amount of coin, you got a machine that could hunt down and destroy exotic hypercars and yet had room for all the family. Acceleration was mind bending—try 0–60 mph in a brisk 4.1 seconds. Although top speed was electronically limited to 155 mph, without a governor more than 175 mph was a reasonable assumption. Outwardly, the FQ360 was distinguished from lesser UK-market Evos by the addition of a carbon fiber front lip spoiler and a roof fairing with vortex generators—harking back to the fearsome Evo VIII FQ-400.

Autocar magazine managed to test one of these beasts, and although it wasn't too fond of the carbon fiber add-ons, it found "the old-fashioned gearbox a treat," with "quick and accurate gear changes. If you think the X is missing a bit of the old Evo spirit, then [the FQ-360] is the one for you, as mad as the last Evo IX, but with an even better chassis."

Continental European Evolution Xs were announced at the 2007 Bologna Motor Show and a black production Euro version, complete with left-hand drive, was on display for all to see. Euro-spec Evo Xs were also displayed at 2008 Geneva Auto Salon in February and deliveries started in May, some two months after the United Kingdom.

The year 2008 ultimately proved to be a very interesting one for auto manufacturers, including Mitsubishi. Although the company announced plans to sell Evolution Xs in China (badged purely as Evolutions), considered by some as a shrewd move at the time, a sputtering economy in the United States soon put a crimp on new car sales as credit dried up and restricted the ability of people to make new automobile purchases. In a somewhat unusual turn, Mitsubishi Motor Sales America (MMSA) elected to keep selling 2008 Evolutions well into the following year. Thanks to a late introduction (January for the GSR and July for the MR model), there was some logic to this, considering that a very short model year run would not have helped sales that were already on a downward slide. Instead, MMSA pressed ahead with plans to launch a slightly updated 2010 model, which made its debut in summer 2009, meaning there was no official 2009 model in the United States.

In other parts of the world, rumors surrounding the 2010 model included the possible introduction of a monster FQ-400 in the United Kingdom. Although Mitsubishi had yet to rejoin the World Rally Championship in any official capacity, privately run Evo Xs were starting to make their way into the Group N production car class. If the success of its predecessors was anything to go by, the X looked set to become just as dominant.

SUBARU: GOING MAINSTREAM

Although archrival Mitsubishi got the jump by launching its next-generation Lancer (Galant-Fortis) at the 2007 North American International Auto Show in Detroit, Subaru decided that the New York show a couple of months later would be the perfect time to reveal the redesigned 2008 Impreza and WRX. On April 3, the wraps came off, with deliveries slated to begin in summer 2007.

Subaru unveiled its true third generation Impreza at the 2007 New York International Auto Show, including the WRX (center). Subaru Global

GROWING UP

True to Subaru tradition, some elements carried over for the new car, namely the horizontally opposed four-cylinder engine, symmetrical all-wheel drive, and all-independent suspension. Styling wasn't that well received, especially from Subaru die-hards. Sure, the car was well proportioned enough, and the new five-door hatchback looked less dumpy than the old wagon, but it somehow seemed a bit generic, with no standout touches. Even the frameless doors, long a Subaru trademark, were a thing of past, as engineers sought to reduce wind noise intrusion.

Not only was the latest Impreza a bit more generic in the looks department, it was also bigger—some 4.5 inches longer, 1.5 inches taller and with a longer 103.4-inch wheelbase. However, it was also put together better, with improved panel gaps, higher-quality exterior paint, and doors that made a more pronounced clunk when you closed them. This improved quality bore out in the cabin, too. The interior was more opulent than before, with upgraded materials and more solid-looking controls. It was also roomier, but like the exterior that quality seemed to come at the expense of character, and the cabin felt less personal and quirky than before.

In a departure from previous versions, the new Subaru WRX was called S-GT in the Japanese market and came in a choice of five-door hatchback or four-door sedan body styles. Subaru Global

Under the skin, the new fourth-generation Impreza was quite different. The new GE chassis was a shortened version of the then-current Legacy and was both stiffer and stronger than the old GD. There was greater use of high-tensile steel and reinforced A-, B-, and C-pillars. Unlike the GD, there was no separate front subframe; instead the suspension attached directly to the unibody via stronger hard points. And, although the front setup was still a MacPherson strut design, elimination of the subframe allowed the engine to be mounted lower in the car, reducing the center of gravity as a gesture toward more neutral cornering. At the back, the previous Mac strut suspension was replaced by a more exotic double-wishbone system, designed for improved packaging (it eliminated the big shock towers, freeing up trunk space), while aiming to improve both ride quality and enhance the car's overall handling. Interestingly enough, this new rear suspension was mounted on a subframe designed to further quell road shocks being transmitted up into the cabin. There was a newer (and quicker) steering system with a faster 15:1 ratio, and the brakes were also changed. Borrowed directly from the Legacy, the new anchors featured dual-piston front and single-piston rear calipers, instead of the previous quad-piston front and dual-piston rear clampers.

As for the engine, the WRX cars shown in New York featured an EJ25, but there were changes to the induction system, namely a new intake manifold assembly and a revised turbocharger and intercooler setup. Changes to the ECU also resulted in slightly different power delivery—the new engine was rated at 224 hp and 226-lb-ft of torque, but it came in at lower rpm (5,200 for max power and a muscle car–like 2,800 for peak torque).

Japanese home-market versions (curiously dubbed Impreza S-GT) continued to use a development of the old EJ20, rated at 247 hp and 246 lb-ft of torque. Although more powerful, the engine also had different characteristics and was peakier—maximum power didn't arrive until 6,000 rpm.

As with previous incarnations, two transmissions were offered on the GE WRX, a five-speed manual and four-speed automatic,

GROWING UP

By this stage, Japanese market cars were the only ones still powered by turbocharged EJ20 engines; the rest adopted the bigger 2.5-liter unit. The JDM models were rated at 247 hp and 246 lb-ft of torque. Subaru Global

though on EJ25-equipped cars the five-speeder got shorter and more widely spaced first and second cogs in an effort to improve low-end acceleration.

Sales of this latest turbocharged Impreza officially began on June 5, 2007 in Japan. North American sales started the following month in Canada and then August for U.S. buyers. Europeans, who also got the EJ25-engined version, had to wait a little longer—UK deliveries didn't begin until November.

A CHANGE IN DIRECTION

So it was clearly more grown up to look at and sit in, but how did this new Impreza drive? In Japan, online resource *NihonCar.com* was given an early S-GT hatchback to flog about and found it quite a bit different to the old WRX. The five-speed gearbox won accolades for its precise shifting, but the new engine was deemed "civilized" and perhaps lacking that raw edge that had characterized these cars for so long.

In the United States, *Car and Driver* got its hands on a local-market WRX and Mark Gillies noted that "wind, engine, and tire

WRX vs. EVO

A brand new S-GT is put through its paces at Fuji Speedway in January 2008. Although the car boasted improved grip over the old WRX, many testers felt the car somehow lacked the character that came to define its predecessor. Huw Evans

Despite a braking system that featured simpler calipers, stopping power was a strong suit of the S-GT. Huw Evans

noise are more muted," and that ride quality was "hugely improved." The retuned EJ25 engine with its lower-rpm peak power delivery meant that "the driver no longer has to shift down two gears to get past that pesky semi." Gillies ultimately concluded that while the new Rex was "more useable in daily driving," the car had somehow "lost the raw edge it used to have when tearing up the back roads."

That sentiment was shared with this author, who drove a new North American–spec WRX, equipped with the automatic, that fall. While the new car was clearly more refined and better put together, it somehow didn't have the same level of personality and driver involvement, despite being supremely tossable and decently fast. While the enthusiast may not have welcomed the change in character, from a sales and marketing standpoint going more mainstream seemed perfectly logical—a strategy that proved well-founded when Japanese home-market deliveries got off to a flying start.

North American-spec GE turbo cars were still badged WRX and came with the EJ25 engine, rated at 224 hp and 226 lb-ft of torque. This was coupled with a five-speed manual or four-speed automatic with select shift feature. Huw Evans

WRX vs. EVO

Styling on the latest Impreza WRX was a lot more mainstream than in the past; in North America the sedan was preferred over the hatchback. Huw Evans

Bigger and torquier than its Japanese market EJ 20 counterpart, max power on the North American 2.5 liter unit came in at a lower 5500 rpm. Equipped with the EJ25, the 2008 WRX was quick and rather satisfying to drive. Huw Evans

GROWING UP

For the 2008 model year, all Imprezas adopted framed doors to replace the earlier frameless-window doors, eliminating another quirk that had previously come to define the marque.
Huw Evans

HATCHBACK ONLY

Still, for the hard-core brigade, there was always the STI. As with previous incarnations, the arrival of the GE Impreza STI was highly anticipated. On October 24, 2007, at the Tokyo Motor Show, the wraps were finally taken off. Unlike the WRX, the new STI came exclusively as a five-door hatchback. The bulging fenders, short rump, and rear roof spoiler made it look very much like a Japanese Ford Focus RS.

Still, there was no questioning the car's technological pedigree. Japanese-market cars featured a 1,994cc EJ20 engine (WRC rally homologation requirements were still a major part of the car's reason for being), which incorporated a new dual active valve control system that hydraulically adjusted timing on both intake and exhaust valves to improve combustion efficiency and reduce emissions. Along with a new intake manifold that incorporated a tumble generator valve

(TGV), a redesigned exhaust system with a revised housing for the Mitsubishi TD05 twin-scroll turbine, and a secondary air injection system that was designed to burn off excess fuel in the exhaust ports, the result was the most torquey and tractable STI motor yet.

Despite the official 280 PS output declared in Japan, power on the new STI EJ20 was an actual 304 hp at a fairly low (by Subaru standards) 6,500 rpm. Torque, which stood at meaty 311 lb-ft, was all in by 4,400 revs—indicating that, at least on the street, this new car looked able to really hold its own.

Bolted to the back of the engine was an exclusive six-speed manual gearbox. Subaru engineers had made some changes, particularly to the

Like its S-GT counterpart, the Japanese domestic market STI featured an EJ20 engine tuned to deliver 304 hp. Torque matched the arch-rival Mitsubishi Evolution at a strong 311 lb-ft. Subaru Global

GROWING UP

Japanese-market STI models came with massive 18-inch BBS alloy wheels, shod in Bridgestone Potenza RE050 tires, plus massive brakes. The fronts were sized at 13 inches, the rears at 12.6. Subaru Global

shifting mechanism, including the adoption of triple-cone syncros on first gear to combat grinding and new shift sleeves designed to make changing gears more fluid and precise (even though Subaru manual gearboxes had improved markedly over the years, they were still, up to that point, notorious for notchy shifting).

As before, the new STI featured a version of Subaru's full-time intelligent all-wheel-drive system, which transmitted power to each tire via front, center, and rear differentials. The front unit was now a Torsen limited-slip unit, as was the rear one, designed to maximize traction at all times. The driver-controlled center differential (DCCD) was also updated, this time being an electro/mechanical unit that, under normal conditions, split the torque 41/59 percent front/rear. It allowed pilots to choose different settings depending on the speed and pavement conditions. A new vehicle dynamics control (VCD) system was also incorporated to prevent overzealous and inexperienced drivers from getting into trouble. It also featured three different modes: Normal, which governed stability, ABS, and traction control; Traction mode, which was designed to optimize grip and give the driver more free reign by delaying the time at which the VDC kicked in; and Off mode, where only the anti-lock braking system functioned, though

Subaru recommended that this feature be used only for emergencies, like getting the car out of heavy snow or muddy bogs. Still, experienced enthusiast drivers were happy to know that they could still have fun.

LESS WEIGHT

Although the new WRX was deemed to be the most generic and mainstream ever, Subaru went to greater lengths than before to distinguish the STI from its somewhat more pedestrian brother. The suspension was one such area. Suspension geometry was specific to the latter, with a wider track both front and rear to improve stability (part of the reason why those monstrous bulging fenders were called for). In addition, there were cast-aluminum lower control arms at the front, plus a unique front sway bar. Out back the double-wishbone arrangement was optimized for STI duty, and although ride quality was noticeably less harsh than past STIs, it was still tauter than the regular Rex.

Braking consisted of a pair of four-piston Brembos up front, clamping big 13-inch discs, while dual-piston units and 12.6-inch rotors were carried out back. In order to effectively harness their ability, vents were incorporated in both the front and rear rotors and ultra-low expansion brake hoses were connected to the master cylinder. A super sports ABS system and electronic brake distribution were also employed, the latter operating in conjunction with the car's driver-controlled center diff to provide effective braking to each wheel independently, ensuring the car stayed on its intended path as much as possible—a boon in slippery conditions.

Gorgeous multispoke 8.5x18-inch BBS alloys were needed to clear the big brakes. Bridgestone Potenza RE050A (P245/40ZR18) low-profile tires were wrapped around them.

Inside, the latest STI featured better-quality materials, though there was still quite a lot of shiny plastic. Still, the instrument panel was simpler, the front legroom in particular was more spacious, and the optional Recaro front seats were comfortable and supportive.

The presence of a 8,000-rpm redline tachometer was certain to dash the hopes of some, including *Automobile* magazine's Jason

GROWING UP

Like the exterior, the new STI's cabin, although ergonomically improved, seemed to somewhat lack the character of its predecessor. At launch, a six-speed gearbox was the only transmission offered. Sporty red-lit gauges offered good visibility at night.
Subaru Global

Cammisa, who found himself taking one of the new JDM STIs for a spin around Fuji Speedway. Cammisa said, "My initial enthusiasm at seeing [the tachometer's] redline start at 8,000 rpm was halved when peak power came in 6,500.... Although the car was very quick around the course, if the right foot is anywhere near the gas pedal, understeer is what you'll get." He praised the car's Brembo brakes and VDC, looking forward to the day when he and other U.S. testers would get their hands on the North American–spec version, which wasn't long in coming.

EXPORT IS BIG

In November, export versions of the new STI began to surface. Unlike the Japanese-market model, European and North American cars got a larger, EJ25 engine that was tuned differently. On paper it advertised less power—305 hp and 290 lb-ft—quite extraordinary, considering the larger displacement. It also featured uniquely calibrated electronics and a single-scroll turbocharger. Still, the consensus among those who had driven both the JDM and North American versions was that the latter car somehow felt faster, perhaps because power came on sooner—max torque was all in by just four grand instead of 4,400.

Although the car was quick, according to some it appeared to be going a bit soft around the edges. This was played out in a comparison test by *Road & Track* magazine, which in its March 2008 issue pitted the new STI against its old adversary the Lancer Evolution, this time in updated X form.

Feature editor Mike Monticello iterated that although the new STI was "lighter (by 195 lbs) than the Evo and has slightly more horsepower, it's far more work to drive around the racetrack, and you're going slower, no matter how hard you push the car." But in comparison with the old GD car, he did say that "in case you're thinking the new STI is a worse performer than the old one, it's not. The new car is a tenth quicker to 60 mph and faster through the slalom."

However, it was interesting to note that while the North American cars also came with Brembo brakes and 18-inch BBS wheels, they rode on different tires: Dunlop SP Sport 600s. The JDM Recaro seats weren't available, even as an option. Still, for the money ($34,995 US), the latest STI was a heck of a buy, especially in view of its 5-second 0-60 mph time and .90 lateral g cornering ability.

European sales of Scoob's new rocket began in Spring 2008. Although the new car's introduction initially met with a lukewarm reception, from an everyday driving perspective it was far easier to live with than the old car. If the regular car's performance wasn't enough, you could always step up to the Prodrive performance pack, which increased power to around 320 hp and torque to 347 lb-ft; thanks to a specially calibrated ECU and performance exhaust system. Although top speed was still limited to 155 mph, these changes hastened acceleration to around 4.8 seconds for the 0–60 mph dash.

GROWING UP

By this time, the regular WRX was also reaching British buyers in healthy numbers. For the go-faster brigade with a bit less money to spend, Prodrive obliged with a performance pack for the Rex and revealed its limited edition WRX-S at the 2008 British International Motor Show.

LAST GASP?

Homologation for the new GE Impreza STI was granted by the FIA on January 1, 2008, and SWRT geared up for another season of action. Two works cars were fielded: one for Petter Solberg and the other for Chris Atkinson, each running with their same co-drivers, Phil Mills and Stephane Prevot. Because the new Prodrive-built cars weren't ready in time for the start of the season, SWRT ran the first five events using updated 2007 machines. Per FIA requirements, they now ran exclusively on Pirelli tires (as did the other teams).

Not surprisingly the new STI's primary raison d'etre was to homologate the GE chassis Impreza for World Championship Rallying. Even though approval was granted at the start of the year, it wasn't until well into the season that the new car actually got a chance to turn a wheel in competition. Subaru Global

In Monte Carlo, Atkinson proved to be a shining star, although he was by no means a tarmac specialist. He drove exceedingly well in this event, which was fraught with tricky conditions, battling with Francois Duval for much of it. Ultimately, he managed to bring his car home in a solid third place, which marked his first podium finish on a tarmac event. Solberg got off to a healthy start, and he, along with teammate Atkinson, was fastest through the infamous Col de Turini stage, which was covered with black ice and snow. Ultimately, he finished fifth behind Duval and ahead of Gigi Galli in the Ford Focus.

Even though it took place on February 8 to 11, there wasn't a whole lot of snow in Sweden for the WRC event, and lots of gravel made the going tough at times. Neither of the works Subaru drivers got off to the greatest start, but Solberg persevered as best as he could, ending the rally in a solid fourth place. Atkinson went off the course on the very first day, ending any chances of a good finish, though he was back in action on leg two and brought the car home to secure a single manufacturer's point.

Unlike Sweden, both drivers got off to a strong start in Mexico. By the end of the first leg, Atkinson was in third place, with this teammate right behind. The Aussie continued his charge on leg two and moved up to second when Jari-Matti Latvala's engine caught fire, and there he stayed to clinch his best ever WRC finish. Solberg wasn't so lucky; the tricky road conditions got the best of him early on leg two, forcing retirement.

Weather proved to be the biggest threat in Argentina. Heavy rains hampered progress for all drivers on the opening leg, but Atkinson and Solberg drove superbly, lying in second and third by the end of the day. The teammates ended up battling it out for much of leg two, but on the last day of competition, Solberg retired when electrical problems caused the car to die just two stages from the finish. That left Atkinson to motor on to yet another second place and his third podium finish in four events.

For the first time, the WRC circus moved to the Middle East for the brand new Rally Jordan. In complete contrast to Argentina, the conditions on this one comprised dry, dusty, and rocky surfaces that proved no less challenging. Solberg, who'd already had experience of the roads thanks to a practice the year before, blasted off and was doing well until some nasty rocks damaged the front suspension and the car caught fire. Atkinson, in fifth after the first day, drove another excellent rally, maintaining an excellent pace to move up two more positions by the end and securing yet another podium.

In Sardinia, changes to the suspension settings appeared to pay off. By the end of leg one, Solberg and Mills were in third place, with Atkinson and Prevot in fifth. However, a puncture early on the second morning cost valuable time for Solberg and Mills; after repairs, the best result they could muster was tenth overall. Atkinson and his co-driver battled to stay ahead of Solberg's brother Henning, in a Ford Focus, and ended the rally in sixth place.

After Sardinia, the teams moved to Greece for the annual BP Acropolis Rally, where the Subaru WRC08 rally cars were finally ready. As always Greece proved a tough event, but the new cars showed tremendous promise. After a strong start, Solberg drove an excellent rally to secure his best finish of the year: second place. Atkinson also drove very well, scoring the fastest time on the opening stage of leg three, but the rocky conditions ultimately got the best of him and he had to retire with damaged suspension.

In neighboring Turkey, Atkinson's progress was halted by rocky conditions on the afternoon of the first leg, with the young Australian on course for a points finish. Solberg and Mills drove solidly, managing to avoid damage to bring the remaining car home in a respectable sixth place.

Up to northern Europe for Finland and again, both Subarus were contenders from the get-go, despite rain on the first leg, which made conditions a bit trying. Solberg and Atkinson were in sixth and seventh by the end of the first day. From there, the Australian cranked up his speed, enough to move him up to third by the end of leg two, where he stayed until the end. Petter battled with younger brother Henning and maintained his sixth-place position.

WRX vs. EVO

As before two primary works cars were fielded, one for Petter Solberg and the other for Chris Atkinson. On the new machine's second outing – a very bumpy Rally of Turkey – Solberg managed to finish in sixth place. Subaru Global

The new Impreza's tarmac debut came in Germany. Unlike years past, conditions were a lot more favorable with largely dry roads, providing much better traction. Solberg and Mills enjoyed a largely trouble-free rally and finished a strong fifth. Atkinson and Prevot also had a largely uneventful run and ended up right behind their teammates. With both cars in the points again, things were looking up for the new car.

New Zealand was a special occasion for the Subaru team, marking not only the 15th anniversary of Colin McRae's famous first win, but

GROWING UP

also the 100th rally since the debut of the Impreza as a WRC machine. Previous heavy rains made some stages quite difficult, particularly in the opening leg, and the Subaru drivers weren't happy with their progress. Atkinson and Prevot ran into trouble on a downhill section during the opening leg and couldn't avoid rolling the car, which caused considerable damage to the front end. Under Super Rally regulations, the Subaru was repaired and they were allowed to restart the following morning, but further engine problems caused them to retire for good. Solberg and Mills drove hard and ended NZ in a strong fourth place, behind former SWRT driver Mikko Hirvonen.

Back to tarmac for Catalunya, where an additional works car was brought in for Frenchman Brice Tirabassi (2003 Junior Rally World Champion). Thanks to minimal testing time and limited tarmac experience with the new WRC08 car, it looked like the odds would be stacked against SWRT. After a tricky start, a change to harder-compound tires on the opening leg improved things for all

The annual Rally de Catalunya proved to be a better one than past years for the Subaru team. All three of the works cars entered managed to finish, with Atkinson coming home a solid seventh after battling Finn Jari-Matti Lavala in the Ford Focus. However, shortly after the season ended, SWRT announced it would be withdrawing from the World Rally circuit. Subaru Global

three drivers. All three cars made it through to the end this time, and to top it off, each driver finished within the top 10. Solberg battled a determined Urmo Aava in the Citroen to finish fifth, while Atkinson ended in seventh, narrowly beaten by Jari-Matti Latvala. Tirbarasi and co-driver Fabrice Gordon finished tenth in an excellent performance.

The Tour de Corse was another event where the Citroens and Fords appeared to have the advantage. Still, the Subaru team pushed hard, and despite conditions that were very hard on the tires, Solberg and Atkinson drove valiantly, battling each other for stage times and ultimately finishing fifth and sixth, respectively. Tirabassi, given another drive, was doing well until the engine died on the second stage of the final leg, robbing him of a decent finish. The team had been making solid progress with the new cars.

Rally Japan, held on the northern island of Hokkaido, proved quite treacherous, with heavy rains making some stages very difficult. Solberg really pushed hard, especially on the second day, setting the fastest time on super-long Stage 12, but on the last stage of the leg (Special Stage 18), he spun and went off the road, causing extensive damage to the car's suspension. Atkinson fared better even though he spun in almost the exact same spot. He kept it together and pushed through to the finish, reaching the line in fourth place.

Rally Wales GB, the last on the calendar, was no less challenging, with even less visibility and ice on some stages, particularly in the forest sections. The latter claimed Atkinson and Prevot this time out. On Special Stage 7, while attempting to negotiate a fast left-hander, the car slid off the road and slammed hard into the bank. Both Chris and Stephane were okay, but the Aussie was lifted to the hospital for observation. Solberg, dealing with the same conditions, remained fairly composed, narrowly missing out on a podium finish this time out. When the 2008 WRC season was all said and done, SWRT finished a strong third in the constructor's cup, behind Citroen and Ford, while in the driver's championship, Atkinson claimed a solid fourth place, behind Jari-Matti Latvala. Solberg took fifth.

GROWING UP

2009

SUBARU: BROADENING APPEAL

As the rally teams began making plans for the upcoming 2009 season, Subaru quite suddenly announced that it had decided not to field a full works effort for the new year. The economic downturn witnessed in 2008 had made market challenges difficult for all automakers, and the company decided to focus its strengths elsewhere for the time being, though it would continue to field Group N machines.

After nearly three decades, three manufacturer's crowns, and two driver's championships, the company that had shown the benefits of symmetrical all-wheel drive both on the street and rally course exited the World Rally stage.

In Japan, the division decided to launch the A-Line, the very first STI to feature an automatic transmission. The A-Line was quite different from the regular Japanese domestic-market STI in that it was

An automatic-transmission version of the STI, dubbed A-Line, debuted in early 2009. A six-speed unit, the new gearbox featured a manual shift mode, activated by paddles on the steering wheel.
Subaru Global

WRX vs. EVO

The A-Line differed from the standard JDM STI in being powered by a 2.5-liter engine, with a different turbocharger. Rated at 300 hp, it was less peaky and developed maximum torque at lower rpm. Subaru Global

powered by the bigger 2.5-liter engine found on export cars, featuring a single-scroll turbocharger and tuned to deliver 300 metric hp. The engine also featured an intelligent drive feature that incorporated three different mapping programs, designed to optimize efficiency depending on the driver's input and road conditions. The transmission, a five-speed unit, incorporated a Prodrive-developed Sportshift feature that allowed the driver to switch between automatic operation and a manual mode that allowed gear selection by pushing the lever or using a pair of paddles mounted on the steering wheel.

As befitting its somewhat more luxurious nature, the A-Line came fully equipped, featuring such items as special leather interior trim and heated front bucket seats, which in the driver's case also incorporated eight-way power adjustment. It was a far cry from the very first GC STI, but it was perfect in keeping with the times. The A-Line went on sale in Japan on February 24, adding yet another interesting flavor to this cult car.

By mid 2009, the STI versus Evolution battle was on the verge of entering its third decade. If the past was any indication, the future looked set to be just as interesting.

APPENDIX A

WRC WORKS RALLY RECORD

LEGEND

(Driver/Co-driver)   Ret = (Retired)   Dis = (Disqualified)

MITSUBISHI

1993 RESULT
MONTE CARLO
5th (Eriksson/Parmander)
6th (Schwarz/Grist)

PORTUGAL
5th (Eriksson/Parmander)
Ret (Schwarz/Grist)

SAFARI
Ret (Shinozuka/Kuukala)

GREECE (ACROPOLIS)
3rd (Schwarz/Grist)
Ret (Eriksson/Parmander)

WRX vs. EVO

MITSUBISHI	SUBARU

NEW ZEALAND
Ret (Dunkerton/Gocentas)

FINLAND (1000 LAKES)
5th (Eriksson/Parmander)   2nd (Vatanen/Berglund)
9th (Schwarz/Grist)   Ret (Alen/Kivimaki)

AUSTRALIA
4th (Dunkerton/Gocentas)

BRITAIN (RAC)
2nd (Eriksson/Parmander)   5th (Vatenen/Berglund)
8th (Schwarz/Thul)   Ret (McRae/Ringer)

1994 RESULT
MONTE CARLO
5th (Eriksson/Parmander)   3rd (Sainz/Moya)
7th (Schwarz/Wicha)   10th (McRae/Ringer)

PORTUGAL
11th (Holderied/Thorner)   4th (Sainz/Moya)
Ret (Recalde/Christie)   Ret (McRae/Ringer)

SAFARI
2nd (Shinozuka/Kuukkala)   4th (Njiru/Sidi)
   5th (Burns/Reid)

CORSICA
16th (Holderied/Thorner)   2nd (Sainz/Moya)
   Ret (McRae/Ringer)

WRC WORKS RALLY RECORD

MITSUBISHI

GREECE (ACROPOLIS)
2nd (Schwarz/Wicha)
Ret (Eriksson/Parmander)

ARGENTINA
5th (Recalde/Christie)
8th (Holderied/Thorner)

NEW ZEALAND
3rd (Schwarz/Wicha)
4th (Eriksson/Parmander)
Ret (Recalde/Christie)

FINLAND (1000 LAKES)
8th (Kytolehto/Kapanen)
10th (Harkki/Virjula)
29th (Holderied/Thorner)
Ret (Recalde/Christie)

SAN REMO
15th (Holderied/Thorner)
Ret (Makinen/Harjanne)
Ret (Schwarz/Wicha)

BRITAIN (RAC)
16th (Holderied/Thorner)

SUBARU

1st (Sainz/Moya)
Dis (McRae/Ringer)

2nd (Sainz/Moya)
Ret (McRae/Ringer)

1st (McRae/Ringer)
Ret (Sainz/Moya)
Ret (Bourne/Sircombe)
Ret (Burns/Reid)

3rd (Sainz/Moya)

2nd (Sainz/Moya)
5th (McRae/Ringer)

1st (McRae/Ringer)
Ret (Sainz/Moya)
Ret (Burns/Reid)

WRX vs. EVO

| **MITSUBISHI** | **SUBARU** |

1995 RESULT

MONTE CARLO
4th (Makinen/Harjanne)	1st (Sainz/Moya)
6th (Aghini/Farnocchia)	8th (Liatti/Alessandrini)
10th (Holderied/Thorner)	Ret (McRae/Ringer)

SWEDEN
1st (Eriksson/Parmander)	Ret (McRae/Ringer)
2nd (Makinen/Harjanne)	Ret (Sainz/Moya)
12th (Backlund/Andersson)	Ret (Jonsson/Johansson)

PORTUGAL
9TH (Madeira/Silva)	1st (Sainz/Moya)
10th (Recalde/Christie)	3rd (McRae/Ringer)
11th (Holderied/Thorner)	7th (Burns/Reid)

CORSICA
3rd (Aghini/Farnocchia)	4th (Sainz/Moya)
8th (Makinen/Harjanne)	5th (McRae/Ringer)
	6th (Liatti/Alessandrini)

NEW ZEALAND
5th (Eriksson/Parmander)	1st (McRae/Ringer)
9th (Recalde/Christie)	7th (Bourne/Sircombe)
10th (Madeira/Silva)	Ret (Burns/Reid)
11th (Ordynski/Stacey)	
Ret (Makinen/Harjanne)	
Ret (Holderied/Thorner)	

WRC WORKS RALLY RECORD

MITSUBISHI

AUSTRALIA
1st (Eriksson/Parmander)
4th (Makinen/Harjanne)
8th (Ordynski/Stacey)
10th (Recalde/Christie)
19th (Holderied/Thorner)
Ret (Madeira/Silva)

SPAIN (CATALUNYA)
5th (Aghini/Farnocchia)
11th (Madeira/Silva)
Ret (Makinen/Harjanne)
Ret (Recalde/Christie)
Ret (Holderied/Thorner)

BRITAIN (RAC)
7th (Madeira/Silva)
14th (Holderied/Thorner)
Ret (Eriksson/Parmander)
Ret (Makinen/Harjanne)

SUBARU

2nd (McRae/Ringer)
Ret (Sainz/Moya)
Ret (Bourne/Sircombe)

1st (Sainz/Moya)
2nd (McRae/Ringer)
3rd (Liatti/Alessandrini)

1st (McRae/Ringer)
2nd (Sainz/Moya)
3rd (Burns/Reid)

1996 RESULT
SWEDEN
1st (Makinen/Harjanne)
14th (Backlund/Andersson)
16th (Nittel/Thorner)

3rd (McRae/Ringer)
5th (Eriksson/Parmander)
10th (Auriol/Occelli)
12th (Liatti/Ferfoglia)

WRX vs. EVO

MITSUBISHI	SUBARU
SAFARI	
1st (Makinen/Harjanne)	2nd (Eriksson/Parmander)
6th (Shinozuka/Kuukkala)	4th (McRae/Ringer)
	5th (Liatti/Ferfoglia)
	8th (Miyoshi/Khan)
	9th (Njiru/Matthews)
INDONESIA	
9th (Alim/Kasiman)	2nd (Liatti/Pons)
10th (Hartono/Baskoro)	Ret (McRae/Ringer)
Ret (Makinen/Harjanne)	Ret (Eriksson/Parmander)
Ret (Burns/Reid)	
GREECE (ACROPOLIS)	
2nd (Makinen/Harjanne)	1st (McRae/Ringer)
14th (Nittel/Thorner)	4th (Liatti/Pons)
	5th (Eriksson/Parmander)
ARGENTINA	
1st (Makinen/Harjanne)	3rd (Eriksson/Parmander)
4th (Burns/Reid)	7th (Liatti/Pons)
	Ret (McRae/Ringer)
FINLAND (1000 LAKES)	
1st (Makinen/Harjanne)	5th (Eriksson/Parmander)
8th (Lampi/Stenroos)	Ret (McRae/Ringer)
AUSTRALIA	
1st (Makinen/Harjanne)	2nd (Eriksson/Parmander)
5th (Burns/Reid)	4th (McRae/Ringer)
10th (Ordynski/Stacey)	7th (Liatti/Pons)

WRC WORKS RALLY RECORD

MITSUBISHI

SAN REMO
8th (Auriol/Giraudet)
Ret (Makinen/Harjanne)
Ret (Nittel/Thorner)

SPAIN (CATALUNYA)
5th (Makinen/Harjanne)
Ret (Burns/Reid)

SUBARU

1st (McRae/Ringer)
5th (Eriksson/Parmander)
Ret (Liatti/Pons)

1st (McRae/Ringer)
2nd (Liatti/Pons)
7th (Eriksson/Parmander)

1997 RESULT

MONTE CARLO
3rd (Makinen/Harjanne)
5th (Nittel/Thorner)

1st (Liatti/Pons)
Ret (McRae/Grist)

SWEDEN
3rd (Makinen/Harjanne)
Ret (Nittel/Thorner)

1st (Eriksson/Parmander)
4th (McRae/Grist)

SAFARI
2nd (Burns/Reid)
Ret (Makinen/Harjanne)

1st (McRae/Grist)
Ret (Eriksson/Parmander)

PORTUGAL
1st (Makinen/Harjanne)
Ret (Burns/Reid)

Ret (McRae/Grist)
Ret (Eriksson/Parmander)

SPAIN (CATALUNYA)
1st (Makinen/Harjanne)
8th (Nittel/Thorner)

2nd (Liatti/Pons)
4th (McRae/Grist)

WRX vs. EVO

| **MITSUBISHI** | **SUBARU** |

CORSICA
8th (Nittel/Thorner)   1st (McRae/Grist)
Ret (Makinen/Harjanne)   5th (Liatti/Pons)

ARGENTINA
1st (Makinen/Harjanne)   2nd (McRae/Grist)
Ret (Burns/Reid)   3rd (Eriksson/Parmander)

GREECE (ACROPOLIS)
3rd (Makinen/Harjanne)   Ret (McRae/Grist)
4th (Burns/Reid)   Ret (Eriksson/Parmander)
6th (Nittel/Thorner)

NEW ZEALAND
4th (Burns/Reid)   1st (Eriksson/Parmander)
Ret (Makinen/Harjanne)   Ret (McRae/Grist)

FINLAND
1st (Makinen/Harjanne)   Ret (McRae/Grist)
7th (Nittel/Thorner)   Ret (Eriksson/Parmander)

INDONESIA
4th (Burns/Reid)   3rd (Eriksson/Parmander)
Ret (Makinen/Harjanne)   Ret (McRae/Grist)

SAN REMO
3rd (Makinen/Harjanne)   1st (McRae/Grist)
Ret (Nittel/Thorner)   2nd (Liatti/Pons)

AUSTRALIA
2nd (Makinen/Harjanne)   1st (McRae/Grist)
4th (Burns/Reid)   Ret (Eriksson/Parmander)

WRC WORKS RALLY RECORD

MITSUBISHI	SUBARU
BRITAIN (RAC)	
4th (Burns/Reid)	1st (McRae/Grist)
6th (Makinen/Harjanne)	7th (Liatti/Pons)
	Ret (Eriksson/Parmander)

1998 RESULT

MITSUBISHI	SUBARU
MONTE CARLO	
5th (Burns/Reid)	3rd (McRae/Grist)
Ret (Makinen/Mannisenmaki)	4th (Liatti/Pons)
SWEDEN	
1st (Makinen/Mannisenmaki)	4th (Eriksson/Parmander)
15th (Burns/Reid)	9th (Liatti/Pons)
	Ret (McRae/Grist)
SAFARI	
1st (Burns/Reid)	Ret (McRae/Grist)
Ret (Makinen/Mannisenmaki)	Ret (Liatti/Pons)
PORTUGAL	
4th (Burns/Reid)	1st (McRae/Grist)
Ret (Makinen/Mannisenmaki)	6th (Liatti/Pons)
SPAIN (CATALUNYA)	
3rd (Makinen/Mannisenmaki)	Ret (McRae/Grist)
4th (Burns/Reid)	Ret (Liatti/Pons)
CORSICA	
Ret (Makinen/Mannisenmaki)	1st (McRae/Grist)
Ret (Burns/Reid)	3rd (Liatti/Pons)

WRX vs. EVO

MITSUBISHI	SUBARU
ARGENTINA	
1st (Makinen/Mannisenmaki)	5th (McRae/Grist)
4th (Burns/Reid)	6th (Liatti/Pons)
GREECE (ACROPOLIS)	
Ret (Makinen/Mannisenmaki)	1st (McRae/Grist)
Ret (Burns/Reid)	6th (Liatti/Pons)
NEW ZEALAND	
3rd (Makinen/Mannisenmaki)	5th (McRae/Grist)
9th (Burns/Reid)	6th (Liatti/Pons)
FINLAND	
1st (Makinen/Mannisenmaki)	8th (Kytolehto/Kapanen)
5th (Burns/Reid)	Ret (McRae/Ringer)
SAN REMO	
1st (Makinen/Mannisenmaki)	2nd (Liatti/Pons)
7th (Burns/Reid)	3rd (McRae/Grist)
AUSTRALIA	
1st (Makinen/Mannisenmaki)	4th (McRae/Grist)
Ret (Burns/Reid)	Ret (Liatti/Pons)
BRITAIN (RAC)	
1st (Burns/Reid)	Ret (McRae/Grist)
Ret (Makinen/Mannisenmaki)	Ret (McRae/Senior)
	Ret (Vatanen/Pons)

WRC WORKS RALLY RECORD

MITSUBISHI	SUBARU

1999 RESULT

MONTE CARLO
1st (Makinen/Mannisenmaki) — 2nd (Kankkunen/Repo)
Ret (Loix/Smeets) — 5th (Thiry/Prevot)

SWEDEN
1st (Makinen/Mannisenmaki) — 5th (Burns/Reid)
9th (Loix/Smeets) — 6th (Kankkunen/Repo)
— 10th (Thiry/Prevot)

SAFARI
Dis (Makinen/Mannisenmaki) — Ret (Burns/Reid)
Ret (Loix/Smeets) — Ret (Kankkunen/Repo)
— Ret (Thiry/Prevot)

PORTUGAL
5th (Makinen/Mannisenmaki) — 4th (Burns/Reid)
Ret (Gronholm/Rautainen) — 6th (Thiry/Prevot)
— Ret (Kankkunen/Repo)

SPAIN (CATALUNYA)
3rd (Makinen/Mannisenmaki) — 5th (Burns/Reid)
4th (Loix/Smeets) — 6th (Kankkunen/Repo)
— 7th (Thiry/Prevot)

CORSICA
6th (Makinen/Mannisenmaki) — 7th (Burns/Reid)
8th (Loix/Smeets) — Ret (Thiry/Prevot)

ARGENTINA
4th (Makinen/Mannisenmaki) — 1st (Kankkunen/Repo)
Ret (Loix/Smeets) — 2nd (Burns/Reid)

WRX vs. EVO

MITSUBISHI	SUBARU
GREECE (ACROPOLIS)	
3rd (Makinen/Mannisenmaki)	1st (Burns/Reid)
4th (Loix/Smeets)	Ret (Kankkunen/Repo)
NEW ZEALAND	
1st (Makinen/Mannisenmaki)	2nd (Kankkunen/Repo)
8th (Loix/Smeets)	Ret (Burns/Reid)
FINLAND	
10th (Loix/Smeets)	1st (Kankkunen/Repo)
Ret (Makinen/Mannisenmaki)	2nd (Burns/Reid)
CHINA	
Ret (Makinen/Mannisenmaki)	2nd (Burns/Reid)
Ret (Loix/Smeets)	4th (Kankkunen/Repo)
SAN REMO	
1st (Makinen/Mannisenmaki)	6th (Kankkunen/Repo)
4th (Loix/Smeets)	Ret (Burns/Reid)
AUSTRALIA	
3rd (Makinen/Mannisenmaki)	1st (Burns/Reid)
4th (Loix/Smeets)	2nd (Kankkunen/Repo)
BRITAIN (RAC)	
5th (Loix/Smeets)	
Ret (Makinen/Mannisenmaki)	

2000 RESULT

MITSUBISHI	SUBARU
MONTE CARLO	
1st (Makinen/Mannisenmaki)	3rd (Kankkunen/Repo)
6th (Loix/Smeets)	Ret (Burns/Reid)

WRC WORKS RALLY RECORD

MITSUBISHI

SWEDEN
2nd (Makinen/Mannisenmaki)
8th (Loix/Smeets)

SAFARI
Ret (Loix/Smeets)
Ret (Makinen/Mannisenmaki)

PORTUGAL
6th (Loix/Smeets)
Ret (Makinen/Mannisenmaki)

SPAIN (CATALUNYA)
4th (Makinen/Mannisenmaki)
8th (Loix/Smeets)

ARGENTINA
3rd (Makinen/Mannisenmaki)
5th (Loix/Smeets)

GREECE (ACROPOLIS)
Ret (Loix/Smeets)
Ret (Makinen/Mannisenmaki)

NEW ZEALAND
Ret (Loix/Smeets)
Ret (Makinen/Mannisenmaki)

FINLAND
4th (Makinen/Mannisenmaki)
Ret (Loix/Smeets)

SUBARU

5th (Burns/Reid)
6th (Kankkunen/Repo)

1st (Burns/Reid)
2nd (Kankkunen/Repo)

1st (Burns/Reid)
Ret (Kankkunen/Repo)

2nd (Burns/Reid)
Ret (Kankkunen/Repo)

1st (Burns/Reid)
4th (Kankkunen/Repo)

3rd (Kankkunen/Repo)
Ret (Burns/Reid)

Ret (Burns/Reid)
Ret (Kankkunen/Repo)

8th (Kankkunen/Repo)
Ret (Burns/Reid)

WRX vs. EVO

MITSUBISHI	**SUBARU**
CYPRUS	
5th (Makinen/Mannisenmaki)	4th (Burns/Reid)
8th (Loix/Smeets)	7th (Kankkunen/Repo)
CORSICA	
Ret (Loix/Smeets)	4th (Burns/Reid)
Ret (Makinen/Mannisenmaki)	7th (Jean-Joseph/Boyere)
	Ret (Solberg/Mills)
SAN REMO	
3rd (Makinen/Mannisenmaki)	7th (Jean-Joseph/Boyere)
8th (Loix/Smeets)	9th (Solberg/Mills)
	Ret (Burns/Reid)
AUSTRALIA	
Dis (Makinen/Mannisenmaki)	2nd (Burns/Reid)
Ret (Loix/Smeets)	Ret (Kankkunen/Repo)
	Ret (Solberg/Mills)
	Ret (Martin/Park)
BRITAIN	
3rd (Makinen/Mannisenmaki)	1st (Burns/Reid)
Ret (Loix/Smeets)	5th (Kankkunen/Repo)
	Ret (Solberg/Mills)

2001 RESULT

MONTE CARLO	
1st (Makinen/Mannisenmaki)	Ret (Burns/Reid)
6th (Loix/Smeets)	Ret (Martin/Park)
	Ret (Solberg/Mills)

WRC WORKS RALLY RECORD

MITSUBISHI	SUBARU

SWEDEN
2nd (Radstrom/Thorner)   6th (Solberg/Mills)
13th (Loix/Smeets)   12th (Martin/Park)
Ret (Makinen/Mannisenmaki)   16th (Burns/Reid)

PORTUGAL
1st (Makinen/Mannisenmaki)   4th (Burns/Reid)
Ret (Loix/Smeets)   Ret (Solberg/Mills)
    Ret (Martin/Park)
    Ret (Arai/MacNeall)

SPAIN (CATALUNYA)
3rd (Makinen/Mannisenmaki)   7th (Burns/Reid)
4th (Loix/Smeets)   Ret (Solberg/Mills)
    Ret (Martin/Park)

ARGENTINA
4th (Makinen/Mannisenmaki)   2nd (Burns/Reid)
6th (Loix/Smeets)   5th (Solberg/Mills)
    8th (Arai/MacNeall)

CYPRUS
5th (Loix/Smeets)   2nd (Burns/Reid)
Ret (Makinen/Mannisenmaki)   4th (Arai/MacNeall)
    Ret (Solberg/Mills)

GREECE (ACROPOLIS)
4th (Makinen/Mannisenmaki)   2nd (Solberg/Mills)
9th (Loix/Smeets)   Ret (Burns/Reid)
    Ret (Martin/Park)
    Ret (Arai/MacNeall)

WRX vs. EVO

MITSUBISHI	SUBARU

SAFARI
1st (Makinen/Mannisenmaki) Ret (Burns/Reid)
5th (Loix/Smeets) Ret (Solberg/Mills)
 Ret (Arai/MacNeall)

FINLAND
10th (Loix/Smeets) 2nd (Burns/Reid)
Ret (Makinen/Mannisenmaki) 5th (Martin/Park)
 7th (Solberg/Mills)

NEW ZEALAND
8th (Makinen/Mannisenmaki) 1st (Burns/Reid)
11th (Loix/Smeets) 7th (Martin/Park)
 14th (Arai/MacNeall)

SAN REMO
12th (Loix/Smeets) 9th (Solberg/Mills)
Ret (Makinen/Mannisenmaki) Ret (Burns/Reid)
 Ret (Martin/Park)
 Ret (Arai/MacNeall)

CORSICA
12th (Loix/Smeets) 4th (Burns/Reid)
Ret (Makinen/Mannisenmaki) 5th (Solberg/Mills)
 6th (Martin/Park)
 Ret (Arai/MacNeall)

AUSTRALIA
6th (Makinen/Hautunen) 2nd (Burns/Reid)
11th (Loix/Smeets) 7th (Solberg/Mills)
 Ret (Arai/MacNeall)

WRC WORKS RALLY RECORD

MITSUBISHI

SUBARU

BRITAIN (RAC)
Ret (Loix/Smeets)
Ret (Makinen/Lindstrom)

3rd (Burns/Reid)
10th (Arai/Sircombe)
Ret (Solberg/Mills)
Ret (Martin/Park)

2002 RESULT
MONTE CARLO
9th (Delecour/Grataloup)
14th (McRae/Senior)

1st (Makinen/Lindstrom)
6th (Solberg/Mills)

SWEDEN
5th (McRae/Senior)
14th (Paasonen/Kapanen)
34th (Delecour/Grataloup)

Ret (Makinen/Lindstrom)
Ret (Solberg/Mills)

CORSICA
7th (Delecour/Grataloup)
10th (McRae/Senior)

5th (Solberg/Mills)
Ret (Makinen/Lindstrom)

SPAIN (CATALUNYA)
9th (Delecour/Grataloup)
13th (McRae/Senior)

5th (Solberg/Mills)
Ret (Makinen/Lindstrom)

CYPRUS
13th (Delecour/Grataloup)
Ret (McRae/Senior)
Ret (Paasonen/Kapanen)

3rd (Makinen/Lindstrom)
5th (Solberg/Mills)

ARGENTINA
8th (McRae/Senior)
Ret (Delecour/Grataloup)

2nd (Solberg/Mills)
Ret (Makinen/Lindstrom)

WRX vs. EVO

MITSUBISHI	SUBARU
GREECE (ACROPOLIS)	
11th (Delecour/Grataloup)	5th (Solberg/Mills)
Ret (McRae/Senior)	13th (Arai/Sircombe)
	Ret (Makinen/Lindstrom)
SAFARI	
9th (McRae/Senior)	Ret (Makinen/Lindstrom)
Ret (Delecour/Grataloup)	Ret (Solberg/Mills)
FINLAND	
8th (Paasonen/Kapanen)	3rd (Solberg/Mills)
Ret (Delecour/Grataloup)	6th (Makinen/Lindstrom)
Ret (McRae/Senior)	
GERMANY	
9th (Delecour/Grataloup)	7th (Makinen/Lindstrom)
Ret (McRae/Senior)	Ret (Solberg/Mills)
	Ret (Arai/Sircombe)
	Ret (Mortl/Wicha)
SAN REMO	
10th (Delecour/Grataloup)	3rd (Solberg/Mills)
Ret (McRae/Senior)	Ret (Makinen/Lindstrom)
	Ret (Mortl/Wicha)
NEW ZEALAND	
9th (Delecour/Grataloup)	3rd (Makinen/Lindstrom)
Ret (McRae/Senior)	Ret (Solberg/Mills)
AUSTRALIA	
9th (Paasonen/Kapanen)	3rd (Solberg/Mills)
Ret (Delecour/Grataloup)	Dis (Makinen/Lindstrom)

WRC WORKS RALLY RECORD

MITSUBISHI | SUBARU

BRITAIN (RAC)
Ret (Delecour/Savignoni)　　1st (Solberg/Mills)
Ret (Dale/Bargery)　　4th (Makinen/Lindstrom)
Ret (Paasonen/Kapanen)

2003 RESULT
MONTE CARLO

　　Ret (Solberg/Mills)
　　Ret (Makinen/Lindstrom)

SWEDEN
12th (Sohlberg/Honkanen)　　2nd (Makinen/Lindstrom)
　　6th (Solberg/Mills)

TURKEY

　　8th (Makinen/Lindstrom)
　　Ret (Solberg/Mills)

NEW ZEALAND
6th (McRae/Senior)　　3rd (Solberg/Mills)
Ret (Sohlberg/Honkanen)　　7th (Makinen/Lindstrom)

ARGENTINA

　　5th (Solberg/Mills)
　　Ret (Makinen/Lindstrom)

GREECE (ACROPOLIS)

　　3rd (Solberg/Mills)
　　5th (Makinen/Lindstrom)

WRX vs. EVO

MITSUBISHI	SUBARU
CYPRUS	
	1st (Solberg/Mills)
	Ret (Makinen/Lindstrom)
GERMANY	
14th (Sohlberg/Honkanen)	8th (Solberg/Mills)
Ret (Pasonen/Kapanen)	Ret (Makinen/Lindstrom)
FINLAND	
	2nd (Solberg/Mills)
	6th (Makinen/Lindstrom)
AUSTRALIA	
	1st (Solberg/Mills)
	6th (Makinen/Lindstrom)
SAN REMO	
	10th (Makinen/Lindstrom)
	Ret (Solberg/Mills)
CORSICA	
	1st (Solberg/Mills)
	7th (Makinen/Lindstrom)
SPAIN (CATALUNYA)	
	5th (Solberg/Mills)
	8th (Makinen/Lindstrom)
BRITAIN (RAC)	
	1st (Solberg/Mills)
	3rd (Makinen/Lindstrom)

WRC WORKS RALLY RECORD

MITSUBISHI	SUBARU

2004 RESULT
MONTE CARLO
6th (Panizzi/Panizzi)   7th (Solberg/Mills)
Ret (Galli/D'Amore)   Ret (Hirvonen/Lehtinen)

SWEDEN
Ret (Panizzi/Panizzi)   3rd (Solberg/Mills)
Ret (Sohlberg/Lindstrom)   9th (Hirvonen/Lehtinen)

MEXICO
8th (Panizzi/Panizzi)   4th (Solberg/Mills)
Ret (Galli/D'Amore)   5th (Hirvonen/Lehtinen)

NEW ZEALAND
Ret (Panizzi/Panizzi)   1st (Solberg/Mills)
Ret (Sohlberg/Lindstrom)   7th (Hirvonen/Lehtinen)

CYPRUS
Ret (Panizzi/Panizzi)   4th (Solberg/Mills)
Ret (Sohlberg/Lindstrom)   5th (Hirvonen/Lehtinen)

GREECE (ACROPOLIS)
10th (Panizzi/Panizzi)   1st (Solberg/Mills)
Ret (Sola/Amigo)   Ret (Hirvonen/Lehtinen)

TURKEY
10th (Galli/D'Amore)   3rd (Solberg/Mills)
Ret (Panizzi/Panizzi)   6th (Hirvonen/Lehtinen)

ARGENTINA
7th (Panizzi/Panizzi)   4th (Hirvonen/Lehtinen)
Ret (Sohlberg/Lindstrom)   Ret (Solberg/Mills)

WRX vs. EVO

MITSUBISHI	SUBARU
FINLAND	
11th (Panizzi/Panizzi)	Ret (Solberg/Mills)
Ret (Sohlberg/Lindstrom)	Ret (Hirvonen/Lehtinen)
GERMANY	
Ret (Panizzi/Panizzi)	8th (Hirvonen/Lehtinen)
Ret (Sola/Amigo)	9th (Sarrazin/Pivato)
	Ret (Solberg/Mills)
JAPAN	
	1st (Solberg/Mills)
	7th (Hirvonen/Lehtinen)
BRITAIN (RAC)	
	1st (Solberg/Mills)
	7th (Hirvonen/Lehtinen)
SARDINIA	
	1st (Solberg/Mills)
	Ret (Hirvonen/Lehtinen)
CORSICA	
	5th (Solberg/Mills)
	6th (Sarrazin/Pivato)
	10th (Hirvonen/Lehtinen)
SPAIN (CATALUNYA)	
6th (Sola/Amigo)	4th (Sarrazin/Pivato)
7th (Galli/D'Amore)	5th (Solberg/Mills)
12th (Panizzi/Panizzi)	8th (Hirvonen/Lehtinen)

WRC WORKS RALLY RECORD

MITSUBISHI	**SUBARU**

AUSTRALIA

    4th (Hirvonen/Lehtinen)
    Ret (Solberg/Mills)

2005 RESULT
MONTE CARLO
3rd (Panizzi/Panizzi)   14th (Sarrazin/Giraudet)
7th (Rovanpera/Pietlainen)   Ret (Solberg/Mills)

SWEDEN
4th (Rovanpera/Pietlainen)   1st (Solberg/Mills)
7th (Galli/D'Amore)   13th (Sarrazin/Giraudet)
     19th (Atkinson/MacNeall)

MEXICO
5th (Rovanpera/Pietlainen)   1st (Solberg/Mills)
8th (Panizzi/Panizzi)   Ret (Atkinson/MacNeall)

NEW ZEALAND
8th (Galli/D'Amore)   3rd (Solberg/Mills)
Ret (Rovanpera/Pietlainen)   7th (Atkinson/MacNeall)

SARDINIA
Ret (Galli/D'Amore)   2nd (Solberg/Mills)
Ret (Rovanpera/Pietlainen)   12th (Sarrazin/Giraudet)
     18th (Atkinson/MacNeall)

CYPRUS
7th (Rovanpera/Pietlainen)   10th (Atkinson/MacNeall)
11th (Panizzi/Panizzi)   Ret (Solberg/Mills)

WRX vs. EVO

MITSUBISHI	SUBARU

TURKEY
8th (Galli/D'Amore)
10th (Rovanpera/Pietlainen)

2nd (Solberg/Mills)
24th (Atkinson/MacNeall)

GREECE (ACROPOLIS)
6th (Rovanpera/Pietlainen)
7th (Galli/D'Amore)

9th (Solberg/Mills)
13th (Sarrazin/Giraudet)
Ret (Atkinson/MacNeall)

ARGENTINA
5th (Rovanpera/Pietlainen)
Ret (Galli/D'Amore)

3rd (Solberg/Mills)
9th (Atkinson/MacNeall)

FINLAND
7th (Rovanpera/Pietlainen)
Ret (Galli/D'Amore)

4th (Solberg/Mills)
Ret (Atkinson/MacNeall)

GERMANY
5th (Galli/D'Amore)
10th (Rovanpera/Pietlainen)

7th (Solberg/Mills)
8th (Sarrazin/Giraudet)
11th (Atkinson/MacNeall)

BRITAIN
4th (Rovanpera/Pietlainen)
13th (Galli/D'Amore)

BRITAIN
1st (Solberg/Mills)
38th (Atkinson/MacNeall)
Ret (Sarrazin/Giraudet)

JAPAN
5th (Rovanpera/Pietlainen)
11th (Panizzi/Panizzi)
Ret (Galli/D'Amore)

3rd (Atkinson/MacNeall)
Ret (Solberg/Mills)

WRC WORKS RALLY RECORD

### MITSUBISHI	SUBARU

CORSICA
9th (Galli/D'Amore)
10th (Rovanpera/Pietlainen)
Ret (Panizzi/Panizzi)

3rd (Solberg/Mills)
4th (Sarrazin/Giraudet)
Ret (Atkinson/MacNeall)

SPAIN (CATALUNYA)
10th (Rovanpera/Pietlainen)
Ret (Galli/D'Amore)

9th (Atkinson/MacNeall)
13th (Solberg/Mills)
Ret (Sarrazin/Giraudet)

AUSTRALIA
2nd (Rovanpera/Pietlainen)
5th (Galli/D'Amore)

4th (Atkinson/MacNeall)
Ret (Solberg/Mills)

2006 RESULT
MONTE CARLO

5th (Sarrazin/Prevot)
6th (Atkinson/MacNeall)
Ret (Solberg/Mills)

SWEDEN

11th (Atkinson/MacNeall)
Ret (Solberg/Mills)

MEXICO

2nd (Solberg/Mills)
Ret (Atkinson/MacNeall)

SPAIN (CATALUNYA)

7th (Solberg/Mills)
8th (Sarrazin/Prevot)
11th (Atkinson/MacNeall)

WRX vs. EVO

SUBARU

CORSICA

    7th (Solberg/Mills)
    11th (Sarrazin/Prevot)
    13th (Atkinson/MacNeall)

ARGENTINA

    2nd (Solberg/Mills)
    6th (Atkinson/MacNeall)

SARDINIA

    10th (Atkinson/MacNeall)
    Ret (Solberg/Mills)

GREECE (ACROPOLIS)

    7th (Solberg/Mills)
    11th (Atkinson/MacNeall)

GERMANY

    8th (Atkinson/MacNeall)
    Ret (Solberg/Mills)
    Ret (Sarrazin/Prevot)

FINLAND

    11th (Atkinson/MacNeall)
    Ret (Solberg/Mills)

JAPAN

    4th (Atkinson/MacNeall)
    6th (Arai/Sircombe)
    7th (Solberg/Mills)

WRC WORKS RALLY RECORD

SUBARU

CYPRUS
    8th (Solberg/Mills)
    9th (Atkinson/MacNeall)

TURKEY
    6th (Atkinson/MacNeall)
    Ret (Solberg/Mills)

AUSTRALIA
    2nd (Solberg/Mills)
    Ret (Atkinson/MacNeall)

NEW ZEALAND
    6th (Solberg/Mills)
    Ret (Atkinson/MacNeall)

BRITAIN
    3rd (Solberg/Mills)
    6th (Atkinson/MacNeall)

2007 RESULT

MONTE CARLO
    4th (Atkinson/MacNeall)
    6th (Solberg/Mills)

SWEDEN
    8th (Atkinson/MacNeall)
    Ret (Solberg/Mills)

NORWAY
    4th (Solberg/Mills)
    19th (Atkinson/MacNeall)

WRX vs. EVO

SUBARU

MEXICO

    5th (Atkinson/MacNeall)
    Ret (Solberg/Mills)

PORTUGAL

    4th (Solberg/Mills)
    Ret (Atkinson/MacNeall)

ARGENTINA

    7th (Atkinson/Prevot)
    Ret (Solberg/Mills)

SARDINIA

    5th (Solberg/Mills)
    11th (Atkinson/Prevot)

GREECE (ACROPOLIS)

    3rd (Solberg/Mills)
    6th (Atkinson/Prevot)

FINLAND

    4th (Atkinson/Prevot)
    6th (Pons/Amigo)
    Ret (Solberg/Mills)

GERMANY

    6th (Solberg/Mills)
    Ret (Atkinson/Prevot)
    Ret (Pons/Amigo)

WRC WORKS RALLY RECORD

SUBARU

NEW ZEALAND

    4th (Atkinson/Prevot)
    7th (Solberg/Mills)
    Ret (Pons/Amigo)

SPAIN (CATALUNYA)

    6th (Solberg/Mills)
    8th (Atkinson/Prevot)
    9th (Pons/Amigo)

CORSICA

    5th (Solberg/Mills)
    6th (Atkinson/Prevot)
    8th (Pons/Amigo)

JAPAN

    Ret (Solberg/Mills)
    Ret (Atkinson/Prevot)
    Ret (Pons/Amigo)

IRELAND

    5th (Solberg/Mills)
    Ret (Atkinson/Prevot)
    Ret (Pons/Amigo)

BRITAIN

    4th (Solberg/Mills)
    6th (Atkinson/Prevot)
    9th (Pons/Amigo)

WRX vs. EVO

SUBARU

2008 RESULT
MONTE CARLO

                                      3rd (Atkinson/Prevot)
                                      5th (Solberg/Mills)

SWEDEN

                                        4th (Solberg/Mills)
                                        21st (Atkinson/Prevot)

MEXICO

                                        2nd (Atkinson/Prevot)
                                        Ret (Solberg/Mills)

ARGENTINA

                                        2nd (Atkinson/Prevot)
                                        Ret (Solberg/Mills)

JORDAN

                                        3rd (Atkinson/Prevot)
                                        Ret (Solberg/Mills)

SARDINIA

                                        6th (Atkinson/Prevot)
                                        10th (Solberg/Mills)

GREECE (ACROPOLIS)

                                        2nd (Solberg/Mills)
                                        Ret (Atkinson/Prevot)

TURKEY

                                        6th (Solberg/Mills)
                                        Ret (Atkinson/Prevot)

WRC WORKS RALLY RECORD

SUBARU

FINLAND

    3rd (Atkinson/Prevot)
    6th (Solberg/Mills)

GERMANY

    5th (Solberg/Mills)
    6th (Atkinson/Prevot)

NEW ZEALAND

    4th (Solberg/Mills)
    Ret (Atkinson/Prevot)

SPAIN (CATALUNYA)

    5th (Solberg/Mills)
    7th (Atkinson/Prevot)
    10th (Tirabassi/Gordon)

CORSICA

    5th (Solberg/Mills)
    6th (Atkinson/Prevot)
    Ret (Tirabassi/Gordon)

JAPAN

    4th (Atkinson/Prevot)
    8th (Solberg/Mills)

BRITAIN

    4th (Solberg/Mills)
    Ret (Atkinson/Prevot)

APPENDIX B

SPECIAL EDITION CARS

The Lancer Evolution and Subaru WRX/STi are not unique among performance cars in spawning special edition versions, but the sheer quantity produced over the years is mind-boggling. Some are mere trim packages, others are commemorative editions and a few are more specialized performance variants. Many comprise specific and unique upgrades, including more powerful engines, sporting suspension packages, and bigger brakes, resulting in some very interesting combinations. Thanks to limited production numbers, today many of these cars are highly desired by enthusiasts and collectors alike. Here we've detailed nearly every significant special edition Lancer Evolution and WRX/STi built between 1992 and 2007.

MITSUBISHI
2000 LANCER EVOLUTION VI TOMMI MAKINEN EDITION (JAPAN/UK & EUROPE)

Perhaps the most desirable of all Evolutions from a collector's standpoint, the Tommi Makinen Edition was built to celebrate the Flying Finn's four World Rally Championship driver's titles between

WRX vs. EVO

2000 Evo VI Tommi Makinen edition. Mitsubishi Japan

1996 and 1999. First revealed at the Tokyo Motor Show in September 1999, Japanese domestic market deliveries began on January 8, 2000. In Japan, the TM Edition was offered in both GSR and RS trim. It came with standard 17-inch Enkei alloy wheels painted in white. Although many GSR cars were painted Passion Red with commemorative graphics, this car was also available in other colors, including Scotia White, Pyrenees Black, Satellite Silver, and Canal Blue. In many respects the TM Edition is a hybrid car, leading some enthusiasts to dub it an Evo VI 1/2. This is mainly due to a revised front air dam, different suspension settings and a lower ride height, and on the GSR version, an updated turbocharger (TD05-15GK2) with lighter blades designed to promote quicker spool up, plus a less restrictive exhaust. The standard Evo VI used a twin-scroll TD05-GD16, shared with the V, though this was fitted to the RS version of the TM edition and a few GSR versions were also installed with it. Although most TM edition cars were sold in Japan, a total of 1,156 were built for export, with both right- and left-hand drive. The most numerous of these were the 295 cars built for Germany and 200 for Sweden. The TM was not officially sold in North America.

2001 LANCER EVOLUTION EXTREME (UK)

Unveiled at the 2001 Autosport International Show, the eXtreme was a tweaked version of the standard, UK-spec 280 hp Evolution VI. The most notable upgrades centered around the 4G63 engine. Revised calibrations resulted in 340 hp and 303 lb-ft of torque, though the power band was similar in shape to the regular Evo, with max power coming in at 6500 rpm and peak torque at 3000 revs. To cope with the extra power and torque, new engine mounts were installed and a front strut tower brace was fitted to reduce torsional twisting under hard throttle. Suspension changes comprised of stronger front and rear sway bar links, special bushings, slightly lower ride height, and massive P225/40ZR18 tires mounted on 18 x 8-inch wheels (regular Evos sported 17s at the time). Different rocker panel extensions, an aluminum hood and front fenders, plus a carbon type rear deck spoiler, stainless exhaust covers, and special "eXtreme" badging were included. To keep the driver and front passenger in place, four-point harnesses were offered. The eXtreme could scoot from 0-60 mph in around four seconds flat. Priced at £41,995 the eXtreme cost a staggering £11,000 more than a regular Evo VI in the UK, but as an all-out performance car, it had few peers at the time of its introduction. Even today, mention of its name still sends shivers down the spines of many died-in-wool Evo enthusiasts.

2002 LANCER EVOLUTION VII FQ 300 (UK)

This was the first of the UK-spec 'super' Evolutions, based on the Cedia chassis VII and 'enhanced' by Mitsubishi's UK Ralliart arm at its facilities in Bristol in the west of England. Its engine was tuned to deliver an extra 29 hp (resulting in 305 brake horsepower) and a monster 321 lb-ft of torque. Boasting a special performance T304 stainless exhaust system, plus real carbon fiber interior panels, the FQ 300 was conceived to combat the sales of unofficial Japanese "gray" imports into Britain. Without the speed limiter fitted to Japanese cars, the FQ 300 was capable of reaching almost 170 mph.

2004 LANCER EVOLUTION VIII FQ 300/FQ 330/FQ340 (UK)

After the Evo VII-based FQ 300, Mitsubishi UK decided to release some more tuned special edition variants on the British market based on the VIII. These included an updated FQ 300 and alongside it the FQ 330, named for its horsepower rating. Featuring a new, specifically tuned ECU and a revised turbocharger, the FQ 330 could sprint from 0-60 mph in less than 4.5 seconds. Special Alcantara seats were fitted as standard. Ralliart UK offered a kit to upgrade the FQ300 to 330 specs at around £1500. Several months later, the FQ330 was supplanted by the even more powerful FQ 340. If you were looking for perhaps the ultimate hooligan car bar none in the U.K. in 2004, the 160 mph-plus FQ 330/340 was probably it.

2005 LANCER EVOLUTION VIII FQ 320/FQ400 (UK)

In Britain, the Mitsubishi Ralliart UK-prepped FQ 300 returned for 2005, but soon gave way to the slightly more powerful (and more expensive) FQ 320. But all eyes were on the FQ 400. So named because of its 405 brake horsepower rating, this 3,200 lb four-door was a complete and utter monster. It was conceived as a flagship special to celebrate 30 years of Mitsubishi in the UK; it could eat supercars and many sports motorcycles for breakfast. It did cost almost £50,000, (approximately $90,000 USD) but for the money it was perhaps the best all-around performance car ever built, not to mention the fastest-ever Mitsubishi. And yet, for all its hypercar performance, the FQ 400 was surprisingly civilized for daily driving duties.

2006 LANCER EVOLUTION IX
FQ 300/FQ 320/FQ 340/FQ 360 (UK)

Based on the updated Evolution IX, these cars followed in the same mode as their predecessors. The FQ 360, launched on July 15, 2006 in the UK at the London Motor Show, was another serious beast. Using similar hop up tricks to the previous VIII-based FQ400, it featured a 4G63 engine tuned to deliver 366 bhp and 363 lb ft of torque via a high-pressure fuel pump, high-flow catalytic converter, and specific engine mapping. Driveability was improved over the FQ400, the peak torque coming at a lower 3200 rpm. This actually made it even quicker to accelerate to 60 mph (a test car was reported to do it in an astounding 4.1 seconds!). Outwardly, the FQ 360 was distinguished by a carbon fiber front lip spoiler, a carbon fiber rear

SPECIAL EDITION CARS

vortex generator mounted on the roof just above the back window, and a set of special Speedline 17-inch alloy wheels that mimicked those found on the tarmac-spec rally cars. These rims were exclusive to the FQ 360 and not available as an aftermarket fitment. The Evolution IX FQ 360 stickered at £35,504 in Great Britain, (roughly $65,000 US), which was still a bargain, considering it could show Porsches, Ferraris, and Lamborghinis its taillights.

2008 LANCER EVOLUTION X FQ 360 (UK)

When the Evolution X was launched in the UK, it was only a matter of time before another ultimate screamer was released. Developed by HKS, the latest FQ 360 was again massaged with specific ECU calibrations and a performance exhaust. Because of the immense power and torque, it came with the IX's old five-speed manual gearbox (the six-speed twin clutch was deemed not strong enough to handle the 363 lb-ft of torque). In the acceleration stakes it was actually slightly quicker than the old Cedia-based car, though nanny laws had finally caught up and the car was electronically limited to 155 mph. Retail price on this beast was £36,499, only slightly more than its predecessor.

SUBARU
1995 SUBARU IMPREZA 2000 TURBO SERIES MCRAE (UK)

Built by Prodrive as a UK-market special to commemorate Colin McRae's win in the 2004 RAC Rally, the Series McRae went on sale midway through 1995. It was based on the British 2000 Turbo, but featured a specifically calibrated ECU, revised exhaust, and a cold air intake kit, delivering a total of 240 bhp (DIN). It also got a revised suspension, with specific spring and shock rates, and featured lightweight Speedline wheels (finished in gold) and Pirelli PZero tires. All series McRae cars were finished in Dark Blue Mica – paying homage to Colin's winning WRC machine– and came fully loaded, with Recaro seats and special interior trim mings. Price was a fairly steep (for the time) £28,300 and just 200 examples were built.

WRX vs. EVO

1996 SUBARU IMPREZA V-LIMITED (JAPAN)

Built to celebrate Subaru's World Rally Championship victories in 1995, the V-Limited was powered by a 260 horsepower version of the turbocharged and intercooled EJ20 engine. It also came in two guises, one based on the WRX, the other on the STi Type RA. The former was limited to a production run of 1,000 cars, with each car serialed via a special plaque. This version also had five-spoke, gold painted STi alloy wheels, standard ABS brakes, special green tinted glass, and a commemorative World Rally Champion appliqué on the trunklid and special embroidering on the seat backs. It was offered in Sports Blue, Feather White, or Black Mica exterior shades. The STi Version II RA took things a few steps further. To begin with, it only came in Sports Blue and production was fittingly limited to 555 units, to correspond with the team's 555 sponsorship. Each car had a special numbered plaque, featured the special World Champion emblem on the decklid and the signatures of Colin McRae and Derek Ringer on the front seatbacks, in addition to the STi logo. Interestingly, the V-Limited STi RA also sported standard air conditioning, an option not offered on "regular" RA models.

1996 IMPREZA WRX RALLYE (AUSTRALIA)

In the spring of 1996, a special edition WRX "Rallye" was released on the Australian market. Mechanically it was identical to the regular Rex but featured special dark solid blue paint, gold finished alloy wheels, and special badging. It was quite rare in that only 120 examples were built.

1997 SUBARU IMPREZA STi V-LIMITED (JAPAN)

In January 1997, another special edition Impreza WRX made its debut in Japan – the STi Version III V-Limited. Like its predecessor, this one featured special Sports Blue paint, gold wheels, standard roof vent, special embroidery on the seats, and a victory emblem on the tail. As before, production was strictly limited to 555 sedans and the same number of wagons.

SPECIAL EDITION CARS

1997 SUBARU IMPREZA WRX CATALUNYA (UK)

This was essentially a British market 2000 Turbo with special Mica Black paint and gold accents, gold wheels, and unique interior trim with specially embroidered seats, floor mats, and carbon fiber inserts for the dash. Plus it came with standard A/C (it was optional on the regular turbo). It went on sale in the UK in March 1997 and just 200 were built.

1997 SUBARU IMPREZA WRX CLUB SPEC EVO (AUSTRALIA)

Because STI models were not available in Australia at this time, in a shrewd marketing move Subaru's local operation decided to release the WRX Club Spec Evo. It was mechanically virtually the same as a regular Rex, but came exclusively with the five-speed manual gearbox. It also featured special Sports Blue paint, unique gold wheels and special "Club Spec" logos.

1998 SUBARU PRODRIVE IMPREZA WR (UK)

At the 1997 British Motor Show in Earls Court, London, Prodrive unveiled a very exclusive Impreza. The WR Sport was an expensive proposition, costing some £7,000 more than the standard Turbo, but it did add some quality upgrades, in particular tweaks to both the engine and suspension. With 240 bhp (DIN) on tap, the WR gave out all the right signals, but despite being lighter, it was actually judged slower in many performance tests. And, with bigger wheels and tires (17-inchers), along with more competition-oriented suspension settings, it delivered a fairly bone shaking ride on the street; this, along with the asking price, meant that the car's appeal was limited.

1998 SUBARU IMPREZA WRX CLUB SPEC EVO 2 (AUSTRALIA)

In 1998, the Aussies got the Club Spec Evo 2. Finished in special in Blue Mica with gold wheels, it paid homage to the SWRT '555' rally cars and also came with special outside ID badging and interior touches. Only 230 were built.

WRX vs. EVO

1998 SUBARU IMPREZA STi 22B
(JAPAN/UNITED KINGDOM)

At the 1997 Tokyo Motor Show, Subaru displayed a muscular, rally inspired concept based on the Retna two-door. Dubbed WRCar-STi, it proved to be a trial balloon for the monstrous STi 22B, which was unveiled a few months later, in March 1998.

Although it appeared to be the next evolution of the STi homologation special and looked very much like the WRC rally cars, the STi 22B was actually powered by a new, bigger EJ22 boxer engine, so it didn't qualify under WRC rules (because the rally cars used modified EJ20 engines).

Still, as a high-performance tour de force, the STi 22B was and still is one of the most prized performance Imprezas ever built. Under the hood, the larger-displacement engine was created using a bigger 96.9mm bore, though stroke was unchanged. A closed-deck cylinder block was employed, as were high-strength forged alloy pistons on an 8.0:1 squeeze. The alloy cylinder heads incorporated metal head gaskets and sodium-filled valves to maximizing sealing ability, combustion, and power delivery. Like 'regular' 1997 STis, the STi 22B engine incorporated a water spray system for the intercooler to further cool the intake charge. An IHI RH5H turbocharger, very similar to that used on 1996 and 1997 regular STi models, was fitted.

Despite the large displacement, the EJ22 was rated at the same 280 bhp as its cousin, as per Japanese requirements. However, there was no denying the extra torque – some 267 lb/ft of it at just 3200 rpm. Coupled with a version of the STi Type RA's close-ratio five-speed manual gearbox but utilizing stronger gears, the STi 22B was an exceedingly quick car on the street, with the wallop of mid-range torque allowing it to scoot to 60 mph in just 4.3 seconds.

The car also featured major suspension changes, including the use of special Eibach springs, specially designed premium Bilstein inverted shocks, stamped aluminum control arms, along with stronger bushings and rose joints on both the front and rear sway bar links. The suspension changes actually increased the car's track by some 0.39-inches up front and 1.57-inches in the rear. Special gold-painted 17 x 8.5 inch BBS spoke rims were fitted, shod in premium P235/40ZR17 Pirelli P-Zero tires. In terms of cornering, the STi 22B was exceedingly impressive, delivering unparalleled amounts of grip and able to routinely pull more than .92 lateral g during skidpad testing. With huge vented disc brakes at all four corners (11.6-in front, 11.4-in, rear) respectively, the STi 22B stopped pretty well too.

Unique front and rear spoilers, bulging fenders, and Sonic Blue Mica paint rounded out the exterior touches. Inside was a special Nardi steering wheel with red stitching, special blue and black trim on the door panels and seats, plus a special plaque on the center console. Even though it came with power windows and air conditioning, a radio wasn't available on the STi 22B, not even as an option. Just 400 cars were built for Japanese domestic market consumption, plus another 25 for export, 16 of which went to the UK as 'official' imports.

1998 SUBARU IMPREZA TURBO TERZO (UK)

Launched hot on the heels of the UK-spec STi 22B, the Terzo was a limited edition Impreza 2000 Turbo that sported its own special "Terzo" Mica blue paint, gold 16-inch five-spoke alloy wheels, and special logos. It came with a whole host of standard equipment, including power locks, windows, and standard anti-theft system – the last an important one, as car theft was reaching epidemic proportions in the UK at the time, pushing insurance rates for cars like this through the roof.

1998 SUBARU IMPREZA WRX TYPE RA/STi V-LIMITED (JAPAN)

At the end of November 1998, Subaru released three special WRX/STi models in Japan, all of them V-Limited models, finished in Sonic Blue Mica, with gold 16-inch wheels. The two sedans, (RA WRX Limited and RA STi Limited) and one coupe (Type R STi Limited) were allocated a production run of just 1,000 units each. They came fully loaded, with standard air conditioning, power windows, locks, and mirrors, and the sedans featured special blue front bucket seats, with special STi and Subaru logos embroidered into the backs. The coupe had somewhat less garish front chairs (in a darker shade of blue) with red inserts.

1999 SUBARU IMPREZA WRX/STi V-LIMITED (JAPAN)

Subaru and Prodrive released a brace of special cars in the latter half of 1999. Four more V-Limited models debuted: three STi Version VI cars and a single WRX Type RA. The STi Version VI cars comprised a coupe, sedan, and wagon. Each came with special Blue Mica paint, blue inserts for the dash and seats, along with a special blue center console, drilled aluminum foot pedals, special ID badging, and a premium convenience package that included standard power locks, windows, and mirrors, along with automatic climate control. The STi coupe featured a WRC-inspired roof vent and aluminum shift knob, while the STi Type RA sedan also got a unique bi-level rear wing and a helical limited-slip front differential.

The WRX Type RA Version featured similar styling touches to its STi counterparts, including the same Mica Blue Paint, 17-inch wheels and tires, and interior upgrades, along with standard ABS brakes and a unique rear spoiler, though it did without the pink grille emblem of the STi cars

The STi Version VI Limited wagon featured similar upgrades to the sedans and coupe, including an interior with blue inserts on the dash, seats, and console, plus the drilled pedals and billet shifter and a premium Kenwood CD sound system. It was the rarest of the group, with just 500 units produced (the STi sedan sold 2,000 copies, and the STi coupe and WRX Type RA version sold 1,000 units each).

1999 SUBARU WRX CLASSIC (AUSTRALIA)

Another "down under" special edition car, this featured special white alloy wheels and came in a choice of Green, Dark Blue, or Black Mica exterior colors. It also featured a very tasteful tan interior with leather-trimmed seats, steering wheel, and shift knob. It was a fully loaded car, coming with standard power locks, windows, air conditioning, plus a premium sound system with CD player and theft immobilizer. Available with either the five-speed manual or four-speed automatic, just 150 were made.

1999 SUBARU WRX CLUB SPEC EVO 3 (AUSTRALIA)

A third Club Spec model was released in Australia, almost at the same time as the WRX classic. Unlike that car, however, it came with the five-speed gearbox only, different alloy wheels (with gold finish), and a special shade of paint called Blue Steel Mica. A remote locking system was fitted as standard and like the Classic, just 150 units were allocated. The car was about a grand cheaper than the Classic in Australia, selling for $41,690 (Aus) versus $42,990 (Aus).

1999 SUBARU IMPREZA TURBO RB5 (UK)

Prodrive introduced two more special edition Imprezas during the course of 1999. The RB5 (the initials in honor of Richard Burns, then driving for SWRT again), came with special Blue Steel exterior paint (it was actually closer to gray) and color-coordinated Alcantara interior trim, along with a STi spec rear deck spoiler and massive rally style foglights (hidden behind covers with special RB5 logos on them), 17-inch Speedline Alloy wheels, and matching ultra low profile Pirelli PZero tires. Although the standard RB5 was mechanically the same as the regular 2000 Turbo, Prodrive offered two tuning upgrades for the car, one delivering 237 bhp, the other an astounding 250 horsepower. With almost 260 lb-ft of torque, the tuned RB5s were rockets, capable of reaching 60 mph in around 5.2 seconds. Thanks to a short throw shifter and stiffened chassis, the RB5 was incredibly fun to chuck about through the corners. Just 444 RB5 models were built.

1999 SUBARU IMPREZA P1 (UK)

Perhaps the ultimate expression of the GC chassis car was the P1, which like the STi 22B used the Retna two-door coupe body. Launched at the 1999 London Motor Show at Earl's Court, London, it had unique body features including a front air dam with a special front chin spoiler and brake cooling ducts, along with tiny Hella driving lights. The whole body was color-coded in Sonic Blue Mica, and that included the rocker panel extensions, door handles, and mirrors. Wheels were unique, gunmetal-finished 17 x 7-inch O.Z. alloys. Unlike the 22B, however, the P1 used an EJ20 engine for propulsion, though it featured a special high-flow exhaust with a single, instead of dual catalytic converters and a specifically programmed ECU. Rated at 277 bhp and 253 lb-ft of torque, the latter in at 4000 rpm, the P1 was a very tractable car, and could scurry to 60 mph in around 4.7 seconds and through the quarter mile in under 14. The P1 also received an STi-derived five-speed manual gearbox with a short throw shifter, massive disc brakes, and specific suspension settings, including WRX rear springs and firmer shock settings. For all its grandstanding performance the P1 was actually very civilized inside, with good use of sound deadening, power everything, standard air conditioning, and tinted glass. Available upgrades included massive Alcon disc brakes (with 18-inch wheels and tires – necessary to clear the big anchors), Recaro front bucket seats, and an even larger bore exhaust system. Entry price for the P1 was a fairly hefty £31,495 (before options), and just 1,000 examples were built.

2000 SUBARU WRX SPECIAL EDITION (AUSTRALIA)

Launched just two days before the end of 1999, this was essentially an update of the WRX Classic, with much the same exterior and interior trim features, but otherwise identical to the standard Australian spec Rex. Like the Classic, the SE was very limited in production, with just 120 built.

2000 SUBARU WRX CLUB SPEC EVO 4 (AUSTRALIA)

The last of the special edition GC chassis cars destined for Australia, the Club Spec Evo 4 parted from previous versions by being offered in shocking Yellow paintwork, with contrasting black 16-inch alloy wheels, rocker panels, and rear bumper extension. Inside, it got a

SPECIAL EDITION CARS

STi-style dash, upgraded sound system, special yellow seat trim and a limited edition plaque. Only 300 examples were built.

2001 SUBARU IMPREZA WRX PRODRIVE UK 300 (UK)

A joint venture between Prodrive and Subaru's UK dealer network, this car featured WRC-style headlights, clear front marker lights, a prominent rear spoiler, and special Prodrive and 'UK 300' logos. Paying homage to the SWRT rally cars, it came exclusively in World Rally Blue Mica, with contrasting gold 18-inch wheels and 225-section Pirelli PZero tires. There were special blue interior trim inserts on the seats and door panels, plus buyers had the option of the Prodrive Performance pack, which added a more aggressive engine tune, less restrictive exhaust, and revised intercooler ducting. With it, the EJ20 engine was rated at 245 bhp and 261 lb-ft of torque, mandating premium-grade fuel.

2000 SUBARU STi S201 (JAPAN)

With a body kit that resembled something out of a Manga cartoon, thanks to a very prominent air dam, aggressive rear fascia, and huge deck spoiler, the S201 boasted a plethora of mechanical upgrades to

2000 Subaru Impreza STi S201. Subaru Global

match the wild styling. Three hundred metric horsepower came thanks to a STi-spec engine control module, larger intercooler, and bigger bore exhaust system. There were also suspension improvements, special gold-finished 16-inch RS-Zero alloy wheels and tires, and a helical limited slip diff up front. All S201s were finished in Artic Silver with contrasting blue interiors, trimmed much like those on the V-Limited cars. The S201 went on sale on April 3, 2000 in Japan.

2001 SUBARU IMPREZA STi PRODRIVE STYLE (JAPAN)

At the 2001 Tokyo Auto Salon, which took place in January, Subaru unveiled the Impreza STi Prodrive Style. In essence, this was a single prototype built in collaboration between the two concerns, finished in the traditional color of World Rally Blue Mica with contrasting gold wheels and massive 'STi Prodrive' graphics carried on the flanks. Most of the changes between this and the regular STi were cosmetic, such as the aero extensions, rear spoiler, bumper covers, and rocker panel skirts, plus O.Z. Rally car-style 18-inch wheels, along with a roof vent and a special interior that housed unique bucket seats and an instrument cluster with blue-faced gauges, very much in the Volkswagen idom. A production version, somewhat more subdued, arrived on September 12, 2001, available in the colors of World Rally Blue Mica or traditional Pure White.

2001 SUBARU IMPREZA STi TYPE RA SPEC C (JAPAN)

A special lightweight version of the STi RA, the Spec C was conceived as a limited production, track-ready monster. It used a thinner roof panel and decklid, less sound deadening, came without air conditioning, power locks, or airbags, and featured special lightweight front seats. The engine was a very special version of the EJ20 that borrowed parts from the old STi 22B mill and was specially tuned to deliver 280 hp and 283 lb-ft of torque. It also featured mechanically operated center and rear differentials with a driver control function and a competition-style suspension with lowering springs and specified 16-inch wheels and tires. It was a hard-riding, virtually no-compromise

SPECIAL EDITION CARS

machine, but highly desirable among hardcore enthusiasts. Every Spec C was built specifically to order.

2002 SUBARU IMPREZA PRODRIVE STi (JAPAN)

Launched at the same time as the regular STi on the British market, this was a special edition car that boasted a few cosmetic alterations, including different aero extensions and a revised front air dam, plus a choice of just blue or black exterior paint and an instrument cluster with blue dials and red needles (the gauges had black faces with white lettering and needles on the standard STi). Just 750 were built.

2002 SUBARU IMPREZA WRX CLUB SPEC EVO 5 (AUSTRALIA)

After a one-year hiatus, a new Club Spec model made its debut in Australia in the spring of 2002. This one, the Club Spec Evo 5, featured orange exterior paint, silver alloy wheels, special badging on the rear doors and decklid, a factory sunroof, a premium sound system, and a special limited edition dash plaque. Just 140 examples were made available to Australian buyers, including approximately 60 wagons. As with previous Club Spec editions, these cars came exclusively with five-speed manual gearboxes.

2002 SUBARU IMPREZA STi S202 (JAPAN)

Based on the WRX STI Type RA Spec C, the S202 was launched on May 7, 2002. It was a very special car, with a highly tuned EJ20 engine that included silicone intake ducting, an ultra high-performance exhaust (which used titanium), and a lightweight aluminum oil cooler. The result was an incredible 320 hp and 283 lb-ft of torque, and a car with lightning-quick acceleration and razor-sharp reflexes. Other high-performance touches included special rear suspension links, lightweight brakes, upgraded brake hoses, and forged 17-inch RAYS alloy wheels with a gold finish. Other exterior elements included a carbon fiber rear deck spoiler, front foglight covers, and projector headlights. Yet for all the lightweight kit, the S202 was a well-equipped car, with standard air conditioning, special interior trim (including aluminum foot pedals) and a limited edition plaque on the center console. Available in Astral Yellow, Pure White, Midnight Black, or World Rally Blue Mica, just 400 were built and they quickly sold out.

2003 SUBARU IMPREZA STi TYPE RA SPEC C (JAPAN)

A hardcore performance variant, the 2003 Spec C was offered in two different configurations, one with big Brembo brakes and 17-inch wheels and tires and another, cheaper model that ran on 16-inch steel wheels and featured smaller anchors. Although mechanically it was very similar to the standard STi, including the 280 hp, 290 lb-ft EJ20 engine, it did feature a different turbocharger and the power curve was a slightly different. This version of the Spec C employed a driver controlled center differential with a fully automatic mode, as well as mechanical front and rear units. The cheapest Spec C was almost 300 lbs lighter than a regular STi and thus the car of choice for serious track or rally enthusiasts.

2003 SUBARU IMPREZA WRX CLUB SPEC EVO 6 (AUSTRALIA)

Launched in the spring of 2003, this as before was based on the regular Australian spec WRX. Available in Graphite Black, Premium Silver, or World Rally Blue Mica, it featured special ID badging on the rear doors and trunk lid. A factory fitted, electrically operated sunroof was standard, as was leather interior trim and side airbags. Only 200 examples were built.

2003 SUBARU IMPREZA WRX/STi V-LIMITED (JAPAN)

Fittingly, after Petter Solberg won the 2003 WRC Driver's championship Subaru released another round of Impreza V-Limiteds, one based on the standard WRX and the other on the STi. These were finished in WR Blue Mica with gold painted wheels and special V-Limited badges, including dash and rear trunk plaques. The WRX

SPECIAL EDITION CARS

featured STi-style exterior pieces, front fascia, skirts, and rear spoiler, while the STi version was appropriately given a production run of 555 units. The most important thing about these cars was the chassis and suspension tuning, which received the personal blessing of legendary Subaru WRC driver Toshihiro Arai.

2004 SUBARU IMPREZA WRX C1 (JAPAN)

Along with the new batch of V-Limited cars released at the end of 2003, Subaru added fuel to the fire by revealing a concept Impreza STi called the Asterope at the 2004 Tokyo Auto Salon, early in the year. This wide-body special morphed into the WRX C1 Wide Body Package released a few months later, which added special flared fenders both front and back, a restyled front fascia and rear bumper, plus revised rear door skins and new rocker panel extensions. The package, at ¥1,100,000, wasn't cheap, but it was distinctive. C1-equipped cars came with standard 18-inch dark gunmetal wheels and were only available in Pure White.

2004 SUBARU IMPREZA WR1 (UK)

In Britain meanwhile, Prodrive dished up the WR1, another special edition car that paid homage to Petter Solberg's 2003 World Rally Championship victory. It was given engine and exhaust upgrades that boosted power to 310 bhp, special suspension settings and wheels, plus a driver controlled center differential. It was offered in just one color – dubbed Ice Blue Metallic – and only 500 examples were built and sold through Subaru UK's dealer network

2004 SUBARU IMPREZA WRX CLUB SPEC EVO 7 (AUSTRALIA)

In many respects, this car was virtually identical to the Club Spec 6 from the previous year, with special badging and trim plus a factory-installed sunroof and standard leather seats. However, it was now offered with an automatic transmission for the first time. Keen-eyed spotters noticed that this version had larger side mirrors and the rocker panel extensions were now body color instead of black. Only 300 were built.

2004 SUBARU IMPREZA WRX PETTER SOLBERG EDITION (AUSTRALIA)

Yet another special edition was launched on the Australian market, hot on the heels of the Club Spec Evo 7. This was the Petter Solberg edition, appropriately finished in World Rally Blue Mica, with special badging outside and in as well as a unique shifter handle. Only 200 were made available (a similar car was later sold with left-hand drive in Italy as a 2005 model)

2005 IMPREZA STi SPEC C (JAPAN)

Alongside the regular STi model, a Spec C variant also debuted for 2005 and remained very much aimed toward all-out enthusiasts and competition style driving. It featured a few changes of its own, including extra chassis stiffening and revised suspension mounts at the rear. It also sported a nice set of BBS 10-spoke 17 x 8-inch alloy wheels on Pirelli tires.

2005 IMPREZA WRX/STi WR (JAPAN)

These were two special edition WR cars, one based on the regular WRX and the other on the STi Spec C. Naturally these featured much of the same hardware as the regular cars did, plus added a few unique touches of their own. Both cars came with World Rally blue exterior paint and logos along with with special gold painted 5-spoke RAYS wheels and other touches.

2005 IMPREZA STi SPEC C TYPE RA (JAPAN)

October saw the launch of the STi Spec C Type RA, another special edition of which just 300 copies were made available. A carbon fiber rear wing, special front splitters, and black Alcantara seats were among its features.

SPECIAL EDITION CARS

2005 IMPREZA STi S203 (JAPAN)

This was perhaps the ultimate expression of the GD chassis Impreza street car. Costing more than ¥4,600,000, it was the most expensive variation on the little road rocket to that time and featured a raft of mechanical improvements. Chief among these were a specially built EJ20 engine that featured a hand-balanced reciprocating assembly, extra-durable silicone air intake hoses, a specially calibrated ECU, and a specific turbocharger with unique plumbing. An oil cooler, high flow catalytic converter, ultra lightweight exhaust system and muffler were additional performance upgrades.

In the chassis deparment, each of the 555 cars featured adjustable struts, lower (and stiffer) springs, pillow ball suspension bushings, plus at the back, lighter aluminum control arms and a thicker sway bar that used ball-mounted bushings to improve rear end stability and traction. Different brake discs provided better and more even stopping power. Other additions included a power steering fluid cooler, special lightweight 18-inch BBS alloy wheels, and Pirelli P-Zero Corsa tires.

Four exterior colors were offered on this car—Crystal Gray, Pure White, WR Blue, and Solid Red—and each S203 featured a carbon fiber front splitter, special mesh grille, adjustable rear wing, tinted glass, and HID headlights. A special black interior included contrasting gray Recaro seats and door inserts, a serialized number plaque on the center console shift boot, STi floormats, a special key fob and leather case, plus a 260 km/h speedometer. Under the hood was an additional plaque signifying each car's exclusivity. The S203 ranks as one of the most collectible of all the GD chassis Imprezas and the survivors are highly sought-after.

2005 IMPREZA WRX V-LIMITED (JAPAN)

This was based on the WRX but looked very much like a STi thanks to the addition of the latter's front fascia, rocker panel extensions, rear bumper cover, and deck spoiler. With SWRT logos on the fenders, spoiler, rear deck, and seats, along with Rally Blue paint and gold RAYS wheels, the '05 V-Limited was a looker, and was well equipped too. Unlike previous versions, its reason for being was to simply highlight the fact that by 2004, Subaru had become the most successful Japanese manufacturer in World Championship Rallying–an incredible feat for a manufacturer that just two decades prior struggled to field cars in the series at all.

2005 SUBARU IMPREZA WRX CLUB SPEC EVO 8 (AUSTRALIA)

Yet another Club Spec model, the Evo 8 was released in Austraila for 2005. This followed the same pattern as the most recent editions, with special ID badging, leather interior, factory sunroof, and air conditioning. An automatic transmission was available and the car was available in a wider variety of exterior colors than previous versions. Still, only 300 were built.

2005 SUBARU IMPREZA WRX 300 (UK)

Painted exclusively in World Rally Blue Mica, this version featured 17-inch gold alloy wheels, special exterior badging, special SWRT-type front bucket seats and a standard five-speed manual gearbox. It also came standard with the Prodrive Performance pack, boosting power to 265 hp, making it a quick and exclusive car (fittingly, just 300 were built for sale in the UK).

2005 WRX TR (USA)

Given the growing popularity of GD chassis among sport compact car enthusiasts in North America, Subaru's US operation offered the WRX TR (Tuner Ready), intending the car to be used as a blank canvas for customization. It came without fog lights, rocker panel extensions, or rear wing, and featured base model Impreza front seats and basic sound and HVAC systems. At approximately $24,000 it was a grand cheaper than the standard stateside Rex.

SPECIAL EDITION CARS

2006 SUBARU IMPREZA STi S204 (JAPAN)

Following on from the previous S203, this was another specialized version of the STI. The EJ20 flat-four engine in this version was tuned to deliver 315 hp, and with the six-speed manual gearbox could reach 60 mph in less than five seconds. Its party piece, however, was a stiffened structure and precisely tuned suspension. Rolling on Pirelli PZero Corsa tires and 18-inch wheels, it was a serious corner carver and faster through the turns than any street-going Impreza built to that point. Outside the S204 was distinguished from the standard STI by a carbon fiber front chin spoiler and rear diffuser. Special lightweight Recaro bucket seats were designed to keep occupants firmly in place during hard driving.

2006 SUBARU IMPREZA RB 320 (UK)

Richard Burns, after battling a brain tumor, sadly lost his life in 2005. One of the greatest rally drivers of his generation, Subaru paid tribute by revealing the RB 320 in 2006. It was a sinister-looking car, finished in a single exterior color, Obsidian Black, with black 18-inch alloy wheels. It featured a special mesh grille treatment, unique front chin spoiler, and a specially trimmed interior with a short throw shifter. The suspension received specific spring and shock settings with a lowered ride height (approximately 1.4 inches at the front and 0.4-inches in the rear). A Prodrive Performance pack was offered on this car, boosting power to an astounding 320 hp and 332 lb-ft of torque. Only 320 examples were built.

2006 SUBARU IMPREZA WRX CLUB SPEC 9 (AUSTRALIA)

Compared to previous editions, the Club Spec 9 (the Evo moniker was dropped) proved a more radical departure, with more aggressive styling and larger 18-inch wheels and tires. Only two exterior colors were offered, World Rally Blue and Obsidian Black. This version featured a unique front spoiler, lowered suspension, leather seats, factory sunroof, and a short throw shifter with an aluminum STI handle. Again, only 300 examples were allocated for production.

2006 SUBARU IMPREZA STi SPEC D (UK)

In late 2005 Subaru UK released the STI Spec D, with the D actually standing for Discreet. This was mechanically identical to the regular STI but featured a smaller rear spoiler, silver instead of gold wheels, increased sound deadening, projector foglights, and a specially trimmed leather interior, with premium sound and entertainment systems, including an iPod adapter and touch screen. Just 300 were built.

2006 SUBARU IMPREZA STi LIMITED EDITION (USA)

With the rest of the world getting an apparently never-ending stream of STI special editions, in 2006 it was time for North American buyers to finally get their own. The STI Limited Edition was a more "mature"-appearing STI and featured a special front fascia with projector style foglights, a unique front splitter, a more discreet rear wing, silver alloy wheels, black interior trim, and special ID badging. Just 800 were built, 400 in Urban Gray Metallic, the rest in Satin White Pearl.

2007 SUBARU IMPREZA STi SPEC C TYPE RA-R (JAPAN)

If you really wanted to build a club racer or rally car, the hardcore, built-to-order Type RA-R (for Radical) was just the ticket. This version featured a fully balanced and blueprinted engine, massive Brembo brakes with six-piston front calipers, and ultra-aggressive suspension tuning, thanks to a generous use of parts from the Japanese STI catalog, including performance springs, shocks, and bushings.

2007 SUBARU IMPREZA STi A-LINE (JAPAN)

Contrasting with the wild RA-R was the A-Line, designed to cater to a more civilized buyer. As a result it featured more restrained styling with a smaller rear spoiler, dark painted brakes, and Enkei alloy wheels. It also featured slightly different suspension tuning, greater use of sound deadening, and a fully loaded interior with air conditioning, premium sound system, and leather seating surfaces.

SPECIAL EDITION CARS

2007 SUBARU IMPREZA GB270 (UK)

A final send-off for the GD chassis WRX was the UK GB270. Launched in 2007, production was strictly limited to just 400 copies, but the lucky few buyers received a car with a great mix of features. This version featured a stainless steel mesh grille (similar to that on the '06 RB320), along with 18-inch alloy wheels and tires, STI-style front bumper and rear spoiler, special exterior badging and a unique numbered plaque on the center console. Also included were a specifically tuned suspension (resulting in a lower ride height) and a Prodrive Performance Pack, increasing power from 227 to 265 hp. Capable of sprinting to 60 mph in just 5.3 seconds, it was a great performer and a surefire collectible.

APPENDIX C

SPECIFICATIONS

Please note that all specifications refer to Japanese domestic market versions of both the Lancer Evolution and Impreza WRX/STi unless otherwise stated.

1993 MITSUBISHI LANCER EVOLUTION GSR

VEHICLE TYPE:
  Compact, front-engined; all-wheel-drive four-door sedan

ENGINE:
  Turbocharged I-4

Construction:
  Cast-iron block with aluminum head
Valvetrain:
  16-valve, operated by dual overhead camshafts
Bore and Stroke:
  85 mm x 88 mm
Displacement:
  1997 cc
Compression ratio:
  8.5:1
Fuel system:
  Sequential electronic injection

1993 SUBARU IMPREZA WRX

VEHICLE TYPE:
  Compact, front-engined; all-wheel-drive four-door sedan

ENGINE:
  Turbocharged H-4

Construction:
  Aluminum crankcase and heads
Valvetrain:
  16-valve, operated by dual overhead camshafts
Bore and Stroke:
  92 mm x 75 mm
Displacement:
  1994 cc
Compression ratio:
  8.5:1
Fuel system:
  Sequential electronic injection

WRX vs. EVO

MITSUBISHI

Max Power
   250 hp @ 6000 rpm
Max Torque
   227 lb-ft @ 3000 rpm

TRANSMISSION
   Five-speed close ratio manual gearbox

RATIOS
   (1st) 2.571
   (2nd) 1.600
   (3rd) 1.160
   (4th) 0.862
   (5th) 0.617

FINAL DRIVE
   5.443:1

DRIVELINE
   Full time AWD system with viscous center differential and limited slip rear differential

CHASSIS
   Steel unibody

SUSPENSION
Front:
   Independent MacPherson struts, pillow ball bushings and stabilizer bar
Rear:
   Independent MacPherson struts, pillow ball bushings and stabilizer bar

BRAKES
Front:
   Vented discs with dual-piston calipers
Rear:
   Solid discs with single-piston calipers

WHEELS
   15 x 6 in aluminum

TIRES
   P195/55VR15

SUBARU

Max Power
   240 hp @ 6000 rpm
Max Torque
   224 lb-ft @ 3500 rpm

TRANSMISSION
   Five-speed close ratio manual gearbox

RATIOS
   (1st) 3.454
   (2nd) 2.062
   (3rd) 1.448
   (4th) 1.088
   (5th) 0.825

FINAL DRIVE
   4.111:1

DRIVELINE
   Full time AWD system with bevel gear viscous center coupling

CHASSIS
   Steel unibody

SUSPENSION
Front:
   Independent MacPherson struts, linear control valve shocks and stabilizer bar
Rear:
   Independent MacPherson struts, linear control valve shocks and stabilizer bar

BRAKES
Front:
   Vented discs with dual-piston calipers
Rear:
   Solid discs with single-piston calipers

WHEELS
   15 x 6 in aluminum

TIRES
   P205/55VR15

SPECIFICATIONS

MITSUBISHI

DIMENSIONS
- Length: 169.7 in (4310 mm)
- Width: 66.7 in (1694 mm)
- Height: 54.5 in (1384 mm)
- Wheelbase: 98.4 in (2500 mm)
- Front track: 57.1 in (1450 mm)
- Rear track: 57.5 in (1460 mm)
- Curb Weight: 2729 lbs (1240 kg)

SUBARU

DIMENSIONS
- Length: 170.9 in (4340 mm)
- Width: 66.5 in (1690 mm)
- Height: 55.3 in (1405 mm)
- Wheelbase: 99.2 in (2520 mm)
- Front track: 58.3 in (1480 mm)
- Rear track: 58.1 in (1475 mm)
- Curb Weight: 2648 lbs (1200 kg)

1994 MITSUBISHI LANCER EVOLUTION II GSR

VEHICLE TYPE:
Compact, front-engined; all-wheel-drive four-door sedan

ENGINE:
Turbocharged I-4

Construction:
Cast-iron block with aluminum head
Valvetrain:
16-valve, operated by dual overhead camshafts
Bore and Stroke:
85 mm x 88 mm
Displacement:
1997 cc
Compression ratio:
8.5:1
Fuel system:
Sequential electronic injection

Max Power
260 hp @ 6000 rpm
Max Torque
227 lb-ft @ 3000 rpm

TRANSMISSION
Five-speed close ratio manual gearbox

1994 SUBARU IMPREZA WRX STi

VEHICLE TYPE:
Compact, front-engined; all-wheel-drive four-door sedan

ENGINE:
Turbocharged H-4

Construction:
Aluminum crankcase and heads
Valvetrain:
16-valve, operated by dual overhead camshafts
Bore and Stroke:
92 mm x 75 mm
Displacement:
1994 cc
Compression ratio:
8.5:1
Fuel system:
Sequential electronic injection

Max Power
250 hp @ 6000 rpm
Max Torque
227 lb-ft @ 3500 rpm

TRANSMISSION
Five-speed close ratio manual gearbox

WRX vs. EVO

MITSUBISHI

RATIOS
(1st) 2.750
(2nd) 1.684
(3rd) 1.160
(4th) 0.862
(5th) 0.617

FINAL DRIVE
5.443:1

DRIVELINE
Full time AWD system with viscous center differential and mechanical limited slip rear differential

CHASSIS
Steel unibody

SUSPENSION
Front:
  Independent MacPherson struts, pillow ball bushings and stabilizer bar
Rear:
  Independent MacPherson struts, pillow ball bushings and stabilizer bar

BRAKES
Front:
  Vented discs with dual-piston calipers
Rear: Solid discs with single-piston calipers

WHEELS
15 x 6 in aluminum

TIRES
P205/60VR15

DIMENSIONS
Length:	169.7 in (4310 mm)
Width:	66.7 in (1694 mm)
Height:	55.9 in (1420 mm)
Wheelbase:	98.9 in (2510 mm)
Front track:	57.6 in (1465 mm)
Rear track:	57.9 in (1470 mm)
Curb Weight:	2751 lbs (1250 kg)

SUBARU

RATIOS
(1st) 3.454
(2nd) 2.062
(3rd) 1.448
(4th) 1.088
(5th) 0.825

FINAL DRIVE
4.111:1

DRIVELINE
Full time AWD system with bevel gear viscous center coupling

CHASSIS
Steel unibody

SUSPENSION
Front:
  Independent MacPherson struts, linear control valve shocks and stabilizer bar
Rear: Independent MacPherson struts, linear control valve shocks and stabilizer bar

BRAKES
Front:
  Vented discs with dual-piston calipers
Rear:
  Solid discs with single-piston calipers

WHEELS
15 x 6 in aluminum

TIRES
P205/55VR15

DIMENSIONS
Length:	170.9 in (4340 mm)
Width:	66.5 in (1690 mm)
Height:	55.3 in (1405 mm)
Wheelbase:	99.2 in (2520 mm)
Front track:	58.3 in (1480 mm)
Rear track:	58.1 in (1475 mm)
Curb Weight:	2648 lbs (1200 kg)

SPECIFICATIONS

MITSUBISHI

1995 MITSUBISHI LANCER EVOLUTION III GSR

VEHICLE TYPE:
 Compact, front-engined; all-wheel-drive four-door sedan

ENGINE:
 Turbocharged I-4

Construction:
 Cast-iron block with aluminum head
Valvetrain:
 16-valve, operated by dual overhead camshafts
Bore and Stroke:
 85 mm x 88 mm
Displacement:
 1997 cc
Compression ratio:
 9.0:1
Fuel system:
 Sequential electronic injection
Max Power
 270 hp @ 6250 rpm
Max Torque
 227 lb-ft @ 3000 rpm

TRANSMISSION
 Five-speed close ratio manual gearbox

RATIOS
 (1st) 2.750
 (2nd) 1.684
 (3rd) 1.160
 (4th) 0.862
 (5th) 0.617

FINAL DRIVE
5.358:1

DRIVELINE
Full time AWD system with viscous center differential and mechanical limited slip rear differential

SUBARU

1995 SUBARU IMPREZA WRX STi Version II

VEHICLE TYPE:
 Compact, front-engined; all-wheel-drive four-door sedan

ENGINE:
 Turbocharged H-4

Construction:
 Aluminum crankcase and heads
Valvetrain:
 16-valve, operated by dual overhead camshafts
Bore and Stroke:
 92 mm x 75 mm
Displacement:
 1994 cc
Compression ratio:
 8.5:1
Fuel system:
 Sequential electronic injection
Max Power
 275 hp @ 6500 rpm
Max Torque
 235 lb-ft @ 4000 rpm

TRANSMISSION
 Five-speed close ratio manual gearbox

RATIOS
 (1st) 3.454
 (2nd) 2.062
 (3rd) 1.448
 (4th) 1.088
 (5th) 0.825

FINAL DRIVE
4.111:1

DRIVELINE
Full time AWD system with bevel gear viscous center coupling

WRX vs. EVO

MITSUBISHI

CHASSIS
Steel unibody

SUSPENSION
Front:
  Independent MacPherson struts, pillow ball bushings and stabilizer bar
Rear:
  Independent MacPherson struts, pillow ball bushings and stabilizer bar

BRAKES
Front:
  Vented discs with dual-piston calipers
Rear:
  Solid discs with single-piston calipers

WHEELS
  15 x 6 in aluminum

TIRES
  P205/60VR15

DIMENSIONS
  Length: 169.7 in (4310 mm)
  Width: 66.7 in (1694 mm)
  Height: 55.9 in (1420 mm)
  Wheelbase: 98.9 in (2510 mm)
  Front track: 57.6 in (1465 mm)
  Rear track: 57.9 in (1470 mm)
  Curb Weight: 2772 lbs (1260 kg)

SUBARU

CHASSIS
Steel unibody

SUSPENSION
Front:
  Independent MacPherson struts, linear control valve shocks and stabilizer bar
Rear:
  Independent MacPherson struts, linear control valve shocks and stabilizer bar

BRAKES
Front: Vented discs with dual-piston calipers
Rear:
  Solid discs with single-piston calipers

WHEELS
  15 x 6 in aluminum

TIRES
  P205/55VR15

DIMENSIONS
  Length: 170.9 in (4340 mm)
  Width: 66.5 in (1690 mm)
  Height: 55.3 in (1405 mm)
  Wheelbase: 99.2 in (2520 mm)
  Front track: 58.3 in (1480 mm)
  Rear track: 58.1 in (1475 mm)
  Curb Weight: 2648 lbs (1200 kg)

1996 MITSUBISHI LANCER EVOLUTION IV GSR

VEHICLE TYPE:
  Compact, front-engined; all-wheel-drive four-door sedan

ENGINE:
  Turbocharged I-4

SPECIFICATIONS

MITSUBISHI

SUBARU

Construction:
 Cast-iron block with aluminum head
Valvetrain:
 16-valve, operated by dual overhead camshafts
Bore and Stroke:
 85 mm x 88 mm
Displacement:
 1997 cc
Compression ratio:
 8.8:1
Fuel system:
 Sequential electronic injection

Max Power
 280 hp @ 6500 rpm
Max Torque
 260 lb-ft @ 3000 rpm

TRANSMISSION
 Five-speed close ratio manual gearbox

RATIOS
 (1st) 2.785
 (2nd) 1.950
 (3rd) 1.407
 (4th) 1.031
 (5th) 0.825

FINAL DRIVE
 4.529:1

DRIVELINE
 Full time AWD system with viscous center differential and limited slip rear differential with electronic active yaw control (AYC)

CHASSIS
 Steel unibody
SUSPENSION
Front:
 Independent MacPherson struts, pillow ball bushings and stabilizer bar
Rear:
 Independent MacPherson struts, pillow ball bushings and stabilizer bar

WRX vs. EVO

MITSUBISHI

BRAKES
Front:
  Vented discs with dual-piston calipers
Rear:
  Solid discs with single-piston calipers

WHEELS
  16 x 6.5 in aluminum

TIRES
  P205/50VR16

DIMENSIONS
Length:	170.5 in (4330 mm)
Width:	66.5 in (1689 mm)
Height:	55.7 in (1415 mm)
Wheelbase:	98.9 in (2510 mm)
Front track:	57.8 in (1470 mm)
Rear track:	57.9 in (1470 mm)
Curb Weight:	2970 lbs (1350 kg)

SUBARU

1997 SUBARU IMPREZA WRX

VEHICLE TYPE:
  Compact, front-engined; all-wheel-drive four-door sedan

ENGINE:
  Turbocharged H-4

Construction:
  Aluminum crankcase and heads
Valvetrain:
  16-valve, operated by dual overhead camshafts
Bore and Stroke:
  92 mm x 75 mm
Displacement:
  1994 cc
Compression ratio:
  8.0:1
Fuel system:
  Sequential electronic injection

SPECIFICATIONS

MITSUBISHI   SUBARU

Max Power
  280 hp @ 6500 rpm

Max Torque
  242 lb-ft @ 3500 rpm

TRANSMISSION
  Five-speed close ratio manual gearbox

RATIOS
  (1st) 3.166
  (2nd) 1.882
  (3rd) 1.296
  (4th) 0.972
  (5th) 0.738

FINAL DRIVE
  4.444:1

DRIVELINE
  Full time AWD system with bevel gear viscous center coupling

CHASSIS
  Steel unibody
SUSPENSION
Front:
  Independent MacPherson struts, linear control valve shocks and stabilizer bar
Rear:
  Independent MacPherson struts, linear control valve shocks and stabilizer bar

BRAKES
Front:
  Vented discs with dual-piston calipers
Rear:
  Solid discs with single-piston calipers
  Four-sensor ABS

WHEELS
  16 x 7 in aluminum

TIRES
  P205/50VR16

WRX vs. EVO

MITSUBISHI

SUBARU

DIMENSIONS
Length: 170.9 in (4340 mm)
Width: 66.5 in (1690 mm)
Height: 55.3 in (1405 mm)
Wheelbase: 99.2 in (2520 mm)
Front track: 58.3 in (1480 mm)
Rear track: 58.1 in (1475 mm)
Curb Weight: 2678 lbs (1215 kg)

1997 SUBARU IMPREZA WRX STi Version III

VEHICLE TYPE:
  Compact, front-engined; all-wheel-drive four-door sedan

ENGINE:
  Turbocharged H-4

Construction:
  Aluminum crankcase and heads
Valvetrain:
  16-valve, operated by dual overhead camshafts
Bore and Stroke:
  92 mm x 75 mm
Displacement:
  1994 cc
Compression ratio:
  8.0:1
Fuel system:
  Sequential electronic injection

Max Power
  280 hp @ 6500 rpm
Max Torque
  253 lb-ft @ 4000 rpm

TRANSMISSION
  Five-speed close ratio manual gearbox

RATIOS
  (1st) 3.166
  (2nd) 1.882

SPECIFICATIONS

MITSUBISHI   SUBARU

(3rd) 1.296
(4th) 0.972
(5th) 0.738

FINAL DRIVE
4.444:1

DRIVELINE
Full time AWD system with driver controlled center differential

CHASSIS
Steel unibody

SUSPENSION
Front:
  Independent MacPherson struts, linear control valve shocks and stabilizer bar
Rear:
  Independent MacPherson struts, linear control valve shocks and stabilizer bar

BRAKES
Front:
  Vented discs with four-piston calipers
Rear:
  Solid discs with single-piston calipers
  Four-sensor ABS

WHEELS
16 x 7 in aluminum

TIRES
P205/50VR16

DIMENSIONS
Length:	170.9 in (4340 mm)
Width:	66.5 in (1690 mm)
Height:	55.3 in (1405 mm)
Wheelbase:	99.2 in (2520 mm)
Front track:	58.3 in (1480 mm)
Rear track:	58.1 in (1475 mm)
Curb Weight:	2720 lbs (1233 kg)

WRX vs. EVO

MITSUBISHI	SUBARU

1998 MITSUBISHI LANCER EVOLUTION V GSR

1998 SUBARU IMPREZA WRX STi Version IV

VEHICLE TYPE:
  Compact, front-engined; all-wheel-drive four-door sedan

ENGINE:
  Turbocharged I-4

Construction:
  Cast-iron block with aluminum head
Valvetrain:
  16-valve, operated by dual overhead camshafts
Bore and Stroke:
  85 mm x 88 mm
Displacement:
  1997 cc
Compression ratio:
  8.8:1
Fuel system:
  Sequential electronic injection

Max Power
  280 hp @ 6500 rpm
Max Torque
  274 lb-ft @ 3000 rpm

TRANSMISSION
  Five-speed close ratio manual gearbox

RATIOS
  (1st) 2.785
  (2nd) 1.950
  (3rd) 1.407
  (4th) 1.031
  (5th) 0.825

FINAL DRIVE
  4.529:1

DRIVELINE
  Full time AWD system with viscous center differential and limited slip rear differential with electronic active yaw control (AYC)

VEHICLE TYPE:
  Compact, front-engined; all-wheel-drive four-door sedan

ENGINE:
  Turbocharged H-4

Construction:
  Aluminum crankcase and heads
Valvetrain:
  16-valve, operated by dual overhead camshafts
Bore and Stroke:
  92 mm x 75 mm
Displacement:
  1994 cc
Compression ratio:
  8.0:1
Fuel system:
  Sequential electronic injection

Max Power
  280 hp @ 6500 rpm
Max Torque
  260 lb-ft @ 4000 rpm

TRANSMISSION
  Five-speed close ratio manual gearbox

RATIOS
  (1st) 3.166
  (2nd) 1.882
  (3rd) 1.296
  (4th) 0.972
  (5th) 0.738

FINAL DRIVE
  4.444:1

DRIVELINE
  Full time AWD system with driver controlled center differential

SPECIFICATIONS

MITSUBISHI

CHASSIS
Steel unibody

SUSPENSION
Front:
 Independent MacPherson struts, pillow ball bushings and stabilizer bar
Rear:
 Independent MacPherson struts, pillow ball bushings and stabilizer bar

BRAKES
Front:
 Vented discs with four-piston calipers
Rear:
 Solid discs with dual-piston calipers

WHEELS
17 x 7.5 in aluminum

TIRES
P225/45ZR17

DIMENSIONS
Length:	171.2 in (4350 mm)
Width:	69.7 in (1770 mm)
Height:	55.7 in (1415 mm)
Wheelbase:	98.9 in (2510 mm)
Front track:	59.4 in (1510 mm)
Rear track:	59.2 in (1505 mm)
Curb Weight:	2992 lbs (1360 kg)

SUBARU

CHASSIS
Steel unibody

SUSPENSION
Front:
 Independent MacPherson struts, linear control valve shocks and stabilizer bar
Rear:
 Independent MacPherson struts, linear control valve shocks and stabilizer bar

BRAKES
Front:
 Vented discs with four-piston calipers
Rear:
 Solid discs with single-piston calipers
 Four-sensor ABS

WHEELS
16 x 7 in aluminum

TIRES
P205/50VR16

DIMENSIONS
Length:	170.9 in (4340 mm)
Width:	66.5 in (1690 mm)
Height:	55.3 in (1405 mm)
Wheelbase:	99.2 in (2520 mm)
Front track:	58.3 in (1480 mm)
Rear track:	58.1 in (1475 mm)
Curb Weight:	2720 lbs (1233 kg)

1998 SUBARU IMPREZA WRX STi 22B

VEHICLE TYPE:
 Compact, front-engined; all-wheel-drive two-door coupe

ENGINE:
 Turbocharged H-4

 Construction:
  Aluminum crankcase and heads

WRX vs. EVO

MITSUBISHI   SUBARU

Valvetrain:
   16-valve, operated by dual overhead camshafts
Bore and Stroke:
   96.9 mm x 75 mm
Displacement:
   2212 cc
Compression ratio:
   8.0:1
Fuel system:
   Sequential electronic injection

Max Power
   280 hp @ 6500 rpm
Max Torque
   267 lb-ft @ 3200 rpm

TRANSMISSION
   Five-speed close ratio manual gearbox

RATIOS
   (1st) 3.083
   (2nd) 2.062
   (3rd) 1.545
   (4th) 1.151
   (5th) 0.825

FINAL DRIVE
   4.444:1

DRIVELINE
   Full time AWD system with driver controlled center differential and variable torque distribution

CHASSIS
   Steel unibody

SUSPENSION
Front:
   Independent MacPherson struts, linear control valve shocks and stabilizer bar
Rear:
   Independent MacPherson struts, linear control valve shocks and stabilizer bar

SPECIFICATIONS

MITSUBISHI

SUBARU

BRAKES
Front:
   Vented discs with four-piston calipers
Rear:
   Solid discs with single-piston calipers
   Four-sensor ABS

WHEELS
   17 x 7 in aluminum
TIRES
   P235/40ZR17

DIMENSIONS
Length:	170.9 in (4340 mm)
Width:	66.5 in (1690 mm)
Height:	55.3 in (1405 mm)
Wheelbase:	99.2 in (2520 mm)
Front track:	58.3 in (1480 mm)
Rear track:	58.1 in (1475 mm)
Curb Weight:	2794 lbs (1270 kg)

1999 MITSUBISHI LANCER EVOLUTION VI GSR

VEHICLE TYPE:
   Compact, front-engined; all-wheel-drive four-door sedan

ENGINE:
   Turbocharged I-4

Construction:
   Cast-iron block with aluminum head
Valvetrain:
   16-valve, operated by dual overhead camshafts
Bore and Stroke:
   85 mm x 88 mm
Displacement:
   1997 cc
Compression ratio:
   8.8:1
Fuel system:
   Sequential electronic injection
Max Power
   280 hp @ 6500 rpm

1999 SUBARU IMPREZA WRX STi Version V

VEHICLE TYPE:
   Compact, front-engined; all-wheel-drive four-door sedan

ENGINE:
   Turbocharged H-4

Construction:
   Aluminum crankcase and heads
Valvetrain:
   16-valve, operated by dual overhead camshafts
Bore and Stroke:
   92 mm x 75 mm
Displacement:
   1994 cc
Compression ratio:
   8.0:1
Fuel system:
   Sequential electronic injection
Max Power
   280 hp @ 6500 rpm

WRX vs. EVO

MITSUBISHI

Max Torque
  274 lb-ft @ 3000 rpm

TRANSMISSION
  Five-speed close ratio manual gearbox

RATIOS
  (1st) 2.785
  (2nd) 1.950
  (3rd) 1.407
  (4th) 1.031
  (5th) 0.825

FINAL DRIVE
  4.529:1

DRIVELINE
  Full time AWD system with viscous center differential and limited slip rear differential with electronic active yaw control (AYC)

CHASSIS
  Steel unibody

SUSPENSION
Front:
  Independent MacPherson struts, pillow ball bushings and stabilizer bar
Rear:
  Independent MacPherson struts, pillow ball bushings and stabilizer bar

BRAKES
Front:
  Vented discs with four-piston calipers
Rear:
  Solid discs with dual-piston calipers

WHEELS
  17 x 7.5 in aluminum

TIRES
  P225/45ZR17

SUBARU

Max Torque
  260 lb-ft @ 4000 rpm

TRANSMISSION
  Five-speed close ratio manual gearbox

RATIOS
  (1st) 3.166
  (2nd) 1.882
  (3rd) 1.296
  (4th) 0.972
  (5th) 0.738

FINAL DRIVE
  4.444:1

DRIVELINE
  Full time AWD system with driver controlled center differential

CHASSIS
  Steel unibody

SUSPENSION
Front:
  Independent MacPherson struts, linear control valve shocks and stabilizer bar
Rear:
  Independent MacPherson struts, linear control valve shocks and stabilizer bar

BRAKES
Front:
  Vented discs with four-piston calipers
Rear:
  Solid discs with single-piston calipers
  Four-sensor ABS

WHEELS
  16 x 7 in aluminum

TIRES
  P205/50VR16

SPECIFICATIONS

MITSUBISHI

DIMENSIONS
  Length: 171.2 in (4350 mm)
  Width: 69.7 in (1770 mm)
  Height: 55.7 in (1415 mm)
  Wheelbase: 98.9 in (2510 mm)
  Front track: 59.4 in (1510 mm)
  Rear track: 59.2 in (1505 mm)
  Curb Weight: 2992 lbs (1360 kg)

SUBARU

DIMENSIONS
  Length: 170.9 in (4340 mm)
  Width: 66.5 in (1690 mm)
  Height: 55.3 in (1405 mm)
  Wheelbase: 99.2 in (2520 mm)
  Front track: 58.3 in (1480 mm)
  Rear track: 58.1 in (1475 mm)
  Curb Weight: 2720 lbs (1233 kg)

2000 SUBARU IMPREZA WRX STi Version VI

VEHICLE TYPE:
  Compact, front-engined; all-wheel-drive four-door sedan

ENGINE:
  Turbocharged H-4

Construction:
  Aluminum crankcase and heads
Valvetrain:
  16-valve, operated by dual overhead camshafts
Bore and Stroke:
  92 mm x 75 mm
Displacement:
  1994 cc
Compression ratio:
  8.0:1
Fuel system:
  Sequential electronic injection

Max Power
  280 hp @ 6500 rpm
Max Torque
  260 lb-ft @ 4000 rpm

TRANSMISSION
  Five-speed close ratio manual gearbox

RATIOS
  (1st) 3.166
  (2nd) 1.882

WRX vs. EVO

MITSUBISHI **SUBARU**

(3rd) 1.296
(4th) 0.972
(5th) 0.738

FINAL DRIVE
4.444:1

DRIVELINE
Full time AWD system with driver controlled center differential

CHASSIS
Steel unibody

SUSPENSION
Front:
 Independent MacPherson struts, linear control valve shocks and stabilizer bar
Rear:
 Independent MacPherson struts, linear control valve shocks and stabilizer bar

BRAKES
Front:
 Vented discs with four-piston calipers
Rear:
 Solid discs with single-piston calipers
 Four-sensor ABS

WHEELS
16 x 7 in aluminum

TIRES
P205/50VR16

DIMENSIONS
Length: 170.9 in (4340 mm)
Width: 66.5 in (1690 mm)
Height: 55.3 in (1405 mm)
Wheelbase: 99.2 in (2520 mm)
Front track: 58.3 in (1480 mm)
Rear track: 58.1 in (1475 mm)
Curb Weight: 2720 lbs (1233 kg)

SPECIFICATIONS

MITSUBISHI | **SUBARU**

2001 SUBARU IMPREZA WRX

VEHICLE TYPE:
  Compact, front-engined; all-wheel-drive four-door sedan

ENGINE:
  Turbocharged H-4

Construction:
  Aluminum crankcase and heads
Valvetrain:
  16-valve, operated by dual overhead camshafts
Bore and Stroke:
  92 mm x 75 mm
Displacement:
  1994 cc
Compression ratio:
  8.0:1
Fuel system:
  Sequential electronic injection

Max Power
  250 hp @ 6000 rpm
Max Torque
  245 lb-ft @ 3600 rpm

TRANSMISSION
  Five-speed close ratio manual gearbox

RATIOS
  (1st) 3.166
  (2nd) 1.882
  (3rd) 1.296
  (4th) 0.972
  (5th) 0.738

FINAL DRIVE
  4.444:1

DRIVELINE
  Full time AWD system with viscous limited-slip center differential

CHASSIS
  Steel unibody

WRX vs. EVO

MITSUBISHI	**SUBARU**

SUBARU

SUSPENSION
Front:
  Independent MacPherson struts, linear control valve shocks and stabilizer bar
Rear:
  Independent MacPherson struts, dual links, linear control valve shocks and stabilizer bar

BRAKES
Front:
  Vented discs with two-piston calipers
Rear:
  Solid discs with single-piston calipers
  Four-sensor ABS

WHEELS
  16 x 7 in aluminum

TIRES
  P205/50VR16

DIMENSIONS
  Length: 173.4 in (4405 mm)
  Width: 68.1 in (1730 mm)
  Height: 56.5 in (1435 mm)
  Wheelbase: 99.4 in (2525 mm)
  Front track: 58.5 in (1485 mm)
  Rear track: 58.1 in (1475 mm)
  Curb Weight: 2764 lbs (1253 kg)

2002 MITSUBISHI LANCER EVOLUTION VII GSR

VEHICLE TYPE:
  Compact, front-engined; all-wheel-drive four-door sedan

ENGINE:
  Turbocharged I-4

Construction:
  Cast-iron block with aluminum head

2002 SUBARU IMPREZA WRX STi

VEHICLE TYPE:
  Compact, front-engined; all-wheel-drive four-door sedan

ENGINE:
  Turbocharged H-4

Construction:
  Aluminum crankcase and heads

SPECIFICATIONS

MITSUBISHI

Valvetrain:
  16-valve, operated by dual overhead camshafts
Bore and Stroke:
  85 mm x 88 mm
Displacement:
  1997 cc
Compression ratio:
  8.8:1
Fuel system:
  Sequential electronic injection
Max Power
  280 hp @ 6500 rpm
Max Torque
  282 lb-ft @ 3500 rpm

TRANSMISSION
  Five-speed close ratio manual gearbox

RATIOS
  (1st) 2.928
  (2nd) 1.950
  (3rd) 1.407
  (4th) 1.031
  (5th) 0.720

FINAL DRIVE
  4.529:1

DRIVELINE
  Full time AWD system with Active Center Differential and limited slip rear differential with electronic active yaw control (AYC)

CHASSIS
  Steel unibody

SUSPENSION
Front:
  Independent MacPherson struts, pillow ball bushings and stabilizer bar
Rear:
  Independent MacPherson struts, pillow ball bushings and stabilizer bar

SUBARU

Valvetrain:
  16-valve, operated by dual overhead camshafts
Bore and Stroke:
  92 mm x 75 mm
Displacement:
  1994 cc
Compression ratio:
  8.0:1
Fuel system:
  Sequential electronic injection
Max Power
  280 hp @ 6400 rpm
Max Torque
  274 lb-ft @ 4000 rpm

TRANSMISSION
  Six-speed close ratio manual gearbox

RATIOS
  (1st) 3.636
  (2nd) 2.375
  (3rd) 1.761
  (4th) 1.346
  (5th) 1.062
  (6th) 0.842

FINAL DRIVE
  3.90:1

DRIVELINE
  Full time AWD system with viscous limited-slip center differential and Suretrac limited slip rear differential

CHASSIS
  Steel unibody

SUSPENSION
Front:
  Independent MacPherson struts, linear control valve shocks and stabilizer bar
Rear:
  Independent MacPherson struts, dual links, linear control valve shocks and stabilizer bar

WRX vs. EVO

MITSUBISHI

BRAKES
Front:
　Vented discs with four-piston calipers
Rear:
　Solid discs with dual-piston calipers
　ABS and Electronic Brake Distribution

WHEELS
　17 x 7.5 in aluminum

TIRES
　P225/45ZR17

DIMENSIONS
Length:	175.4 in (4455 mm)
Width:	69.7 in (1770 mm)
Height:	57.1 in (1450 mm)
Wheelbase:	103.3 in (2625 mm)
Front track:	59.6 in (1515 mm)
Rear track:	59.6 in (1515 mm)
Curb Weight:	3080 lbs (1400 kg)

SUBARU

BRAKES
Front:
　Vented discs with four-piston calipers
Rear:
　Vented discs with dual-piston calipers
　Four-sensor ABS

WHEELS
　17 x 7.5 in aluminum

TIRES
　P205/45ZR17

DIMENSIONS
Length:	173.4 in (4405 mm)
Width:	68.1 in (1730 mm)
Height:	56.5 in (1435 mm)
Wheelbase:	99.4 in (2525 mm)
Front track:	58.5 in (1485 mm)
Rear track:	58.1 in (1475 mm)
Curb Weight:	2770 lbs (1256 kg)

2004 MITSUBISHI LANCER EVOLUTION VIII GSR

VEHICLE TYPE:
　Compact, front-engined; all-wheel-drive four-door sedan

ENGINE:
　Turbocharged I-4

Construction:
　Cast-iron block with aluminum head
Valvetrain:
　16-valve, operated by dual overhead camshafts
Bore and Stroke:
　85 mm x 88 mm
Displacement:
　1997 cc
Compression ratio:
　8.8:1
Fuel system:
　Sequential electronic injection

2004 SUBARU IMPREZA WRX STi

VEHICLE TYPE:
　Compact, front-engined; all-wheel-drive four-door sedan

ENGINE:
　Turbocharged H-4

Construction:
　Aluminum crankcase and heads
Valvetrain:
　16-valve, operated by dual overhead camshafts
Bore and Stroke:
　92 mm x 75 mm
Displacement:
　1994 cc
Compression ratio:
　8.0:1
Fuel system:
　Sequential electronic injection

SPECIFICATIONS

MITSUBISHI

Max Power
  280 hp @ 6500 rpm
Max Torque
  289 lb-ft @ 3500 rpm

TRANSMISSION
  Six-speed close ratio manual gearbox

RATIOS
  (1st) 2.909
  (2nd) 1.944
  (3rd) 1.434
  (4th) 1.100
  (5th) 0.863
  (6th) 0.693

FINAL DRIVE
  4.583:1

DRIVELINE
  Full time AWD system with Active Center Differential and limited slip rear differential with electronic active yaw control (AYC)

CHASSIS
  Steel unibody

SUSPENSION
Front:
  Independent MacPherson struts, pillow ball bushings and stabilizer bar
Rear:
  Independent MacPherson struts, pillow ball bushings and stabilizer bar

BRAKES
Front:
  Vented discs with four-piston calipers
Rear:
  Solid discs with dual-piston calipers
  ABS and Electronic Brake Distribution

WHEELS
  17 x 8 in aluminum

TIRES
  P235/45ZR17

SUBARU

Max Power
  280 hp @ 6400 rpm
Max Torque
  290 lb-ft @ 4400 rpm

TRANSMISSION
  Six-speed close ratio manual gearbox

RATIOS
  (1st) 3.636
  (2nd) 2.375
  (3rd) 1.761
  (4th) 1.346
  (5th) 1.062
  (6th) 0.842

FINAL DRIVE
  3.90:1

DRIVELINE
  Full time AWD system with viscous limited-slip center differential and Suretrac limited slip rear differential

CHASSIS
  Steel unibody

SUSPENSION
Front:
  Independent MacPherson struts, linear control valve shocks and stabilizer bar
Rear:
  Independent MacPherson struts, dual links, linear control valve shocks and stabilizer bar

BRAKES
Front:
  Vented discs with four-piston calipers
Rear:
  Vented discs with dual-piston calipers
  Four-sensor ABS

WHEELS
  17 x 7.5 in aluminum

TIRES
  P225/45ZR17

WRX vs. EVO

MITSUBISHI

DIMENSIONS
- Length: 176.8 in (4490 mm)
- Width: 69.7 in (1770 mm)
- Height: 57.1 in (1450 mm)
- Wheelbase: 103.3 in (2625 mm)
- Front track: 59.6 in (1515 mm)
- Rear track: 59.6 in (1515 mm)
- Curb Weight: 3102 lbs (1410 kg)

SUBARU

DIMENSIONS
- Length: 173.4 in (4405 mm)
- Width: 68.1 in (1730 mm)
- Height: 56.5 in (1435 mm)
- Wheelbase: 99.4 in (2525 mm)
- Front track: 58.5 in (1485 mm)
- Rear track: 58.1 in (1475 mm)
- Curb Weight: 3060 lbs (1388 kg)

2006 MITSUBISHI LANCER EVOLUTION IX GSR

VEHICLE TYPE:
   Compact, front-engined; all-wheel-drive four-door sedan

ENGINE:
   Turbocharged I-4

Construction:
   Cast-iron block with aluminum head
Valvetrain:
   16-valve, operated by dual overhead camshafts
Bore and Stroke:
   85 mm x 88 mm
Displacement:
   1997 cc
Compression ratio:
   8.8:1
Fuel system:
   Sequential electronic injection
Max Power
   280 hp @ 6500 rpm
Max Torque
   295 lb-ft @ 3000 rpm

TRANSMISSION
   Six-speed close ratio manual gearbox

RATIOS
   (1st) 2.909
   (2nd) 1.944
   (3rd) 1.434

2006 SUBARU IMPREZA WRX*

VEHICLE TYPE:
   Compact, front-engined; all-wheel-drive four-door sedan

ENGINE:
   Turbocharged H-4

Construction:
   Aluminum crankcase and heads
Valvetrain:
   16-valve, operated by dual overhead camshafts
Bore and Stroke:
   99.5 mm x 79 mm
Displacement:
   2457 cc
Compression ratio:
   8.0:1
Fuel system:
   Sequential electronic injection
Max Power
   227 hp @ 5600 rpm
Max Torque
   236 lb-ft @ 3600 rpm

TRANSMISSION
   Five-speed close ratio manual gearbox

RATIOS
   (1st) 3.45
   (2nd) 1.95
   (3rd) 1.37

SPECIFICATIONS

MITSUBISHI

(4th) 1.100
(5th) 0.863
(6th) 0.693

FINAL DRIVE
4.583:1

DRIVELINE
Full time AWD system with Active Center Differential and limited slip rear differential with electronic active yaw control (AYC)

CHASSIS
Steel unibody

SUSPENSION
Front:
 Independent MacPherson struts, pillow ball bushings and stabilizer bar
Rear:
 Independent MacPherson struts, pillow ball bushings and stabilizer bar

BRAKES
Front:
 Vented discs with four-piston calipers
Rear:
 Solid discs with dual-piston calipers
 ABS and Electronic Brake Distribution

WHEELS
17 x 8 in aluminum

TIRES
P235/45ZR17

DIMENSIONS
Length:	176.8 in (4490 mm)
Width:	69.7 in (1770 mm)
Height:	57.1 in (1450 mm)
Wheelbase:	103.3 in (2625 mm)
Front track:	59.6 in (1515 mm)
Rear track:	59.6 in (1515 mm)
Curb Weight:	3102 lbs (1410 kg)

SUBARU

(4th) 0.97
(5th) 0.74

FINAL DRIVE
3.90:1

DRIVELINE
Full time AWD system with viscous limited-slip center differential and Suretrac limited slip rear differential

CHASSIS
Steel unibody

SUSPENSION
Front:
 Independent MacPherson struts, linear control valve shocks and stabilizer bar
Rear:
 Independent MacPherson struts, dual links, linear control valve shocks and stabilizer bar

BRAKES
Front:
 Vented discs with dual-piston calipers
Rear:
 Vented discs with single-piston calipers
 Four-sensor ABS

WHEELS
17 x 7 in aluminum

TIRES
P215/45ZR17

DIMENSIONS
Length:	173.4 in (4405 mm)
Width:	68.1 in (1730 mm)
Height:	56.5 in (1435 mm)
Wheelbase:	99.4 in (2525 mm)
Front track:	58.5 in (1485 mm)
Rear track:	58.1 in (1475 mm)
Curb Weight:	3070 lbs (1395 kg)

*Refers to European specification model

WRX vs. EVO

MITSUBISHI	SUBARU

2007 SUBARU IMPREZA WRX STi*

VEHICLE TYPE:
  Compact, front-engined; all-wheel-drive four-door sedan

ENGINE:
  Turbocharged H-4

Construction:
  Aluminum crankcase and heads
Valvetrain:
  16-valve, operated by dual overhead camshafts
Bore and Stroke:
  99.5 mm x 79 mm
Displacement:
  2457 cc
Compression ratio:
  8.0:1
Fuel system:
  Sequential electronic injection

Max Power
  276 hp @ 6000 rpm
Max Torque
  289 lb-ft @ 4000 rpm

TRANSMISSION
Six-speed close ratio manual gearbox

RATIOS
  (1st) 3.64
  (2nd) 2.23
  (3rd) 1.52
  (4th) 1.14
  (5th) 0.89
  (6th) 0.71

FINAL DRIVE
  3.90:1

DRIVELINE
  Full time AWD system with viscous limited-slip center differential and Suretrac limited slip rear differential

SPECIFICATIONS

MITSUBISHI

SUBARU

CHASSIS
Steel unibody

SUSPENSION
Front:
  Independent MacPherson struts, linear control valve shocks and stabilizer bar
Rear:
  Independent MacPherson struts, dual links, linear control valve shocks and stabilizer bar

BRAKES
Front:
  Vented discs with four-piston calipers
Rear:
  Vented discs with dual-piston calipers
  Four-sensor ABS

WHEELS
17 x 8 in aluminum

TIRES
P225/45ZR17

DIMENSIONS
Length:	173.4 in (4405 mm)
Width:	68.1 in (1730 mm)
Height:	56.5 in (1435 mm)
Wheelbase:	99.4 in (2525 mm)
Front track:	58.5 in (1485 mm)
Rear track:	58.1 in (1475 mm)
Curb Weight:	3298 lbs (1495 kg)

*Refers to European specification model

2008 MITSUBISHI LANCER EVOLUTION GSR* (X)

VEHICLE TYPE:
  Mid-size, front-engined; all-wheel-drive four-door sedan

2008 SUBARU IMPREZA STI**

VEHICLE TYPE:
  Compact, front-engined; all-wheel-drive five-door hatchback

WRX vs. EVO

MITSUBISHI

ENGINE:
  Turbocharged I-4

Construction:
  Cast-iron block with aluminum head
Valvetrain:
  16-valve, operated by dual overhead camshafts
Bore and Stroke:
  86 mm x 86 mm
Displacement:
  1998 cc
Compression ratio:
  9.0:1
Fuel system:
  Sequential electronic injection

Max Power
  291 hp @ 6500 rpm
Max Torque
  300 lb-ft @ 4400 rpm

TRANSMISSION
  Five-speed close ratio manual gearbox

RATIOS
  (1st) 2.855
  (2nd) 1.944
  (3rd) 1.446
  (4th) 1.105
  (5th) 0.763

FINAL DRIVE
4.69:1

DRIVELINE
  Full time AWD system with Active Center Differential and limited slip rear differential with electronic active yaw control (AYC)

CHASSIS
  Steel unibody

SUSPENSION
Front:
  Independent MacPherson struts, pillow ball bushings and stabilizer bar

SUBARU

ENGINE:
  Turbocharged H-4
Construction:
  Aluminum crankcase and heads
Valvetrain:
  16-valve, operated by dual overhead camshafts
Bore and Stroke:
  99.5 mm x 79 mm
Displacement:
  2457 cc
Compression ratio:
  8.2:1

Fuel system:
  Sequential electronic injection

Max Power
  305 hp @ 6000 rpm
Max Torque
  290 lb-ft @ 4000 rpm

TRANSMISSION
  Six-speed close ratio manual gearbox

RATIOS
  (1st) 3.64
  (2nd) 2.24
  (3rd) 1.52
  (4th) 1.14
  (5th) 0.87
  (6th) 0.67

FINAL DRIVE
3.90:1

DRIVELINE
  Full time AWD system with viscous limited-slip center differential and Suretrac limited slip rear differential

CHASSIS
  Steel unibody

SUSPENSION
Front:
  Independent MacPherson struts, linear control valve shocks and stabilizer bar

SPECIFICATIONS

MITSUBISHI

Rear:
    Independent multi-link with coil springs, shocks and stabilizer bar

BRAKES
Front:
    Vented discs with four-piston calipers
Rear:
    Vented discs with dual-piston calipers
    ABS and Electronic Brake Distribution

WHEELS
    18 x 8.5 in aluminum

TIRES
    P245/40ZR18

DIMENSIONS
Length:	177.0 in (4496 mm)
Width:	71.3 in (1811 mm)
Height:	58.3 in (1480 mm)
Wheelbase:	104.3 in (2649 mm)
Front track:	60.8 in (1544 mm)
Rear track:	60.8 in (1544 mm)
Curb Weight:	3555 lbs (1612 kg)

*Refers to North American specification model

SUBARU

Rear:
    Independent double wishbones, coil springs, linear control valve shocks and stabilizer bar

BRAKES
Front:
    Vented discs with four-piston calipers
Rear:
    Vented discs with dual-piston calipers
    Four-sensor ABS

WHEELS
    18 x 8.5 in aluminum

TIRES
    P245/40ZR18

DIMENSIONS
Length:	173.8 in (4414 mm)
Width:	70.7 in (1795 mm)
Height:	58.1 in (1475 mm)
Wheelbase:	103.3 in (2623 mm)
Front track:	60.2 in (1529 mm)
Rear track:	60.6 in (1539 mm)
Curb Weight:	3360 lbs (1524 kg)

**Refers to North American specification model

BIBLIOGRAPHY

Autocar Magazine
    Mitsubishi Evolution V vs Subaru WRX STi, May 13, 1998
    Mitsubishi Evolution VI Road Test, March 24 1999

Auto Express Magazine (www.autoexpress.co.uk/carreviews)
    Mitsubishi Evo VI Makinen: First Drive
    Mitsubishi Evo VII GT-A: First Drive
    Mitsubishi Evo VIII FQ-300: First Drive
    Mitsubishi Evo VIII 260: First Drive
    Mitsubishi Evo VIII FQ400: First Drive
    Mitsubishi Evo X: First Drive

BBC Sport
    www.news.bbc.co.uk/sport2/hi/motorsport/world_rally (2003-2008 Rally seasons)

Drive Subaru
    www.drive.subaru.com (Subaru History, the early years)

Edmunds.com
    Mitsubishi Evolution VIII vs Subaru STi (July 31, 2003)
www.insideline.com/mitsubishi/lancer-evolution
    Mitsubishi Evolution IX vs Subaru WRX STi (Jan 31, 2006)
www.insideline.com/mitsubishi/lancer-evolution/2006

Evo Magazine
    "Choose Your Weapon," David Vivian, June 2003

Hot Rod Magazine
    USA vs Japan: Mustang Cobra vs Subaru STi, Matt King, 2003

Long, Brian, *Impreza: the Road Car and WRC Story*, Veloce Books 2005

Long, Brian, *Evo: the Road Car and WRC Story*, Veloce Books, 2006

Mitsubishi Motors Japan
    www.mitsubishi-motors.co.jp. (Lancer Evolution information)

Mitsubishi Motors Japan/motorsports
    www.mitsubishi-motors.co.jp/motorsports/e/archive.html (1995-2005 Rally seasons)

Mitsubishi Cars UK (Mitsubishi Evolution VIII/IX/X – FQ)
    www.mitsubishi-cars.co.uk/evolution

Mitsubishi Lancer Evolution VI press pack (issued London Motor Show, Earl's Court October 1999)

Mitsubishi Evolution VI (Author test, December 2009)

Mitsubishi Lancer Evolution IX press pack (issued NYIAS April 2005)
    www.media.mitsubishi-motors.com

BIBLIOGRAPHY

Mitsubishi Media (Global Site) (Lancer Evolution VII-X press releases)

Mitsubishi Motors Web Museum
   www.mitsubishi-motors.com/corporate/museum/history (mitsubishi history)

Mitsubishi Motors South Africa
   www.mitsubishi-motors.co.za/featuresites/mm_history (mitsubishi history 1870-1990)

Motorsport News Channel (1994-2009 Rally seasons) www.motorsport.com/

Rallye-Info
www.rallye-info.com (1992-2008 WRC Rally results and commentary)

Road & Track Magazine
   STI versus Evo, Next Gen Street Warriors, June 2007
   Lancer Evolution versus Impreza STI, March 2008
   2002-2006 Subaru Impreza WRX and STi "Choosing Performance over Styling," March 2008

Robson, Graham, *Rally Giants: Subaru Impreza*, Veloce Books, 2006

Subaru Global
   www.subaru-global.com/history.html (Subaru history 1917-2005)

Subaru Global Media
   Impreza 2002-2008 press releases

1993 Subaru Impreza Turbo Brochure and Specifications (issued London Motor Show, Earl's Court October 1993)

Subaru Impreza/2000 Turbo Brochure and specifications information 1997 London Motor Show, Earl's Court

1998 Subaru Full-line UK model Press releases – issued to Midsummer Books

1999 Subaru Full-line UK model Press releases – issued to Midsummer Books

2000 Subaru Full-line UK model Press releases – issued to Bright Star Publishing

2005 Subaru Impreza WRX and STi Press Pack, issued NAIAS, January 2005

2006 Subaru Impreza WRX and STi Press Pack, issued NAIAS, January 2005

Subaru P1 Prodrive Specification Sheet (issued London Motor Show, Earl's Court, October 1999)

Subaru World Rally Team
www.swrt.com (Subaru Rally information – 1994-2008)

Subaru WRX Author Test, September 2007

Top Speed
    www.topspeed.com (Lancer Evolution History)

World Rally Championship
    www.wrc.net (2005-2008 Rally seasons)

World Rally.net
    www.worldrally.net (1994-2002 Rally seasons)

BIBLIOGRAPHY

World Rally Championship.net
   www.worldrallychampionship.net (1999-2008 Rally seasons)

World Rally Championship season highlights, BBC Top Gear, Tony Mason 1989-1994

World Rally Championship Season Review (1992) Duke Video

World Rally Championship Season Review (1993) Duke Video

If you enjoyed this book, spread the word.

Go to www.amazon.com and write a review on the book's page.

Visit the book's home page (www.wrxvsevo.com).

Become a fan on the book's Facebook page
and suggest it to your friends.

Email info@671press and tell us directly.

* * *

671 Press is an independent publishing company,
created and operated by enthusiasts like you.

We encourage your suggestions ideas, and even corrections.
Your input helps us improve our publications and make better ones
in the future. Please send any feedback to info@671press.com.

Become a fan of 671 Press on Facebook
(www.facebook.com/671press) or check us out at www.671press.com.

Send an email to info@671press.com to receive information about our
upcoming publications and other news from 671 Press.

www.ingramcontent.com/pod-product-compliance
Lightning Source LLC
Chambersburg PA
CBHW022056150426
43195CB00008B/160